KERRERA
Mirror of History

LONG SERPENT
OF HAAKON'S FLEET

Whence came wars and fightings amongst you?
Violence in the land, ruler against ruler

KERRERA

Mirror of History

Hope MacDougall of MacDougall

EWAN'S
GALLEY

British Library Cataloguing in Publication Data
A catalogue record of this book is available from the British Library

ISBN 1 899863 94 X

First published by the author as *Island of Kerrera: Mirror of History* in 1979
This edition published by House of Lochar 2004

Typeset by XL Publishing Services, Tiverton
Printed in Great Britain by Bell & Bain, Glasgow
for House of Lochar
Isle of Colonsay, Argyll PA61 7YR

CONTENTS

ILLUSTRATIONS

Sources of Illustrations
Half-title verso adapted from watercolour by the late Dr Donald G. Duff; title page adapted from design based on Coat of Arms and architect's reconstruction of Gylen Castle (pp.29–32) specially drawn for me by my late brother in law, Leslie Grahame MacDougall. All other line drawings are my own. Black and white photographs are from family albums and other friends.

Colour photographs on cover by Martin J. Haddlington, Architect © 2004

ACKNOWLEDGEMENTS

Over long years Dr I.F. Grant has given generous help and encouragement, and this contribution to local history owes much to her.

I am grateful to Dr W.D. Lamont for advice with chapter I, and to Dr A.G. MacGregor for valued and constructive assistance with chapter XIV; to Miss Dickson, since retired, of the Reference Department, Edinburgh Public Library, and to Mr Alexander Fenton, of the National Museum of Antiquities of Scotland.

Special thanks are due to the many, mostly with Kerrera connections, past and present, who have enriched these pages with stories and information; and not least to my sisters, Coline MacDougall of MacDougall (30th Chief) and Jean Hadfield, whose support has included delving deep into family papers.

Note to the Third Edition
House of Lochar is grateful for help and advice from Nancy Black, Catherine Gillies and from the author's niece, Morag MacDougall of MacDougall of Dunnollie. We have been unable to refer to Hope MacDougall's original MS and notes and some detailed references have been irrevocably lost; any errors or omissions new to this edition are entirely ours.

Margaret Hope Garnons MacDougall of MacDougall, 1913–1998

Miss Hope MacDougall was born on 21 January 1913 in Athlone, Ireland, where her father, Chief of the Clan MacDougall, was stationed with the Royal Army Medical Corps.

With the advent of the First World War, the family returned to the Clan seat at Dunollie in Oban, and Miss Hope settled into the life of an aristocratic Highland girl. She and her two sisters Coline and Jean were educated by a governess before a short, and apparently unpopular spell at a French school in Edinburgh. From there the girls went to Bulcote boarding school in Yorkshire, which Hope loved, and where she rose to be head girl.

Through a scattering of travel notebooks and other snippets of information, a picture emerges of Hope as a young woman with an abiding love of her own land-scape – both in terms of family and history, and of Argyll. At the age of 20 she was travelling to Coll and Tiree, making detailed records of bird life and other natural history. Tantalisingly, the diary entries are interspersed here and there with obser-vations of the life of islanders; the description of a farm tool; a note on an old building – clues to what later became the great passion and legacy of her life.

But before pursuing these interests, the intervention of another war led her into work as a nursing assistant at Cortachy Castle, at Kirriemuir in Angus, and then to part-time work on a farm, where she learned to drive a tractor. After the war, Hope worked as a gardener at Westerogil, near Forfar in Angus, for six years.

She returned home to Dunollie House on her father's death in 1953, and cared for her mother until her death ten years later. In the meantime, the succession of the Chiefs of Clan MacDougall had passed for the first time to a woman, Hope's eldest sister Coline, who came home in 1966 with her husband Leslie Graham MacDougall to live at Dunollie.

For the first time now, Hope moved into a home of her own at Ganavan House, less than a mile from Dunollie. Almost immediately, she began the serious pursuit of a hobby which had clearly exercised her through most of her life.

Over the next forty years, Miss Hope MacDougall amassed a social history museum collection of national significance, relating to the working and domestic lives of the people of the Highlands and Islands, with comparative material from else-where in Britain and overseas. She gathered around 4,000 objects, plus an extraordinary archive of anecdote, research, photographs and more. It is not over-working the term to describe the Collection as unique – her position as the daughter of a Clan chief gave her an unrivalled perspective of the breadth of Highland life across the social divides. She befriended crofters and travelling people, learned trades off weavers and dairymen, and dined at the best houses North and West of the

Highland line. The Collection reflects these diverse worlds, from peat spades and pack saddles to silver snuff boxes and a silk parasol.

Critically, it was during this period of her life that she wrote this book, *Island of Kerrera: Mirror of History*. The same impetus which led her to record the social history of the Highlands and Islands was at work when it came to family history and archive. She made full use of her access to MacDougall records to unravel the life and work of the parishes of

Kerrera – and for those lucky enough to have had access to her Collection archive, the same combination of eclecticism and academia can clearly be seen to run through the pages of *Mirror of History*. The book displays her joy at obscure facts, her serious-ness in recording detail, and her complete inability to resist a really good story or anecdote.

To read the book is to know more than a little of the woman herself.

Alongside these activities, Miss MacDougall was fulfilling another role as Clan historian; supporting her sister, the Chief, and ensuring records were kept and main-tained in some order. Given that the family can trace an unbroken line back to Somerled, Lord of the Isles (Dunollie and lands were a gift to his son Dougal), that was no mean responsibility.

While she lived quietly and frugally on her own in the big house at Ganavan, she was also a notable local figure. Her Collection guided much of her activity: she was renowned for clearing old shops as they closed, for beachcombing, rifling through refuse middens, attending farm sales, and charming people on her extensive collecting tours from Arran to Shetland. She was a devout church attender, did volun-tary work with the elderly, and is still spoken about for her habit of taking snowdrops and daffodils to people in hospital whether she knew them or not. She made only three trips abroad: two to the Holy Land, and one to the Faeroes. She was a bird-watcher and naturalist, keeping a wild garden at Ganavan, and she invited birds into the house freely – one Great Tit used to help himself to her hair as nesting material. She was a keen dawn bather in the sea from the small beach by her house, which she did all year round and well into her seventies, frightening the postman as she emerged from the water in the half light of a winter morning. She never married, drove only Minis, and invited many local children to her house, by whom she was known univer-sally as 'Miss Hope'.

She died suddenly, in her garden, on 22 December 1998.

Catherine Gillies

For more information about the MacDougall Collection, write to Catherine at the MacDougall Collection, Ganavan House, Oban, Argyll.

INTRODUCTION

Let sixteenth-century Timothy Pont, cartographer, introduce Kerrera.

> Kerrera is ane Illand pertaining to MacCoul of Lorne next to Dunnoligh forgainst the Northend of that Illand. This Illand is verie fertil and profitable of come and abundance of milk, fishes also in the neighbour sea. It is of two mylls and ane half in length or therby between the two ends of it, and not one myll in breadth.
>
> In this Illand there are many foxes … and they are somewhat bigger than the foxes that are on mainlands and more bold in killing sheep, for upon the mainalands the foxes doeth no harme to anie kind of cattle sheep nor goats but the wolfes which is the destruction of horses cattell sheep goatee Deare and Rae.[1]

The foxes have gone; gone also are the little meal mills, the corn kilns, the crops of flax, the 'abundance of milk'. Gone are the changehouses, which did business with the great ferry traffic of black cattle – gone too is the cattle-swim to the mainland, and the mail ferry to Mull. Because the island still 'pertains' to MacCoul (MacDougall) of Dunnoligh (Dunollie) it is possible to glean from the documents, rent books, letters and diaries which have accrued, a harvest of records of Kerrera's past to set against the wider canvas of West Highland history.

A Kerrera farmstead

For small as it is – four and a half miles in length, less than two across – Kerrera grandly reflects the image of Highland life down the years. Lying off the Argyllshire coast and sheltering Oban Bay, it formed an important stepping stone between the mainland and the Island of Mull.

The eight farms, or former townships, which figure in early maps still have their place in modern surveys. With one exception, they have belonged to successive McDougall chiefs since Somerled founded the clan in the twelfth century. 'Dunnolith', remarks Pont, 'the principall dwelling, Castle and toun of MacKoul of Lorne ... is builded on ane heigh Craig or Rock above the sea. It is a very strong castle'.

Although ruined, Dunollie still stands very strong on its high rock overlooking the lands of Kerrera which divide the Firth of Lorn and the Sound of Kerrera, as they make their way to the Atlantic ocean.

Pont described Kerrera in his own characteristic style. Equally characteristic, the last Minister of the old charge of Kilmore and Kilbride chose words from the Bible:

A good land, a land of brooks of water, of depths that spring out of valleys and hills.

Biblical words rest happily upon the texture of Kerrera's fabric.

I HISTORICAL

It was in Ewen's time that Kerrera was involved in the clashes between the Scots and Norwegian Kings. Ewen of the thirteenth century, was son of Duncan, son of Dugall, eldest son of Somerled, and his wife Ragnhild from the Isle of Man. His grandfather, Dugall, was the first Chief of the clan MacDougall whose main seat was, and is, Dunollie.

Many royal occasions are recorded on the map of Scotland by the place name *Dalrigh* – the field of the king. Kerrera's Dalrigh earned its name in 1249; The Horseshoe Bay, beside which it lies, was visited at least three times by Royal fleets, contesting the ownership of the Western Isles.

In previous centuries the Vikings from the north had swept through the Isles down to the Isle of Man, not only raiding but conquering, so that the Islands were under Norwegian ownership. When Alexander II became King of Scotland (1214–1249) he reigned over a more united kingdom than his predecessors – thanks to their efforts, and he had the ambition to reclaim the Western Isles to Scotland.

He tried three diplomatic approaches; the story is recounted in the Norwegian Sagas[1]

> Alexander sent from Scotland in the Western Sea two Bishops to King Haco. At first they begged to know if King Haco would give up those territories which Magnus Barefoot had unjustly wrested from Malcolm, predecessor to the Scottish King – but King Haakon could not agree to this.
>
> The Commissioners then said that the King of Scotland was willing to purchase all the Hebrides from King Haco and intreated him to value them in fine silver. The King replied, he knew of no such urgent want of money as would oblige him to sell his inheritance.

After repeated attempts to negotiate with Norway, Alexander tried nearer home. The Isles, under Norwegian Sovereignty, were held partly by the descendants of Somerled, and partly by the Kingdom of Man. At the time of Alexander's negotiations, Mull, Coll, Tiree and other isles down to and including North Jura were held by Ewen, already mentioned, and South Jura, Islay and Colonsay by his cousin Dugall.

Ewen is variously described in the old accounts – Eoghann, Eugenius, Bon or Johannes of Argyll. To the Norwegians he was 'King John' and his cousin 'King Dugall'. Part of his lands, those on the mainland, he held under the King of Scotland; part – the islands – under the King of Norway.

It was King Alexander's intention to win over these 'Kings' who owed allegiance to Norway to relinquish their loyalties due to their island overlord, and join him in his efforts to recover the islands. In return he offered greater estates in Scotland.

The situation was difficult, but Ewen's creed was simple; he stuck to it in spite of much persuasion from both sides and from 'relations and friends'. As long as he held land and loyalty to a king, he could not fight against him. If, as he did, he had loyalties to two kings, he must remain unshaken in his refusal to join in battle with either against the other. 'No man can serve two masters' they told him. Ewen was, in fact, willing to resign his Norwegian territories and withdraw his homage from Norway, but this would still have left the islands in Norway's hands, and not have helped Alexander.

Curiously enough, considering the times he lived in, when heads were easily lost, his creed was justified. He kept the respect of both monarchs and regained his lands when the sovereignty of the Isles eventually returned to Scotland. He is recorded as being 'righteous and trustworthy'.

Since diplomatic negotiations had failed, Alexander collected forces throughout all Scotland, and prepared for a voyage to the Hebrides, and determined to subdue those islands under his dominion. 'He made it manifest to all his subjects he would not desist till…. he had reduced under himself all the provinces which the Norwegian monarch possessed to the westward of the German ocean.'

In the summer of 1249 he arrived at the Sound of Kerrera and anchored in The Horseshoe Bay. That he apparently met with no opposition was presumably due to Ewen's policy: if he could not help him against Norway, he would not oppose him. At the time he was away from Dunollie, being in the Island of Lewis.

The Saga continues:

That summer, Alexander King of Scotland, then lying in Kiararay Sound, dreamed a dream. He thought that three men came to him; one was in royal robes, but very stern, ruddy in countenance, something thick and of middling size. Another seemed of a slender make, but active, and of all men most engaging and majestic. The third again, was of very great stature, but his features were distorted, and of all the rest he was the most unsightly. They addressed their speech to the King, and enquired whether he meant to invade the Hebrides. Alexander thought he answered that he certainly proposed to subject the Islands. The Genius of the vision bade him go back; and told him no other measure would turn out to his advantage.

The King related his dream; and many advised him to return. But the King would not and a little after he was seized with a disorder and died.

The Hebridians say that the men whom the King saw in his sleep were St. Olave, King of Norway, St. Magnus Earl of Orkney, and St. Columba.

The previous spring the King had been so unwell that his clerk Abel had obtained from Pope Innocent IV an indulgence for him during Lent of that year: 'The constant eating of fish was so distasteful to him that he was ill during almost the whole of Lent' and the Pope's indulgence 'permitted him to eat eggs, cheese butter and meat on the advice of his confessor and physician when necessary.'[2] Whether or not this indisposition of the King had any connection with the 'disorder' which resulted in his death at Kerrera, most of the brief contemporary accounts suggest his passing was sudden. The *Chronicles of Man* reports: 'When Alexander King of Scotland arrived at the island that is called Kerrera he was seized with a fever there and died.'

There are, however, one or two pointers which might perhaps suggest that his stay on Kerrera, or on board his ship in The Horseshoe Bay, was not so brief. *Origenes Parochiales Scotiae* records a document granting the church of Kilbride (nearby on the mainland) to the See of Argyll, and this is dated that year 'in Keruerhey'. It also records among documents found in Edinburgh Castle in 1292 and ordered by King Edward I to be delivered to King John Baliol, one entitled 'a letter of the abbot and monks of Cupar, binding themselves to build a chapel at their own expense in the isle of Karuelay in Arkadia (evidently Kerrera in Argyll) – and find three monks to perform divine service there for the soul of the deceased Alexander King of Scots, for a certain sum of money which they had beforehand received from that King.' Even if nothing more came of this, it is perhaps suggestive that the King realised death might be approaching. He had also expressed a wish to be buried in Melrose.

The *Chronicle of Melrose* records he 'was attacked by a serious infirmity while he was upon his way to pacify the district of Argyle, and he was conveyed to the island of Kerrera, where after receiving the ecclesiastical Sacraments his happy soul was taken from this light … and his body transported (as he had commanded before he died) to the Church of Melrose and was committed to the bosum of the earth in it in royal fashion … He departed from this life in the fifty first year of his age and the thirty fifth of his reign on Thursday the eighth of July 1249.'

The Bodleian version of the Verse chronicled in Skene's *Picts and Scots* records the king as a 'noble and pious man': 'when he had completed thirty and five years of his reign he died in Argyle; but he lives without end … since the honour of his uprightness lives in fame. He died in Argyle … and Melrose holds his bones in burial.'

Kerrera certainly holds in memory his arrival and death at The Horseshoe Bay, and commemorates it in the name of the field beside the shore – Dalrigh. His tomb may be seen in the 12th-century church of Melrose Abbey near the high altar.

The Saga concludes the story, after his death: 'The Scottish army then broke up; and they bare the King's body to Scotland.' Perhaps to us, looking from the mainland across the narrow Sound of Kerrera, this is the most remarkable statement of the whole story – that Kerrera, as one of the Western Isles, belonged to Norway.

Fourteen years later, Alexander's son Alexander III (1249–86) made another, and eventually successful, bid to regain the Western Isles for Scotland. This time, however, it was the Norwegian fleet that anchored in the Sound of Kerrera.

Hearing news in the summer of 1263 that 'the Scottish King purposed to subdue all the Hebrides if life were granted to him' (that dream had made him nervous) gave King Haco 'much uneasiness' and he summoned his Council in Bergen to consider confirming his ownership by an expedition to the Isles. He had now been King of Norway 'for six and forty winters' and Prince Magnus of Man begged to command the expedition instead of King Haco, who should stay at home. He thanked him in very courteous words; but he observed that he himself was older, and had longer aquaintance with the Western lands, and that, therefore, he himself would go this voyage.'

On July 4th King Haco 'set sail for the German ocean with all his fleet; he had a favourable breeze; the weather was fair, and the armaments beautiful to behold'.

Snorro Sturlson, the King's Bard, paints a vivid word-picture of the scene as the great fleet swept towards the Hebrides:

> The Leader of his people unmoored the ploughers of the ocean
> and raised aloft the expanded wings
> From the stern of his snorting steed adorned with
> ruddy gold he viewed the retiring haven
> And soon they were in sailing order, and the beautiful
> fleet proceeded out to sea.
> A glare of light blazed as the sea-borne wooden
> coursers broke the roaring waves
> Gold glanced against the clear heavens from the
> bright shields fastened round the ships
> The swelling sails of keels that ride the surge reflect
> the beams of an unsullied sun –
> The abyss returned the flaming gleam of war – darted
> from the bright glittering concave shields of
> the goddess of battle
> the passage of the magnificent princess fleet of
> ships was as a streak of lightning as he proceeded
> with his adorned ships by the seaways of the
> Hebrides.

During this voyage King Haco had that great vessel (the Christsudan) which he had caused to be constructed at Bergen. It was built entirely of oak, and contained twenty seven banks (benches) of oars. Probably the planks were caulked with cow's hair and tar; certainly it was ornamented with 'heads and necks of dragons beautifully overlaid with gold. He also had many other well appointed ships.'

At four minutes past one there was an eclipse, and 'while Haco lay in Ronaldsvo in the Orkneys a great darkness drew over the sun, and it continued so for some hours.' Haco had already sent word to the Hebrides and told 'King Dugal' – Ewen's cousin – that 'he might expect an army from the east. King Dugal therefore spread abroad a report that forty ships were coming from Norway and by this means he prevented the Scots from making a descent.'

Doubtless as the Norwegian fleet sailed along the north coast of Scotland, then headed south for Mull 'this voyage by the bands of the troubler of peace through the sea that streams round the world was unwelcome to the foe – they dreaded the extraction of tribute.'

The people of Kerrera must have had mixed feelings when King Haco 'proceeded to the Sound of Mull, and then to Kiararey where King Dugal and the other Hebrideans were assembled with their troops. King Haco had now above a hundred vessels for the most part large and all of them well provided both with men and arms.' Imagine the sight in The Horseshoe Bay!

The description continues:

> While King Haco remained at Kiararey he divided his forces, and sent fifty ships south to the Mull of Kintyre. The Captains he appointed over them were King Dugal, Magnus King of Man and five others. He also ordered five ships for Bute.

Haakon himself sailed to the island of Gigha off Kintyre, and it was here that Ewen (King John) met him, arriving in a galley with Bishop Thorgil.

> King Haco desired him to follow his banner… but King John excused himself. He said he had sworn an oath to the Scottish King, and held of him more lands than of the Norwegian monarch; he therefore entreated King Haco to dispose of all those estates which he had conferred upon him. King Haco kept him with him some time and endeavoured to incline his mind to fidelity… After King Haco had sailed south from Gud-ey (Gigha) he set King John at liberty; and bidding him go in peace, wherever he would, gave him several rich presents. He promised King Haco to do everything in his power to effectuate a peace between him and the Scottish King.

It was after the Norwegian fleet had sailed south to the coast of Ayr, and had been defeated by the Scots that Haakon sailed north again, passing the Mull of Kintyre:

> King Haco set sail again on the first Sunday of winter; and met a fog and a storm so violent that few of the ships could carry their sails. The King therefore made

for Kiararay; and about this time messages passed between him and King John but to little purpose.

Was King John back at home at Dunollie, by this time?

While he was in The Horseshoe Bay King Haco 'was imformed that his troops had made depredations in Mull and that some of the Mull-men, with two or three Norwegians, had been killed'. No mention of the Kerrera-men. To feed his troops King Haakon had levied many tributes from several communities – a thousand head of cattle from Kintyre on his way south, and on his return he laid a charge on Islay of three hundred, but part of this was to be paid in meal and part in cheese

King Haco next set sail to the Calf of Mull, where he stayed some nights. There King Dugal and Allan his brother took leave of the King, who gave them those estates which King John formerly possessed.

On his way home King Haakon was taken ill in Orkney, where he died. Before long Ewen's lands were restored to him and there was an agreement (1266) between the two countries in which 'all the inhabitants of the said Islands which are thus ceded to the King of Scotland, both old and young shall be subject to the laws and usages of the Kingdom of Scotland... but should it happen, which God forbid, that people belonging to the King of Norway suffer shipwreck upon the coasts... they shall be allowed in peace and quietness to take up their shattered or damaged ship as well as their property'.

Ewen, 3rd Chief, was succeeded by his son Alexander, who, with his heir Iain Bacach, 'lame John' clashed with King Robert Bruce. They met in 1306 near Strathfillan in Perthshire (the spot was afterwards named Dalrigh) and gained in combat his shoulder clasp – the famous Brooch of Lorn. Two years later they met him again in the Pass of Awe, and, being defeated, for a period lost much of their lands.

It was in the time of John (11th) who died in 1480 that Kerrera was the scene of a kidnapping, as recorded in the Auchinleck Chronicles.

The Year of God 1460, the erll of Argyle Colyne Campbell passit in Lorn for the redemption of his cosing John Keir of Lorne, the quhilk was tane be his brother Allan of Lorn, sister's son to Downe Balloch, and shortlie this Erll with his oist come to the Isle of Kerervira quhair this Allane had his brother in festynans – his intent was to destroye hime that he mycht have succeedit to the heretage. He had Jhon Keir bound. Alan was surprised, many of his men killed... redeemed his cosing and restorit him to his Lordship.

Gylen Castle appears to have been built in the time of Dugall (15th), and his son Duncan, who married firstly a MacLean of Duart and secondly a MacLauchlan of

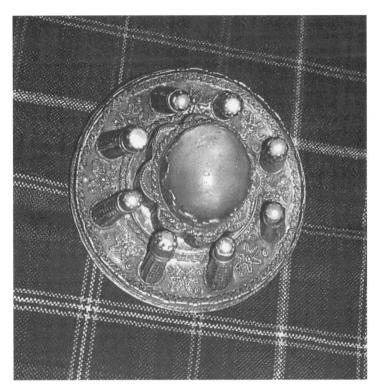

The Brooch of Lorn

Castle Lauchlan. The marriage stone is dated 1587. His son John (17th) succeeded, and the 'Valuation of the Parish of Kilbryde by the Subcommissioners of the Presbytery of Argle' dated 1629/30 includes 'The land and Yle of Corivoray or Kerreray ... pertaining to the said Sir Johne Mcdougal of Dunnoleych knyt'.

After his death in 1643 his son Alexander succeeded, and marched at the head of his clan and the Kerrera men during the wars of the Covenant to defend the Castle of Dunaverty in Kintyre. In this treacherous massacre of 1647, by troops under General Leslie's orders, he and his followers lost their lives; only his young son, John (Iain) was saved, and succeeded as the 19th Chief. According to Acts of Parliament of the reign of King Charles II, this John sought redress for the wrongs suffered during the reign of the late King; this was perhaps the darkest period in the history of Kerrera's people.

They record:

> In the years of 1643–47 in ane or other of the moneths thereof James Marquis of Montrose and Sir James Lawmond of Inveryre Knight being comissignate by his Majesty to ryse in armes ... and to raise all men friends and followers and others who would adhere to him against the Marquis of Argyle and his followers who were then in rebellion against his Majesty ... John McDougall and Alexander his

father having risen in armes with all their followers to the number of five hundred men of their friends, kindred and tennants and joyned themselves to Sir James Lawmond during the war and being still in armes in his most royall Majesties service, wher invaded by the Marquis of Argyle and David Leslie and these in armes with them, and pursued to the fort of Dunavertie in Kintyre, which not being able to hold out ther being ane message sent into those within the fort that if they did not come forth again ten hours the next day they should not have quarters and if they came out they sho uld have quarters. And Johne McDougall being within the fort, with his friends who haveing punctually as desired at the verie hour of the day come forth and rendered themselves they were all at the instigation of the Marquis of Argyle … to the number of fyve hundreth men, officers and soldiers cruellie and inhumanellie butchered in cold blood (the said Joun McDougall being then a child and in nonage was only spared).[3]

There is a list of 'The Names of the Men who wes murthered at Dounavertie in Kyntyre and several others not to be remembered of in 1646 or 47.' A commentator adds a footnote: 'No less than 49 MacDougalls are given in this first list, and 41 of various other names presumably dependent on them. The first column undoubtedly represents the blood relations of the Old House of Lorne sprung from the race of Dougall, son of Somerled…'

The long list only specifies one Kerrera man with his home – Dougall McDougall of Ardmore; but the specific details of other names suggest they could be identified in contemporary times with their homes. They also suggest the adoption of the clan name by dwellers in clan territory. A few examples:

Duncane McDougall brother to the Laird of McDougall
Allane McDougall his brother
Alister McDougall cousing germane to the said Laird
Iain McDougall his brother
Dougall McDougall of Ardmoir.
Sorlee McConochie alias McDougall
Allane McAllane alias McDougall
Alexander McEwine Vc eun Vc ewin alias McDougall …

and so the list continues indicating both male and in places female descent a generation of the clan massacred.

The Acts continue – vague as to dates, less so as to details.

In ane or other of the said years Archibald Campbell Marquis of Argyle did ryse fyre and brunt … the thirty merk land of Kerrerie and cruellie robd and took away the haill bestial goods comes and plenishings… In the year 1646 in ane or other of the moneths therof a party of Campbell officers at the command of the Marquis of Argyle went with a partie under their command to the yle of Keirrara and ther by forthought, fellonie most cruellie murthered with swords and dirks

Johne Oig McDougall of Slatera	Johne McIlmichell
Dougall MacDougall	Duncan McAulay
Angus McDougall	Lauchlane McCannoch
Duncan McDougall	Vivineoch
Alexander MacDougall	Johne McKeirrick
Johne McVartine	alias Leich
John McIlcheon	John McKeag
Duncan McCallane	Donald McIlvernak

innocent persons his Majestie's free leidges liveing under his Majesties protection and authority and that under cloud and silence of night and took sex others captive viz –

Hew McDougall Ewen MacDougall Duncan MacDougall Ronald MacDougall Donald McGillespie Johne O'conocher and even after quarter given for life at least in cold blood and being his Majesties free leidges carried them prisoners to Inveraray and ther cruelly murthered and hanged them to death.

A tradition has been handed down that a MacDougall defended himself and killed his seven attackers as he stood on the jutting out ledge of sandstone in a conglomerate rock pillar below Gylen Castle near the west shore.

Young John MacDougall (19th) having miraculously survived the Dunaverty massacre, had the hard task of trying to defend his castles of Dunollie and Gylen against the Government troops; during the attacks the Brooch of Lorn was taken, and remained hidden in Campbell hands for nearly two centuries.

The account is continued in the Act:

Johne McDowgall and some of his said ruined friends in the years 1644–47 … for the good of our Soverane Lords deceast most royall fathers service and for the safety of himself and his friends from the crueltie of the late Marquis of Argyle and his friends, did fortifie their house of Dunollie and after the … Marquis… had caused burn Johne McDowgall his house of Gyland in the Yle of Kerrera having threatened those that were therin with hanging to death if they did not burne the same. The said house was accordingly at his command brunt, and thereeafter being forced to make capitulation with David Leslie and Collonel

Holbourne the leaders of the forces of the Marquis of Argyll for the house of Dunollie ... And at last for the saifing of the wyves and children of those who wer murthered at Donnaverty and Kerrera being then all destitute of subsistence, and the said Johne McDougall of Dunollie deducted to great miserie... wes forced to give over and quyte to the Marquis his heritable Bawllierie of Lorn.

By an Act of Parliament in 1661, in the reign of Charles II, John's lands were restored to him; he was succeeded by his brothers, firstly Duncan, and then the younger Allan (21st). Allan received a charter of land in 1686 from James VII, and in that year he married Mary MacLachlan of Kilbride.

Tradition has it that for the birth of her first-born Mary went to the little cottage which overlooks the Kilbride Church, and there the heir was born. John, usually known as Iain Ciar, thus first saw light in the little house whose ruins still mould the turf, and which overlook the walled enclosure beside the Church where he was buried in 1737 because a storm prevented the cortege crossing Loch Etive to the family burial ground at Ardchattan.

Partly because of his involvement in the Fifteen Rising and the events following it, Iain Ciar became an almost legendary figure. His long enforced exile caused one of his tennants to exclaim, it is recorded, 'Would that Iain Ciar were back among us; he would be a tower of strength in himself; even his presence would hearten us, if it did nothing more.'[4]

In 1712 he married Mary MacDonald, grand-daughter of Sir Donald MacDonald of Sleat (twelve MacDougalls fetched his bride from Skye in Galleys) and three years later set out in support of the Jacobite cause.

After the horrors which overtook the Kerrera people in the seventeenth century it is a relief to learn that they emerged, apparently, from their part in the 'Fifteen' at the battle of Sheriffmuir 'very well, without losing a drop of blood'.

The story of the royal fleets in Horseshoe Bay has been gleaned mostly from quotations from translations of the Norwegian Sagas; the deeds of the religious wars from Acts of Parliament; and now something of Kerrera's support to the claim of the Jacobite King to the British throne from the personal letters of the Chief to his young wife whom he had left at Dunollie to defend the castle – 'Keep the house and cause line the door with turf on the inside' he told her.

There were many rumours during the year of 1715 of the expected arrival of James Stewart in Scotland to make his bid for the crown. At one time there was the suggestion that he might land at Dunstaffnage Castle nearby – then it was learned that the castle was garrisoned by Hanoverian troops.

In late September Iain Ciar received the following letter from Dunstaffnage:

Dunstaffnage
23rd Septr. 1715

Sir,

　　His Grace, as heritable Lord Lieut. of this shyre has been pleased to nominate and appoint me as one of the deputy lieutenants of this shyre, and it being necessary that such men as I formerly nominated to join the militia be in readiness to march with me to Inveraray against Monday next, I hereby order and desire that you and your men do meet me at Kilmore against eight of the clock forenoon Monday next being the 26th instant, and that each of your men take along a fortnights provision, and be sure all your men take along all their defencible arms as you'll be answerable to the Duke of Argyll as our Lord Lieutenant and to his deputes from Kilmore to march on Monday ….

　　from Sir, Your humble servant g Campbell.

I request you to see that the people of Kerrera or any other you are concerned in be not deficient; and consider what I told you formerly, a word to the wise is enough. I hope you will pardon my freedom.

yours sincerely – H. Cll Dun.

You'll sycilie (surely) inform your men of this call.[5]

The Duke of Argyll was, of course, commander of the Hanoverian forces.

　　Dunstaffnage's personal postscript to his circular letter suggests that he had reservations as to Dunollie's loyalties, and was warning him where prudence lay. In this he was fully justified, for traditionally the family had not given prudence much priority when supporting a cause. Iain Ciar was full of dedication and enthusiasm for the Stewart claim, and not only the 'people of Kerrera' but Iain himself were 'deficient' at the rendezvous at Kilmore – now a small village but then the centre of the community.

　　On the other hand, the enthusiasm of the leaders was not necessarily shared by all the tenants – the awful losses of the previous century can hardly have been out of mind, and also adherence to the two sides was locally divided. If the Kerrera people were not over anxious to leave their homes, they were not alone in this. The Earl of Mar, head of the Jacobite forces, writes bitterly concerning his Aberdeenshire tenants in September of that year:

It is a pretty thing, when all the Highlands of Scotland are now rising upon their King and Country's account, that my men only should be refractory. Is not this the thing we are now about, which they have been wishing for twentysix years and now when it is come and the King and the Country's cause is at stake, will they for ever sit still and see all perish?'[6]

After the years of destitution following the civil wars of the seventeenth century, several of the Kerrera farms were pledged in wadset. These names appear on the rent roll:

> In Gylene – John Mcurchrein, John McPherson, Coll McDougall Gilbert McIlichoan, John McKulloch, Gilbert McChruim, Allan McDougall, John McKeire,
> In Slachterach – Alexander MacDougall, Donald McCulloch alias Mconochy, John McDougall, Donald McCulloch, Angus McCulloch, Duncan MacCulloch Also Archibald McCulloch, miller of Oban and Gylyne.

The miller's son, Neil is mentioned as a messenger between Iain Ciar at Perth and his wife at Dunollie.

Iain Ciar set out for Perth to join the Earl of Mar, and on November 6th he wrote to his wife:

> Dearest and only Comfort,
> This day I was in company wt Earl of Marr … and I hop in God in few days you will hear a good account of this army. I'm to joyne Sir Donald (MacLean) who cam throi days ago. What was reported formerly they are not out of hops of itt as yett … if anny body come to you be very kind to ym. I wish you saw Coull and the tutor and if they concur wt you itts good in sending all the men of Korvora (Kerrera) and anny others they can get with ane of Coulls sons or anny body who will take in hand to come wt them.
> Keep good hearts and be noo ways concerned aboutt me for I am in noo danger nor do I see anny danger in our undertaking believe nothing you hear aboutt us accept what you hear to our advantage. You shall hear from me very shoone hast back Donald and say him travel night and day till he comes up with this army …
> perth novor the 6 1715.

This letter was written just a week before the battle of Sheriffmuir – the next a few days after it. During the battle both right wings of the two armies had success; their left wings defeat. Although later events proved the battle to have been disastrous for the Jacobite hopes, at the time, Iain Ciar's exaltation, was quite in line with the well known jingle recording the battle:

> There's some say that we wan
> And some say that they wan …
> But one thing I'm sure, man

> That at Sheriffmuir …
> We baith did fight and both did beat
> And baith did run awa', man.

Iain Ciar wrote again to Mary at Dunollie:

I doubt not but ye have got a duleful account of me and the whole of the King's party. But blessed be God, our behaviour, at least a part, is known by this time in most of Britain.

The matter of fact was this, on Sunday being the thirteenth instant, about twelve o'clock we engaged the enemy; we had my Lord Argyle's left wing. We were placed on our own right wing – viz Glengarry, Clanranald, Sir Donald MacLean's and a small battalion commanded by the Earl Merischal. The enemy being unanimously attacked by us whom I name, was utterly defate, for of five regiments of foot and Black horse, there never entered Stirling of them five hunder men, but the whole was killed or taken. For I can ssure you such as engaged, I mean Sir Donald's men, there was never a score that left the field of them.

Our left wing was indeed put in a confusion and was a good way geses (dispersed) by the enemy; and then our horses made extraordinary good resistance and kept their ground and artillery and camped that night where they had fought it and so kept the field of battle. My Lord Argyle was obliged to betake himself to Stirling that night with the loss of eight or nine hunder killed and two hunder at least taken prisoner. Blessed be to God, our loss need not be recorded, for Sir Donald yr was not twenty of his whole men killed nor twenty wounded – and I have the honour, my dearest, to be reckoned amongst the wounded for I received a slight one through the right thigh….

Our Army in England consiste of about fifteen thousand and meets with no opposition as yet. I will not be fashing you with all the news we have, but all are good, but begs you may not give ear to the country clashes (gossips) for I know the country will quean news to dishearten you, but God is still in heaven on whom I have still my dependence, God give you grace to do the same.

The few that came with me are very well, without losing a drop of blood except Hugh Krekanich's son got in the arm. There are four of them away home with a full handful but and please God I go home, some of them shall not escape the widdie as they diserved.

I admire (wonder) what keepid little Donald, I durst not send you anything for fear to lose the haill by reason that there is robbers on the way. Haste back the bearer, and let little Donald come along with him by all means, so likewise send Neil the Miller's son in your company that he may return with the things I'll not name at present.

Later Mary received a letter from Iain Ciar written from Perth on December 29th, full of excitement at the arrival of Prince James Francis Edward on the east coast on December 22nd. He writes:

> Blessed be God, I have the best news to give you since ever you was born. This morning the King arrived with a throng train your unkoll Allan is come with him and many of greater note, and I have sent you the King's Declaration – as printed in France, I would not wait the reprint of it here.
>
> I write this so as you may not doubt what your dearest says, had I not seen his face and kissed his hands. I bless God that we are very hearty and I hope this will encourage you to give all your company the King's health and success to his arms. I hope you will not neglect mine, for I debosh myself by drinking yours. I trust your couching neighbours will now think shame on themselves. I doubt not that my last will prevail upon my friends in sending up men with my brother. I know it is uneasy for him to have passage, but willing people will still fall on the means. Let one and all of them depend if they disobey this, and if it is our Lord's will to place our undoubted Sovereign on his ancestor's throne … they shall have their reward, and please God I see an end to his wars.

Jacobite optimism, however, was short lived, and as history records, within a few weeks the Rising was over. The Prince, the Earl of Mar and others sailed for France; the Highlanders made for home, if they thought they could safely do so, or into exile if they feared being made prisoner. So far as is known, any Kerrera man who was 'out' returned home. For Iain Ciar it was different; he had to face twelve long years of exile, a threat of execution or deportation, before he was pardoned and able to return to Dunollie, his wife and his family. Part of the time was spent in Ireland, much of it in France, and several interludes in Scotland – he took part in the 1719 attempted Rising. He was also locally in hiding, and through the years able to make several secret meetings with his wife. Dunollie was garrisoned by Government troops and for a time Mary took refuge in a cottage in Gylen. There is a strong tradition that Iain Ciar for a time was in hiding locally, sometimes in a cave in the Lerags district but more probably in a cave high in the Gallanach cliffs, above the Sount of Kerrera and looking over towards Gylen. From this cave, it is said, he managed to make the crossing by night, and come to Mary.

In a list of North Argyll men concerned with the Forty-five rising, three Kerrera men are mentioned: John MacLauchlan, brewer at Kerrera Ferry; John MacLauchlan, weaver, and Neil MacLauchlan, both from 'Balemore'.

Iain Ciar, who died in 1737, was succeeded at Dunollie by his son Alexander, but is was a younger son, Duncan, who led the Clan at Culloden. The above list marks

Dunollie Castle (from an old print)

the Kerrera men as 'soldiers, not known where they are now', but there is reason to think that the weaver, at least, got home safely to Balliemore.

The aftermath of Culloden brought a famous visitor, as a Jacobite prisoner, to The Horseshoe Bay. For the part she played in helping the escape of Prince Charles Edward in the months following the battle, Flora MacDonald was taken prisoner in Skye on 11 July 1746, and placed on board the *Furnace*. Later in the month the *Furnace*, with General Campbell, Flora and a few other prisoners sailed south for the Sound of Mull. The General received a message from Commodore Smith of the *Eltham* that he was sailing 'for Horseshoe Harbour between Kerrera and the main.'[7]

Here, at 11 a.m. on 1 August the *Furnace* joined her, and the General handed over the prisoners he had brought with him – all except Flora MacDonald, who was to be more comfortably confined at Dunstaffnage Castle, once more garrisoned with government troops. Ever since she was taken prisoner, General Campbell 'treated here with the utmose respect', and he himself admitted 'he had a great compassion for the younge lady.' 'Her courage, modesty and sincerity' won her friends wherever she went, but it was through General Campbell's orders that she received gentle treatment.

From the *Furnace* he wrote to the Captain of Dunstaffnage:

On his Majesty's Service to Neil Campbell Esq. Captain of Dunstaffnage, from Major-General Campbell.

Horseshoe Bay Augt 1st
1746

Dear Sir,

I must desire the favour of you to forward my letters by an express to Inveraray, and if any are left with you let them be sent by the bearer. I shall stay here with Commodore Smith till Sunday morning, and if it is not inconvenient should be glad to see you. If you can't come I beg to know if you have any men now in Garrison at your House, and how many. Make my compliments to your lady and tell her that I am obliged to desire the favour of her for some days to receive a very pritty young Rebell; her zeal and the perswasion of those who ought to have given her better advice, had draun her into a most unhappie scrape by assisting the younge Pretender to make his escape. I need say nothing further till we meet, only assure you that I am, Dear Sir, your sincere friend and Humble Servant,

John Campbell.

I suppose you have heard of Miss Flora McDonald.

On the back of the letter: 'If Dunstaffnage is not at home his Lady is desired to open this letter.'[8]

A few days later the General and the Commodore paid a visit to the castle, and were entertained by Neil Campbell and his wife, who were treating Flora MacDonald as guest rather than prisoner. It has been recorded that local ladies paid social calls on Flora MacDonald whilst she was at Dunstaffnage.

After nearly a fortnight the General sent a request to Dunstaffnage for her return to the ship:

Wednesday evening.

Sir,

You will deliver to the bearer, John McLeod, Miss MacDonald, to be conducted her(e) in his wherry; having no officer to send, it would be very proper you send one of your Garrison alongst with her,

I am, Sr, your most obedient Humble Servant,
John Campbell.

To the Captain of Dunstaffnage.

Commodore Smith had proposed to sail from The Horseshoe at 'tine first spirt of wind' but he was still wind-bound there until 22nd August. Before this the General had left for Inveraray, but on his way wrote to Dunstaffnage with a message for the Commodore. He evidently knew of the difficulty of attracting the ship's attention from the mainland for he writes:

Dear Sir,

The packet I send you for Commodore Smith requires the utmost despatch so I must beg you'll send a careful fellow with it by hand. Let him haill either the Commodore or the *Furnace*, that he may not be detain'd on the shoar which had happened sometimes I should think the messenger had best take his firelock and two charges or cartrages of pouder to fire so as to make himself hear'd on board the ships.

John Campbell.

Whilst politically unlikely, it would be interesting to know if Mary MacDonald, Iain Ciar's widow, ever met Flora. The two women might have had something in common; both had given much to the Jacobite cause, both were renowned for courage, charm and loyalty. Both were Skye women, and not too distant neighbours. At the time of Flora's enforced visit, Mary was spending her long widowhood in Kerrera.

Her eldest son Alexander married in the autumn of 1737, and shortly after his father's death in December, Alexander and his mother drew up an agreement concerning her future. Two years later she decided to take up the terms of the agreement and to live on Kerrera:

Be it known to all men … me Mary MacDonald Relict of the deceased John McDougall of Dunollie fores much by articles of agreement entered into betwixt me and Allexr MacDougall now of Dunollie my son … on the fifteenth day of December seventeen hundred and thirty seven years … (it was agreed) should we incline to separate our living together in one family … I was to restrict my liferent provision and joynture to the sum of four hundred merks scots money of annuity yearly to be paid me att Martimas and Whitesunday by equal portions out of the first and readiest of the rents of the lance (of) Slaterich and Geyline and assigned the superplus of my said joynture to ye said Allexr MacDougall …

It was also agreed … in the event of our separation families upon his own expence to stock the fourth part of Geyline in Kerera with labouring horses cows and sheep and seed corn conform to the souming and rooming of the place and give me possession of the said fourth part during my life time in satisfaction of soe much of the said annuity of four hundred merks as the rents therof will amount to on the same terms and conditions that the other tenants therof possess it.

It was further agreed that in the case of our separation I was to have the thrid part of the Household plenishing and furniture … that pertained to my deceast husband … and now seeing I have thought it more to my interest to live separate than to remain in one family with Allexander my son … therefore wit ye me, the said Mary MacDonald, to have exhonoured claim…

Signed by me at Geyline in Kerera the nineteenth of October one thousand seven hundred and thirtynine years …

Mary MacDonald.

Alexander (23rd) was born two years before his father joined the Rising, and spent most of his boyhood with a family in Dunbarton, whilst his father was in exile and his mother and the younger children were suffering the difficulties of that period. When Iain Ciar was pardoned, and the family united at Dunollie in 1727, Dugald McDougall of Ardmore, a year before he died, presented young Alexander with his family Bible. It has the inscription: 'Gift Dugd McDougall of Ardmore to Alexr of Dunollie in the year 1728. And ye date of my Birth is the fifth of July 1713 & theirto is subjoined ane account of the Birth of my children & of date of my marriage qch was September 15th 1737.'

Those were the days of large families, and Alexander and his wife Mary, third daughter of Patrick Campbell of Barcaldine, were industrious in filling the large front page of the Bible. Before the arrival of the thirteenth child the Gregorian Calendar had come into use in Brittain and an adjustment made so that in 1752 September 2nd (old style) was followed by September 14th (new style). The births were carefully entered:

Lufsie was born Dec 26 1738 (added – old style) followed by John, Mary, Patrick, Allan, Duncan, Jean, Alexander and Allan (twins) Anna, Jean, Elizabeth, Coline Feb. 19th new style, Alexander and finally James, September 1756.

As can be seen from the repetition of names, not all the children survived early youth. Of them all, it was the fourth son, Duncan, who rented Ardantrive farm from the Earl of Breadalbane, built himself a new house there, and also farmed, as tacksman to his father, Balliemore, Port Kerrera, and for a period Gylen Park.

Alexander himself was not out in the Forty-five, the Clan being led by his younger brother Duncan; legend has it that his wife poured a kettle of boiling water over his foot to prevent his taking part, and possibly again losing the lands which had recently been restored to him.

Be that as it may, he, unlike his father, had the opportunity to concern himself with his home and farmlands, and like contemporaries all over Scotland to try to benefit himself and his tenants by improved farming practices. Perhaps his most notable action was to transfer his rapidly growing family from the old castle which had housed his ancestors for so many centuries and generations to the new house he built nearby on the lower ground, making additions to existing older buildings.

Calf-bound books on farming gathered on the Dunollie shelves, then and later. Among them was the 1727 *Country Gentleman and Farmer's Monthly Director* containing 'Necessary Instructions for the Management and Improvement of a Farm in every month of the Year. Wherein is directed the Times and Seasons proper for Ploughing and Sowing all sorts of Corn or Grain'. The book ends with a piece of charming advice to the farmer:

> And I now leave him to conclude the Year in Hospitality and harmless Mirth, and to begin the New Year with Courage and Conduct, that the End may be crowned with Riches.

Other books followed – *The Farmer's Calender* (of many editions) 'Containing the Business Necessary to be Performed on Various Kinds of Farms during Every Month in the Year' by Arthur Young Esq, and Sir John Sinclair's *Code of Agriculture*.

Alexander died in 1801 and was succeeded by his second son Patrick (24th), As a boy, Patrick had been fostered with the MacCulloch family, onetime Millers of Gylen and the Oban Glenshellach mill, when they moved to Morvern. It had for long been a custom among Highland lairds to send at least some of their sons to be fostered by certain of their tenants, thus building up a lifelong interest and friendship between the two families. Patrick belonged to the last of Dunollie generations to be fostered in this way before the custom died out. In his *Records of Argyll* (1885) Lord Archibald Campbell quotes from an account given him by John MacDougall, Selma Villa, Oban, concerning Patrick's early upbringing:

> … the child (Patrick) was reared for several years by the MacCullochs, where he would hear no language but Gaelic or see manners other than those of the Highland peasantry. When the time came for him to return home MacCulloch sent with him thirteen head of cattle including a bull, on condition his father would add an equal number to them to form a stock for his son. It was usual for the father to send with his child a certain number of cattle, to which the fosterer added an equal number. When the period of fostering expired, these cattle, with their increase, were sent home with the child to form a nucleus of a portion for it. When his father saw them landing at Port Mor, below Dunollie he was delighted, and said what a fine lot of cattle MacCulloch has sent with our son!

Patrick married Louisa Maxwell, a Campbell of Achalader, and returned to Dunollie at the end of the nineteenth century to manage the estate for his aged father.

Twice a year the mainland and Kerrera tenants gathered at Dunollie, not only to pay their rents, but to discuss problems, renew leases, sign agreements. Rent days were about mid June and mid December, a couple of weeks or so after the Whitsunday and Martimas terms. They met in what came to be known as the 'old dining room' after additions were made to the house in the late 1830s. On what was called the 'rent table' – a round pedestal table with four drawers set in the edge – were laid out ink, quill pens, sandbottle, Patrick's blue-steel rimmed spectacles in rolled cardboard case, spare paper, and the rent books.

Alexander's rent book – 1746 to 1797 – was nearly twelve inches high and only three and a half inches across the page, rough skin covered and tied with thongs. The faded brown ink entries have many of the usual abbreviations, when the letter 'y' stood for 'th' or 'the', as in 'oyr' for other, 'fayr' for father, 'yr' for their or there, and 'ye' for the.

Skin-covered rent book

The next books, covered with a rough surfaced brown paper were soon succeeded by calf-backed books whose hard boards were covered with the coloured 'marbled' paper beloved by the legal profession.

Receipts and agreements were headed Dunollie, and written out for the tenant to sign, latterly with his full signature. Older papers were usually signed by his 'mark' – a cross or initial inserted between the christian and surname.

In the eighteenth century unpaid rents came under the heading 'rests' – later the column was headed 'arrears'. On 22nd June 1822 a note shows how the money was paid:

£5	notes 2,	£10		
40/-	do 2,	£4	Gold	£1 10/-
21/-	do 22	£23 2/-	Silver	£2 5/-
20/-	do 19,	£19		

For a period after 1797 the Bank of England issued £2 as well as £1 notes, but local Scottish Banks issued various denominations.

Rent day was a social occasion, and the account books show entries of Whisky for Rent (or Collection) Day, and possibly more solid refreshment was offered.

Among the tenants were the two Ground Officers, one for the mainland and one from Kerrera. Apart from acting as go-between with landlord and tenant, the Groundsman had a variety of duties; dividing the riggs, the peat mosses and other communial rights, settling the seaware boundaries, controlling the heather burning, to say nothing of distributing whisky on Old New Year's day.

In Kerrera, MacDougalls from Slaterach held this office for three generations. Allan MacDougall, then in his late thirties, recalled in 1842 that he 'had been Ground Officer in Kerrera since his Father's death upwards of eight years ago; his father was Ground Officer for the period he thought of about forty years, and he understood

Gylen Castle; in the foreground, 29th Chief Col. A.J McDougall of MacDougall 1872–1953

his grandfather was also Ground Officer for some time'. It was surely daughters of this family who married into the MacIntyre (school teacher) and MacKinnon (Leac houses) families.

Before Patrick's death in 1826, the missing Brooch of Lorn, raided in the 1640s, was restored to Dunollie. Campbell of Lochnell, a trustee for the family who had held it in secret, arranged to hand it back at a private celebration at Inveraray Castle; but since Patrick was too aged to make the journey, his second son John, deputised for him. Alexander, the eldest son was killed in the Peninsular war in 1812; his mother confided the news of her recent loss to Sir Walter Scott as they walked along the shore near Dunollie.

John (25th) married Sophia Elisabeth Timins, and entered the Navy, and later became Admiral. Sophia had a deep concern for the tenants – especially during the hard years of the potato famine. Since much of John's sea service was spent in the Far East, many were the letters, beginning 'My Dearest MacDougall' full of Kerrera news and problems, which crossed the seas in the sailing ships.

II GYLEN CASTLE & SINDRIE HOUSES

The oldest standing building on the island is Gylen Castle, and like many of the lesser dwellings it was probably built on the site of an earlier fort. A traveller visiting Kerrera wrote that 'its southern extremity is a promontary exhibiting noble cliff scenery, and crowned with the strong tall roofless tower of Gylen Castle.'[1]

Built as a fortified residence, fortification has obviously been given priority, both in the choice of the near impregnable site, perched across the narrow neck of high cliffs, and its construction as a tower of defence, with trebly guarded entrance, gunloops and gunholes, and observation outlooks on all approaches.

Gylen Castle is also gloriously sited for scenery, and being a small tower built of local stone with a beauty of proportion, it fits well with its surroundings. In their *Castellated and Domestic Architecture of Scotland* (1887) MacGibbon and Ross describe it as 'a little architectural gem' and this seems so fitting that it has been quoted ever since.

The stonework itself gives satisfaction, and the walls are a mosaic of the varied rocks of Kerrera, and banded black limestones, slates, breccia quartz and granite boulders from local conglomerates are set among the more predominant shales and sandstones. The latter, quarried from exposures along the south coast, has been used for the lintels, stairway and corner stones. At one time much of the exterior stonework was hidden when the walls were ivy-clad.

There is also beauty in the varied details of the exterior carving and sculpture. Delicate chequered corbelling caps the walls of the north-west turret; revived dog-tooth carving surrounds the oriel window on the north wall, with a line of cable moulding below the window-breast, suggesting craftsmen in love with their work.

This north wall is further ornamented with carved faces and figures, becoming increasingly weather-worn. It used to be said that the masks best showed their characteristic moods when the slanting rays of an early morning sun lit up the features. A fine stone figure with an Elisabethan ruff, and three-inch circular brooch below, was removed for safety when it became liable to fall. There is another figure on the right of the oriel window, with arms akimbo, and a head, with winged coif, below the inscription on the window-breast.

The castle is entered through a vaulted passage which goes under the building to the grassy courtyard in front, bounded by now ruined walls which include the small limits of the cliff top, with a sheer drop on three sides to what was the sea level before, geologically speaking, it became a 'raised beach'. Remains of two or three sea-stacks, now partly grass grown, among the jumble of rocks below, have gathered the tradition that they were used as pulpits in times of religious unrest.

Seen from the courtyard is a grand and often sparkling sea-scape – Mull to the west, mainland to the east, and ahead the islands of Seil, Luing, Scarba, Jura and the Isles of the Sea.

Stone figure from north face, Gylen Castle

At the re-entrant angle of the passage a doorway leads into the building, giving access both to the vaulted cellar alongside the passage, and to the stair way. Unlike Dunollie Castle, the great wedge steps of the stairs spiral up in a sunwise turn, giving access to the three main rooms, one above the other; and also to the small south-west turret which housed a spiral stair to the gabled caphouse of the main stair tower. The larger north-west turret contained a small apartment, and from it what a view there must have been! This district, in the seventeenth century, was a busy part of the island, with cattle from Mull landing at Ardmore on their way to the marts, an inn for the drovers, and the meal mill near the shore below the castle, powered by water from Gleann Mor and Gleann Beag. Much nearer, outlines still to be seen in the moulded turf suggest a community of little homes beside the castle.

On the first floor is the main hall and kitchen combined. Dominating it, against the east gable wall, the arched fireplace has stone jambs over two feet thick. Here stood a large iron firebasket, with its pair of swees, on which hung chains and hooks so that the big cooking pots could be raised or lowered, or swung away from the heat of the glowing peat fire.

Opposite, in the thickness of the west wall, is a small stone sink whose drain neatly connects with the privy on the left, and both to the latrine drain running down the outside of the wall to the rock below, and adding, incidentally, to the architectural interest of this western face.

Probably the main hall was simply furnished; the floor strewn with rushes, and cruisie lamps with peeled rush wicks and fueled with fish oil, supplemented the glow of firelight at night. It has good windows to the east, south and north, and a peep-hole to the west. The window of this room and the one above, both of which have gunloops, are attractively set in a recess, which, in the upper room is capped by an arch. This upper room has the additional feature in the north-west corner of the arch supporting the turret on the north-west angle of the tower. Each of the three main rooms had its fireplace, and in the present ruined condition it is interesting to see the arrangement of these in the east wall.

The top room had the oriel window projecting over the main entrance, and it is suggested that stones etc. could be dropped on attackers below, or boiling liquid rushed from the nearby fireplace and tipped over. But in spite of the castle's apparent strength, and the skill of its defence, its life of human occupation was seemingly barely sixty years.

Above the oriel window was a stone with the date 1587, and below, the initials

D MD . D

V.B.M.

It is assumed that this indicates the date of the building, and the initials on the marriage stone of the first occupants. It has been suggested, more recently, that the date on the stone could read 1582.

It was therefore apparently built in the time of Dougall MacDougall of Dunollie and his son Dunacn, 15th Chief, who obtained a charter from James VI in 1596. Timothy Pont, map maker of the time has marked on his map showing Kerrera, the castle as 'Dun Donachy' – Duncan's Fort, suggesting that at first it may have gone by the name of its owner, rather than the district.

Below the window is the inscription, now probably too weathered to read, but earlier in this century a rubbing was taken; parts of some of the letters were missing but the meaning was:

> Trust in thy God, and in not men,
> My son do well and let them say.

At the time when the castle was burnt, the people of Kerrera and the Clan MacDougall had little heart to trust in men. Not long before many of them had been

TRUST · IN · THY
GOD · AND · IN
ME · ME · MY
SIN · DO · VEIL ·
& LAT · THAME · SA

Inscription on Gylen Castle

in Dunaverty Castle, Kintyre when it was successfully besieged by General Leslie. When his troops cut a trench to draw off the castle's water supply so that 'there was not a drop of water but fell from the clouds' the garrison were forced to seek conditions of surrender. Accepting these, they were in fact 'inhumanlie butchered in cold blood John MacDougall being then a child and in nonage was only spared.'

It was this same John, by now the 19th Chief since his father was among the five hundred massacred at Dunaverty, but not very much older, who was in Gylen Castle in about 1647 when Leslie and his men arrived to besiege it.

It seems possible that it was the position of the water supply that was the weak spot in the castle's defence, and the cause of its failure to withstand attack. It has been thought that there was a well in a small hollow on the left of the approach before the passage walls are reached, and in 1960 this was confirmed by a professional water diviner, Mr. Robert Ballantine of Markinch, Fife. Here his cane indicated water, and he felt sure it would spring at the level where the conglomerate of the castle cliff rested upon the lower sandstone, such as is indicated in a rock pillar above the shore northwest of the Castle.

Whether or not Leslie commanded the water supply, he was evidently in a position to dictate terms. Tradition has it that when the castle was burnt the Campbells took possession of the Brooch of Lorn which had been in MacDougall possession since they took it from King Robert Bruce on August 11 1306.

Two centuries later, a visitor to the castle wrote that 'the edifice appears as if it

GYLEN CASTLE, ISLE of KERRERA

BUILT 1587 BY DUNCAN MACDOUGALL, 16ᵗʰ of DUNOLLIE,
RECONSTRUCTION (BELIEVED TO BE AS AT THE ORIGINAL DATE
EXCEPT FOR WINDOWS, WHICH WOULD HAVE TIMBER SHUTTERS)

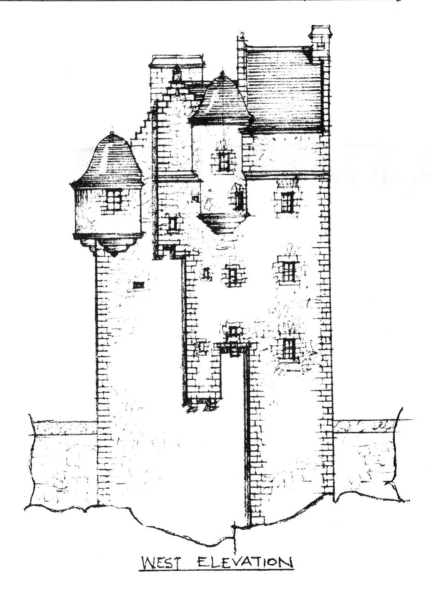

WEST ELEVATION

(This and following 3 pages): Architect's reconstruction of Gylen Castle, believed to be as at original date: west, north, east and south elevations

NORTH ELEVATION

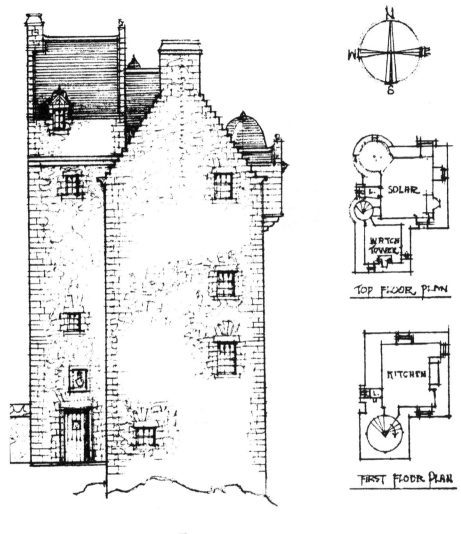

TOP FLOOR PLAN

FIRST FLOOR PLAN

EAST ELEVATION

Leslie Grahame MacDougall.
RSA · FRIBA · PPRIAS · PSA(SCOT.)

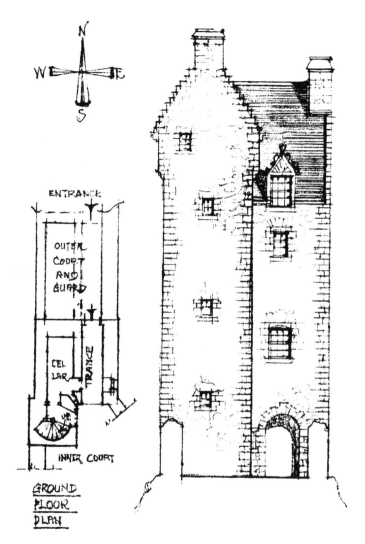

N
W   E
S

ENTRANCE

OUTER
COURT
AND
GUARD

CEL
LAR

ENTRANCE

INNER COURT

GROUND
FLOOR
PLAN

SOUTH   ELEVATION
SCALE for ELEVATIONS ⅛ inch = 1 foot
SCALE for PLANS 1/16 inch = 1 foot

had been dismantled by fire', for the building was never restored. From time to time it has been repaired, notably in the 1850s and in World War 1, when restoration was being considered before the war made it impossible.

There is a small cave below the castle in the cliff and tradition claimed that this had been used as a dungeon or a hidden store. Investigation has shown nothing to confirm this.

Old maps mark Kerrera's townships and old documents refer to the 'sindrie houses'. The sites of the dwellings have mostly remained traditional. Buildings, made from materials at hand in the landscape by the people who were going to use them, have been succeeded by buildings partly or wholly constructed of imported materials, built by men whose profession was building.

Eight names of Kerrera habitations have for long remained constant; their spellings have not. In some cases the least used spelling is the one on contemporary maps.

In the following brief notes, no attempt has been made towards conformity, which would be uncharacteristic of the variations in documents, formal and informal, of different centuries and decades. But in these brief notes the modern map spelling is given first, followed by some others used or in use.

Starting at the ferry from the mainland, and moving sunwise round the island:

Ferry House
Portnymichar (1660) Portinmicher (1790) Port Kerrera.

Formerly there was an inn or changehouse, with brewing and distilling; boat-building and boat repairs. From 1879 the island's Post Office.

Ardchoirc
Ardchoiric (1654), Ardchoirk, Ardchork (1660) Ardichork, Ardawhork – 'height of the cornfield, 'hill of the oats'. The farm overlooks The Horseshoe Bay, and Dalrigh, 'the field of the King' (Alexander II).

More recently a row of houses for slate quarriers, followed by lobster traders, at The Little Horseshoe Bay.

Gylen
1572 Geylen Gerlan (1654) Gyllan (1669), Ghealin, Geylin, Geyline, Geulan. On an 1849 gravestone – Gaylen.

Sixteenth century Castle (marked in Blaeu's 1654 map as Doun Donachy – Duncan's fort, but named Gylen Castle). Three farm dwellings, old meal mill, weaver, quarries, an inn or changehouse which served the neighbouring Ardmore ferry traffic, brewing and distilling, salmon fishing.

Ardmore

Ardmor (1654) Ardmoir – the 'great height', 'high hill'.

An old ferry to Auchnacraig, Mull, and fanks for collecting the droves of cattle and sheep; salmon fishing.

Barr nam boc

Barnabuck (1654) Barnabock, Barnambock.

Old ferry to Auchnacraig, Mull (1750s) for passengers, beasts, cargo and mail. Changehouse, brewing and distilling.

Slaterach

Slaterich (1654) Slatterich, Slaterach, Slatragh, Slatrich, Slaughterach.

Eighteenth century meal mill, eighteenth century Dunollie dower-house. Bronze age burial site.

Ardantrive

Ardentryve (1654) Ardentrive, Ardintra – 'Hill of the swimming'.

Cattle-swim across to mainland. During part of eighteenth, nineteenth and part of twentieth centuries belonged to Earls of Breadalbane. Boatbuilding, repairs and harbour. Seaplane servicing station for a time in World War II.

Balliemore

Ballemore (1654) Ballemoir (1660) Balliemore, Ballymore, Ballimore Balmoir, Baillemore, 'the great township' – blacksmith, weavers, tailor, school, and later school/church.

It is interesting to try to trace the changes in the eighteenth and nineteenth centuries, as suggested by rental agreements, estimates, accounts, diaries and letters – buildings to house humans and beasts, crops, kilns and watermills, inns, schools and Church; walls to enclose land, piers to receive boats.

> All and haill the sex merklands of Gyllan with the milne thairof, together with all and sindrie houses, biggings, yard, tofts crofts grasseings sheallings annexis part pendicles and partinents of the same lyand in the isle of Kerrarie within the Lordship of Lorn and the Sheriffdom or Argyle.

So runs the legal jargon of April 18 1669.

What were they like, these sindrie houses and biggins which clustered in the 'wintertowns' of Balliemore, Slaterach, Barr nam boc and Gylen, the homesteads of Ardmore, Ardchoirc, Portnymichar and Ardantrive?

Two and three centuries ago there were many small thatched buildings to house the several families who each had a quarter or sixth share of a farm, and the cottars with their small crofts, as well as the men who served the community – millers, change-house keepers, ferrymen, blacksmith, weaver, tailor, and later school and school teacher. And the families had their own little barn, byre and their share of the kiln.

1773 – all six barns and six byres with the kiln in Bailmor.
1786 – the oyr small houses annexted to the publick house at Barnabuck.

Successive clauses in tenants' agreements bring the picture more clearly into focus.

1760 – N.B. All the tenants at their removal, both on Kervera and the Main are obliged to leave their whole biggies sufficient in timber, stone and thatch, and yr kail gardains sufficient under comprisement, Twelve merks is the allowance for each insufficient couple or that which is quite ruinous in timber stone or thatch.

More details of the buildings themselves in 1779 and 1786:

to leave yr dwelling house and barn consisting the house of three couples with two stone gewells or gewell trees worth 20 sh the couple and the barn of two couples and two gewells of stone or two gewell trees worth allso 20sh the couple and the two gewells to be computed as a couple. Doors of the house and barn worth 2sh each, and to leave 40sh worth of a kiln, and a door to it worth 2sh.

Before an outgoing tenant removed, there was a valuation by certified 'comprisers', and the following account indicates both the type of buildings and their worth. Both were a part of the Dunollie estate, near Kilmore, and suggest similar conditions to those on Kerrera.

Houses compraisement the year 1794.

Dalnanaines	Change hous	8/-
do	barn	3/6
do	byre	15/-
do	kiln	3/6
do	brewhous	5/6
Cleigh	brewhous	9/-
do	peathous	16/3
do	byre	£1 9/-
do	kiln	13/2
do	stable	2/-
do	barn	0 /0

We, Hugh McLugash miller at Oban and Dugald MacDougall in Molie Sworn compraisers did view and examine above the mentioned houses and find the Dificienties to be just the sum as above this we did according to the best of our knowledge as witness our hand.

    Dugall // MacDougall   Hugh McLugash
         his mark

The agreement requires the buildings to be 'sufficient' in timber stone and thatch, and these were the three building materials locally procurable.

Kerrera's varied outcrops of rock, as well as the stony shores and screes, provided material suitable for building the biggins, usually of partly dressed stone. Quarries were opened in different parts of the island, of slate, lava and sandstone. There are ruins of houses and huts built entirely of slate in the Gylen district. Massive slates or flagstones were carefully chosen as lintels above doorways and fireplaces.

Of the three building materials perhaps the most difficult to come by was wood. There was a period in Scotland when the efforts of owners of land to grow wood were frustrated by people who were against tree-planting, and who pulled up by night saplings planted by day. Perhaps this accounts for the seemingly stiff clause in the 1779 Kerrera setts:

> they are to save the growing timber or to pay each five pound scots for each tree or breech of a tree cutt or to discover the transgresser.

Wood was needed for the 'couples' to support the roof. As the stone walls of the building were rising, the bases of couples were built into them; these were pairs of stout branches, usually with a natural curve so that they arched towards each other to meet at the apex of the roof. If suitable complete arches were not to be found, two pieces were pegged together to give the same result. They were also pegged with wooden pegs where they met at the top, or both pegged to a short joining cross-bar. Sometimes the wood was artificially bent to give the right curve, as shown in an account for a mainland farm:

> 1731 Jan 12 – three oaken couples of timber imployed in Colgine, cutt in Ardoran and bending said couples £15 scots.

The same account refers to 'timber got att two different times for the houses at Ardmore.' By 1840, when wooden pegs and nails were giving way to blacksmith made iron nails and bolts, the smith supplied: '... four screwbolts for couples 10½ lbs @ 5d – 4/4½'.

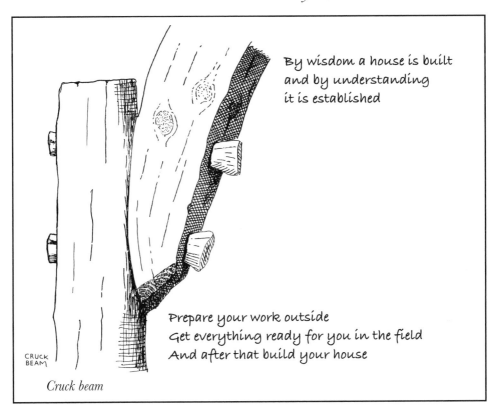

By wisdom a house is built
and by understanding
it is established

Prepare your work outside
Get everything ready for you in the field
And after that build your house

CRUCK
BEAM

Cruck beam

Couples were precious – the most precious part of the building since they were the most difficult, as a rule, to replace. In some districts a man leaving a house might take the couples with him for building his next house; hence the clause in the Kerrera setts that they must remain. Support was needed for the roof about every seven feet, so a house twenty-eight feet long might need three couples between the supporting gables. In 1830 it was complained that the front wall of the byre of Balliemore was 'a little bulged on account of the couples being placed too far apart in the middle of the byre.' The initial framework for the roof covering was strengthened by fixing less substantial branches and sticks between the couples.

Hugh MacLucas and Duncan MacDougall comprised the following materials at Ardantrive at a valuation of the roof in 1776:

4 oaken joists @ 10d	3/4
6 side sticks of birch @ 4d	2/-
8 birch or aller (alder) joists @ 4d	2/8
The whole cabers of the lofts	3/-

Chambers's Scots Dialect Dictionary defines 'Cabers – the small wood laid on the rafters under the roofing'. In 1798 Ardantrive was referred to 'as the only good house' but that was after it had been rebuilt in 1783.

Over the framework of branches, heather turf or sods were laid, often skilfully sliced off the ground with the flachter spade so that thinner edges neatly overlapped the thicker. The roof was then ready for thatching.

Kerrera has a plentiful supply of rushes, and before the extensive draining, it probably had more. It is said to take about two days cutting to get enough for one days thatching.

The last house to be re-thatched with rushes was the old house among the trees above Slaterach mill, lived in at one time by Iain Ciar's widow from Dunollie, and later kept watertight by rethatching for use as a potato store. It is said that about the time of the last war a group of campers abused the hospitality which the island had extended to them by setting fire to the thatch. Since many of the houses were thatched with straw, special provision was made for this in the rent agreements.

How much straw was needed to thatch the house? In 1786 Mr. MacGregor of the Barnabuck public house was to receive from the other Barnabuck tenants 'yearly thirty-two fathoms of straw for thatching the dwelling house and his portion of the kiln, and eighty straw roaps alongst with the thatch'. A fathom seems to have been as much straw as a man could embrace with his outstretched arms.

The straw for the 'roaps' was twisted with the help of a 'thrawcock' or some such simple device with a handle that revolved, twisting the rope as it was fed from the fathom. The ropes were made of a length suitable to throw over the roof to hold down the thatch against the winter gales; sometimes they crossed it from side to side. Usually the rope ends were weighted with stones hanging in a row along the eaves, tied to lengths of wood, or to pegs or stones jammed into the wall of the house. There is an account of 1862 'to thatching & repairing houses on farm of Ardmore £3 10/- Heath ropes 10/-'.

The little houses were mostly put up by the families who occupied them, and repaired and re-thatched as required. There was, however a professional builder, one John MacMartine, who is mentioned as having made several buildings on Kerrera about the middle of the eighteenth century.

1746 Nov. – Compted with John MacMartine for building ye kiln, and ows him 7 merks of qch he has gott a wedder. All since paid.
1748 – John MacMartine built the Ferry house and milk house, Port Kerrera.

He was, as was customary, paid 'in kind' and drew his meal etc. over a period of about three months. The items include:

Oatmeal – 14 stone, 1 furlett.

Barleymeal – 3 stone, 3 furletts and 5 lippies
Cheese – 4 stone, 6¹/₂ pounds.
Butter – 4 stone.
A fou.quet of salt.

Some, at least, of the meal was got from the Slaterach Mill; there was also a cash payment of £1 1/-, the whole account valueing £4 11/2.

In 1749 he built the house at Barr nam boc at £3 10/- and in 1751: 'John McMartin his accost for building fishing hous qch I agreed for 10 pound Scots.'

Dr. Garnett, in his *Observations on a Tour through the Highlands and part of the Western Isles of Britain in 1778,* passed briefly across Kerrera, and recorded that 'the island which is very hilly, contains seven hamlets, or groups of miserable huts, and is divided into as many farms.' Such a superficial view of passing travellers was not unusual at the time – especially if they had not been privileged to experience the very real quality to be found in the homes of the fine type of Highlander who met hardship and poverty with dignity. Nor could they appreciate the beauty of the traditional building materials which blended with the landscape from which they were drawn.

Often the household plenishings were few; one man's possessions in 1841 were 'two bedsteads with bedding, two chests, one table, one dresser and wrack with stoneware; two pots, one boyne (flat milk basin) a churn, one chair and two stools.'

About the middle of the nineteenth century the prevalent mood of change was seeping into Kerrera, and with it new methods and imported materials in dwelling houses and farm buildings. Slate roofs began to replace the thatches, and some of the new houses built upon old sites had an upper story. Walls were lime washed, windows had sashes, floorboards laid across sleepers replaced the traditional hardbeaten earth floor, often covered with a layer of fresh sand.

When Mr. Archibald Livingstone moved from Ardchoirc to Gylen in 1854 'he was exceedingly urgent ta have flags for the floor of his new house'. He was therefore authorised to 'get the house flagged after ascertaining the reasonable expence of it'. Seemingly 'Caithness Flags were very difficult to be got at present and would cost about 5/6 a yard' so Mr. Livingstone 'was to try to get flags at the slat quarries at Gylen, and failing that at Easdale.'

The earliest references to farm buildings concern the barns. Whether they were alongside the dwelling house or separate they were built in the same way as the dwelling house, with two or more wooden couples, their bases built into the walls, about half way up, their uppers arching across to hold the roof. In 1756 the outgoing tenant must either leave '20sh sterling in lieu of his barn, or a barn equate to that sum'.

The doors to the barn were 'computed' as worth 2 shillings each, and very often

Cruck beam and ventilation hole in a Kerrera byre

the barn had two doors exactly opposite each other. This allowed for a through draught, which was important for flailing the corn. The corn sheaves were laid on the floor, a few at a time, their heads overlapping inwards, between the two doors. With the wind in the right direction, and the right strength to blow through the barn and carry away the chaff, thrashing could begin. The flail was made very simply of two pieces of wood hinged together, very often with a thong of sheepskin. The longer piece of wood was the handle, and with a skilful twist the shorter rod was swung behind the head and brought down on the sheaves to knock out the grain. Although the flail was a simple and effective implement it needed much energy and skill to use. Yet a lady of ninety-two said recently she believed if she had one she could still use it, as she enjoyed the work. In her younger days she used to sneak out to the barn when the men were on the hill, and flail a pailful of grain for the hens, to make them lay better. People differed in the way they laid the sheaves for flailing – some in a circle, heads inwards, some in facing lines.

In 1856 a tenant at Dunolliebeg wrote 'the corn… here has been secured in excellent condition, and the sample of proof sheaves may be thrashed any day. On examining the floor of the barn, however, I find that it is in a very bad state, and any corn thrashed upon it will be much injured. Instead of patching it up it would be better to have a wooden floor put in, which would be a permanent improvement.' The Roup Roll of sale of farm implements belonging to the previous tenant showed among the items 'thrashing floor 5/-'. Apparently portable threshing floors were not unusual at the time.

The older barns had no windows, but when ventilation holes were made in the Kerrera barns, byres and stables they were often triangular openings, lined with three slates or shale flags. The base made a useful ledge for the odd horseshoe or bottle of archangel tar. Some of the farm buildings have their walls pierced with tubular drainage tiles; haybarns have long vertical slits to allow good draught.

In 1868 Duncan Cowan sent an account for 'making group and causing Byer at Ardmore' – that is for making the open drain (group) which ran behind the cows' tails through the muck hole to the midden outside, and for flooring the byre with pavings or cobbles.

About the end of the nineteenth century some of the Kerrera farms installed threshing machines powered by one, or a pair of horses, which walked round and round a circular platform outside the barn, attached to a rotating arm connected to the gearing of the threshing mill inside. Traces of these circular walks can still be seen.

A little building, then so important in the lives of the Kerrera communities, slipped out of use and even out of sight, from the farming scene during the nineteenth century. This was the Corn Kiln, and although there are many references to it in the eighteenth century, it is difficult to trace even the ruins now. Before grain could be ground into meal it had to be dried to a hardness suitable for grinding. Oats taken to the mill was usually dried there on the perforated metal floor over the kiln, but most of the farming communities shared the little corn kiln on their farm. When the barley had to be 'kiln drayed at harvest' and when the mainland miller was 'to send to receive it in the tenants' kilns' it was in the farm kilns that it was dried.

In 1746 Dunollie 'compted with John MacMartin for building ye kiln'. In the following year, when there was a new tenant at the Barr nam boc Change House, he promised 'to put sufficient timber and stone upon the ground for a kiln before the 1st of July next, and the said John MacDougall (changekeeper) is to bild it.'

As mentioned elsewhere, the innkeeper at Barr nam boc was to receive from the other tenants sufficient straw to thatch the inn and 'his portion of the kiln,' the other tenant was obliged to thatch and keep in repair the 'oyr half.'

1779 – keep sufficient the kiln at Ballemore and also at Port Kerrera.
1786 – Slaterich to leave 40sh worth of a kiln, and a door to it worth 2sh.

Corn kilns varied in different districts, but perhaps this description from Loder's

Colonsay and Oransay of the Colonsay kilns may be suggestive of the Kerrera Kilns.

'Colonsay's new mill provided facilities for drying the corn; the kilns belonging to individual holdings ceased to be used. These kilns were circular, six to eight feet in diameter, with dry built stone walls, thatched roofs and one or two doors according to size. The floor was excavated two or three feet into the earth. Here the peat fire was lighted under cross timbers, over which straw was laid, and the corn was spread above this to dry.'[2]

Beautiful examples of corn kilns are to be seen in Shetland, and these were in use within living memory. The well-built little towers, open to the sky, were attached at one end of a barn, and the flue from the fire in the barn ran up through the tower to dry the grain. Apparently Kerrera's kilns were free standing. Presumably they went out of use about the time when it was more convenient to buy meal from the mainland than to thresh it with the flail and grind it at the watermill.

III MERKLANDS

Formerly the lands of Kerrera were measured in *merks*. The merk was a measure of value rather than of area, dating back to the thirteenth century and based on how much land could be valued at one merk, that is 13/4.

The acre, now in use as a land measure, was established in the reign of King George IV, and in 1835 his successor abolished local and customary measures. An acre originally indicated the amount of land a plough could work in a day. Kerrera's twenty-nine merklands were thus divided:

Gylen	5 merkland	Balliemore	6 merkland
Ardmore	3 merkland	Ardchoirc	3 merkland
Barnabuck	3 merkland	Ardantrive	5 merkland
Slaterach	4 merkland		

For the purpose of letting the farms were reckoned in horsegangs. It required four horses to pull a plough, and if it was a four horsegang farm it was likely to have four tenants, each of whom would provide a horse to pull his share of the plough, and who would himself pull his share of the work.

As can be seen from examples from 1747 tacks, the shares could be allotted to suit tenants.

The four merkland of Slaterach, a four horsegang farm was rented in four equal shares:

Lauchlan McDonald	$^1/_4$ share,	Allan McDougall Sen.	$^1/_4$
Hew McDougall	$^1/_4$ do	Allan McDougall Jun.	$^1/_4$

Ardchoirc, a three horsegang farm was shared between two brothers, who took a horsegang and a half each:

Dugald MacPherson the one half
Duncan MacPherson ye oyr half.

Gylen was a five horsegang farm, but in 1747 was shared among seven tenants, in the following proportions:

Ronald MacDougall	1/6th	Donald McPheterich	1/6th
Duncan MacDougall	1/6th	Angus MacDougall	1/12th
Sorle MacDougall	1/6th	Dun. MacIllichoan	1/12th
Dugald McCoan	1/6th		

the last two tenants only having half a horsegang each.

On the other hand, Balliemore, an eight horsegang farm was shared among six tenants:

Duncan MacDougall senior 1/4th
Duncan MacDougall youd (younger) 1/8th
Dougall MacDougall 1/8th
Donald McLauchlane (3 horse gans equally betwixt them).
John MacLauchlane

In 1786, the Port Kerrera ferryman had a quarter share of Balliemore, and 'he pays rents equal to two horsegangs of Balemore, and all oyr services and prestations in the same proportion.' Sometimes the rent book refers to portions of farms, or to other tenants in the words 'as oyr plews'.

Before considering some of the details of Kerrera's farm tacks, it is perhaps worth noting the farming situation of one of her island neighbours.

After the disturbances of the first half of the eighteenth century more attention was being given to the cultivation of land, improvement of stock, and experiments into more productive methods.

Patrick MacDougall, younger of Dunollie wrote his views in 1780 to his father Alexander:

If I may be forgiven to say so, most of the landlords with us pay too little attention to the breed of their cattle by having proper bulls, a proper kind, and properly
stocked. Everyman, I am satisfied, must attend to his estate as he does his family.
If production of the lands are capable they should be suited to the crops and articles for which there is a demand. Therefore two principles I would lay down –
moderate rents and keeping the land in good heart.

In this respect, one of the most successful of the Western Isles was Colonsay and its smaller tidal neighbour Oransay, lying south of Kerrera. About this time there was a connection by marriage between Dunollie and these islands. Mary MacDougall of Dunollie, born 1741, was the last daughter to be born in the old castle, before the family removed to the modern dwelling below. She married Alexander MacNeill, whom Pennant described as 'the go-ahead tenant of Oransay' and also remarked that the small island impressed him as being better managed than Colonsay, although the soil inferior.

Their eldest son John, later known as 'the Old Laird', was given 'a sound agri-
cultural education which enabled him to become one of the foremost agriculturists of Scotland'.[1] In 1805 he bought Colonsay from his cousin, and it was later said that

the forty years during which he was laird were the most prosperous Colonsay and Oransay had ever known.

There was much correspondence between Dunollie and these islands over several decades, and it seems possible that some of Colonsay's successful methods may have been reflected in Kerrera's search for improved farming methods.

Oransay 12 March 1802

Dear Uncle,

… The seed corn is very much at your service if I knew how to send it – the *Martin* goes immediately to Liverpool with a cargo of potatoes, and if they meet with a good market will most probably bring another there. If there is any opportunity before the 25th of this month I will send the oats, if not it will be needless to think of it.

All here are well and join in best wishes to all at Dunollie and Ardintrive & I am,

Dr Uncle, yours affectly
John MacNeill.

As was usual in the West Highlands, the Kerrera arable lands were divided into 'infields' and 'outfields'. The infields were nearest the township, within the 'winter-town' and most accessible to the community. They received the most attention and manure. The outfields lay beyond, at some distance from the farmsteads, and although frequently cropped received little manure and required periods of rest before they could be induced to produce a fresh crop. However, in the latter decades of the eighteenth century the Kerrera leases encouraged tenants to manure the outfields and bring them gradually up to the standard of the infields.

1779 – to lay yearly on either outfield or infield shell sand or some oyr kind of manure.
1786 – to labour two outfields yearly and two parts of yr infield.
1793 – to add one of the outfields to yr infields.

The infields were shared by the tenants of the farm, and divided into strips – rigs – for different crops; oats, barley, potatoes and flax. Each man's strips were not necessarily adjacent, since the intention was to share the good and less good lands fairly among the tenants. On an appointed day the strips were measured out by line and allocated amongst the tenants by the groundsman.

1779 – Slaterach … and divide your infields if not already done.

A few years later, at this period of changing agricultural methods, two documents suggest interesting landmarks in the island's farming history.

The first is a short note in a Dunollie account book of 1798:

> to joining the Riggs to be sowing with oats in the mass 4 men @ 9d per day –
> £1 2/2.

Thus it took four men seven and a half days to level the ground ready for a whole crop of oats. As fewer families tenanted the farm, and carts and improved implements made a larger area workable the rigs of the 'runrigg' systen were flattened to make a field of a single crop.

The second interesting landmark concerned tenant's use of the land. Previously they had lived in houses clustered together, as a small township, their beasts sharing the common grazing, their crops growing on adjacent strips. In 1812 a new agreement was drawn up between Dunollie and the three tenants of Slaterach, by which the land was divided into three parts, on which each tenant was to build a house and barn and byre, and enclose his portion:

> Conditions upon which Patrick MacDougall of MacDougall setts the lands of Slatrich in the Island of Kerrera to the present possessors of this Farm. He agrees to give them a lease of above form for twelve years, from Whitsunday eighteen hundred and twelve … As they made out their different allotments by dividing the farm into three divisions *Sloch* possessed by John MacDougall seer. *Drimcock* by John MacDougall jun. *Runalich* possessed by Lachlan MacKinnon the money rents paid by each of them is well known by themselves and is marked in my Rental book, and as to the Victual and other Prestations they are to pay and return jointly. In regard to John MacDougall seer. in Sloch has built a dwelling House and Byre attached thereto, likewise a Barn, which I am informed is sufficient and how soon he finishes a sufficient fence round his lot of the farm with a stone wall of three feet and a half high with a double feel Turff upon the Dyke, but where stone cannot be got but at a very great expence the Fences are to be made in the most substantial manner they can be done.
>
> John MacDougall junr. has built a Barn upon his lot of the farm and so has Lachlan MacKinnon built a fuelling house and a Byere attached thereto on his division which I am informed is sufficient, when John MacDougall junr. builds a sufficient dwelling house and Lachlan MacKinnon a sufficient Barn and when both John MacDougall and Lachlan MacKinnon performs and Implements the Building of their Dykes and fences in the manner described to John MacDougall seer. in Sloch, then they shall have their leases upon Stamp paper at the Proprietor and their mutual expences upon the terms set forth. They are to be allowed two

years from Whitsunday eighteen hundred and thirteen to finish their dykes and houses and no longer. They are to Plough and Mannure their lands in a proper and regular manner and upon no account to take three crops following on the sane ground unless the third is to be a green crop, that is to say potatoes, grass seed or turnips… No cottars or householders are be be admitted to reside upon any of the above three lots without the consent of the Proprietor…

Signed at Dunollie the sixteenth of March eighteen hundred and thirteen.

    Patrick MacDougall

    John X MacDougall Sen.

    his mark

    John MacDougall Bun, (own writing)

    Lachlan X MacKinnon

    his mark

Writing in the seventeenth century, Martin Martin remarks about the Lewis cultivations:

> the best increase is commonly from ground manured with seaware … the natives … dig the ground with spades and in most places they turn the ground so digged upside down and cover it with seaware; which certainly produces a greater increase than digging or ploughing otherwise.

A hundred years later, it was said of Mull 'the chief manure made use of in this island is seaware, and in some parts shell sand.'[2]

In the early nineteenth century, the 'Old Laird' on Colonsay was having great success with improved crops for feeding his fine cattle stock, and it is recorded:

> in order to produce such crops, and also to reclaim the quantities of waste ground, Collansay must have a good supply of good manures. These consist of shellsand, seaweeds, common dung and composts made of those materials. One third dung and seaweeds, and two thirds peatmoss with the scourings of ditches made a very goad compost, and frequently serve Mr. MacNeill's needs for his greencrops.

The use of seaware still continues in many places for the simple reason that potatoes grown in the old island methods are so very delicious – large clean tubers of excellent flavour.

The right to gather the seaware for dressing the land was carefully apportioned among tenants at the north end of Kerrera. It fell to the groundsman to see that the people of Barnabuck and Slaterach gathered the ware within their allocated boundaries. Included with the shores of Balliemore lands were the offshore islands,

Fraoch Eilean in the Sound, *Eilean na Gamhna* and *Eilean nan Uan* to the north-west.
   Much effort was also made to make up the deficiency of lime.

> 1768 – they are yearly to lay out 600 loads of lime shellsand or of composition of dung in lea ground.
> 1779 – to lay yearly, either outfield or infield 400 loads of shell sand or some oyr kind of manure.

With lack of roads and wheeled carts, the seaware, the shell sand and the dung, unless pulled by sledge or slyp had to be carried on the back of man, woman or beast.
   Much is made of the necessity of liming in the 1810 Kerrera leases:

> As both the proprietor and tenants suffer greatly from the manner the farm is managed, and neglecting to manure the same properly, the tenant is obliged possessing a markland to lay out during this lease three pounds ten shillings sterling or to the value thereof in sheal sand or line in the wintertown or in the outfield as thought most advantagious in the sight of the proprietor, and should it not be convenient at the time for tenant to pay the money, the said proprietor will give the cash or his credit to the extent required for six months … and should the tenants lay out more than the above in sheal sand and lime, the proprietor will give them a credit for a twelve month without interest.

In a letter of July 1817, Dunollie wrote to his son:

> It was one of my agreements with the Tennants in the Mainland to give them sheal sand for manure. I freighted a vessil at Oban to go to Collonsay for sand, and Peter, Lucy and Mary took the Benefit of this Conveyance to see their friends eight days ago.

Lime was also imported from Lismore, where the old lime kilns and buildings can be seen, especially by the shore at Kilcheran seven miles across the water to the north west.
   In 1842, Allan MacDougall, Ground Officer, stated that 'it was the practise on Kerrera for the incoming tenant to pay the outgoing tenant for any lime he might put on the outfield to be cropped the year of his removal; the outgoing tenant being only bound to cart the lime from the shore to the lands.' He went on:

> The practice on Kerrera is to put sixty Bolls of slocked (slaked) lime on the acre of lea land … A boll of shell lime yields two of slocked lime. The price of a boll of lime in shall, delivered in Kerrera, is ninepence unslocked. Carting of the neces-

sary quantity of lime for say $2^1/_2$ acres of lea land on the farm of Ballemore would occupy two days of two horses and two carts in carting it from the shore to the said lands.

At the beginning of the twentieth century artificial fertilisers were regarded with distrust, and this injunction was included in all the Kerrera leases: 'Tenants shall not top dress their crops with nitrate of soda or other stimulating manures'. There was also the usual clause: 'Tenants shall not sell any straw or manure raised on the land'.

The shepherd and the herdsman would seem to have an older history than the cultivator of crops; and few parts of the world have such fine all the year round grazing as Britain. It has been suggested that grain growing only makes much profit in abnormal times of overseas crop failure and in time of war. Many old farm leases had a clause deterring the tenant from ploughing up existing grass land, and thus reducing the value of the farm.

On Kerrera the little crops were the lifelines of the people and in times of poor transport it was essential to have the food growing close at hand. There were, however, in different periods, some injunctions concerning ploughing the tacks.

1779 – they are to plew no third field unless they divide yr outfields into seven parts;
1812 – they are to plough and manure their lands in a proper and regular manner.

At this time there was a regulation concerning the 'outgoing tennant and income in the farm of Balemore: The Crofts – two thirds of the arable land to be in tillage and one third to be left lea. The Park – two fields in tillage; Ealarly and Lagchinnich and the Wintertown, reserving Duchnapuch for the income tenant to plant his potatoes.' It is evident that much thought went into trying to make the best use of the land in the period following the old runrig system.

Again concerning Balliemore in 1818 the tenant:

shall have liberty to plough and break up one third of the Winter town that is within the limits of the present tenants possession of the farm, and one outfield, and no more during the period; that the said third of the wintertown and field shall be properly manured and cultivated yearly, that they shall have liberty to take a small part of the field of Ellary close to what is called the Hay Park nearly bounded therewith, but in the event that they will take on the said piece of ground in Ellery then when they break up a field they are to leave out an equal portion of land in that field unbroken.

1834 – in year of his removal shall not have more land under crop than the average of the three years preceding … not to break up any new land beyond the regular lea break.

Now most of Kerrera's cultivated land has gone back to grazing, to carry a fine stock of cattle and sheep. Human food is imported; the making of meal and butter a thing of the past.

The growing of specific crops, or varieties of crops, are occasionally directed in the Kerrera farm tacks. As mentioned elsewhere, encouragement was given in the West Highlands to the growing of flax, and this was reflected on the Kerrera farms:

1768 Slaterach … to sow four pecks of lintseeds.

In that year, and in following tacks throughout the island: 'to sow no small (or grey) oats'.

After an alleged misuse of land by the outgoing Balliemore tenant, in 1842 Angus MacKinnon, tenant in Slaterach was called among witnesses. In giving evidence he describes his methods on the wintertown of his own farm:

It is the practice for a field to be in grass for one year; on the following year he takes a crop of oats therefrom, and the next year a crop of potatoes, the next year bear, barley or oats sown down with grass seeds. After which he allows it to lie out a year in grass, and then follows the rotation already mentioned.

He went on to say that, as far as he recollected, he was the first tenant in Kerrera who commenced to sow grass seeds, and this was nearly twenty years ago. Within that same period he was in the habit, where he did not sow grass seed, to take two white crops (barley or oats) in succession after the potato crop in the same field, in the wintertown – previous to the introduction of sowing grass seed.

Formerly, he explained, the practise on Kerrera in regard to the outfield land, was to teathe them by letting the cattle and sheep lie out in them at night, and also after being milked for some hours during the forenoon, and then to take two white crops off the outfield in close succession 'Generally', he said, 'a farm consists of six outfields and two of them are yearly under crop, having the crop taken off each in succession, after which they lie out in natural grass or pasture until it again comes to their turn to be broken up, which would be in four year's time. It was within the last twenty years the practise began of using lime for the outfields before being broken up, instead of teathing (teath – a cattle dropping).'

By the middle of the century a five-crop rotation seems to have been in operation

– not without its critics, as the elderly tenant of Port Kerrera croft explained. He had three sons at home, but two were required at the ferry, and it was as much as the third could do to work the land, as he himself was too frail to do much, and since he had been housebound, to adhere to the five-crop rotation had not paid so well as it used to do.

The new century leases for the island stipulate that

> The tenants shall be at liberty to pursue any system or rotation of cropping which shall not waste or deteriorate the land, but during the last five years of the lease they shall be bound to cultivate on the five-shift rotation and leave the land under that rotation at the termination of their lease. Outgoing tenants shall be bound at their removal to leave on the land all the growing grain, ryegrass, turnip and potato crops … The incoming tenant shall have liberty to sow grass seed among all grain crops …
>
> The outgoing tenant shall have no claim for any sown grass above one year old, which with all hay ground he shall be obliged to hain or preserve from April 1 preceeding the Whitsunday of removal.

(The word 'Hain' means to preserve grass for hay.)

In 1934 the 'tenant obliged himself to cultivate the arable land according to the most approved method of husbandry … and in the last year of tenancy to harrow, free of charge, the ryegrass and clover seed properly sown with the corn of that year the said seed being provided by the ingoing tenant at the time.'

'There are no enclosures, so that herds are continuously employed to keep cattle from the corn, and from encroaching on the different farms, a mode very prejudial to Agricultural improvements', commented the traveller who rode across Kerrera for the Mull ferry in the July of 1798.[3] Possibly his anxiety to catch the ferry made his observations somewhat casual, for his impressions are misleading.

As the rent and account books show, there was quite a programme of dyke building in Kerrera, begun some decades before his visit. Feal walls, that is walls built of turf, were built in many parts of Kerrera, for various reasons, among them to influence the path of cattle when they had landed from the Mull ferry and were being driven across the island to the point where they were forced into the sea to swim to the mainland. Strategically placed turf walls not only eased the job of the drovers but did something towards saving the tenants' lands.

A brief reference, in 1768, to the 'Kerrera Dick' may perhaps suggest the start of building the long drystane dykes, which later spread across the farmlands.

In all the 1768 new eleven-year leases there comes a clause, not previously mentioned; 'leave in sufficient repair at yr removal march dicks that will be built about any part of the farm.' And in this same year there is an account for 'the expence of Dick of Gylen being a hundred and ninty roods thirty-one pounds.'

In the next year was built the 'Mile park Dick qch measures ninety-four roods. Duncan McInish for building, leading and quarrieing the stones at 3sh 9d per rood, seventeen pounds, nineteen shillings and two thirds penny'. Payment was made, as was customary, in a mixture of cash, meal, money for shoes, a horse, a filie, a bull and eight pecks of barley.

At the start of the new leases in 1779, some, if not all of the march dykes had been built: 'Gylen … and leave all yr march dicks sufficient to preserve the planting upon yr farm.' The tenant of Balliemore was to 'leave the march dick between Ardantrive and Balliemore sufficient,… and to leave the haill stone dykes upon the said lands hinging and standing and the ditches and Earthen dykes in sufficient repair.'

The next concern was to enclose the cultivated ground within the farms themselves, and in the leases of 1786 comes the injunction to 'leave yr corn fences sufficient, as also yr kaille garden dicks,'

There is some indication in the account books of the type of dykes that were built, and the cost of the labour.

> 1790 – James MacColl, undertaker for building the Dick in Dunollie –
> three foot and a half, stone two rows caping
> leading, quarrying and building 4sh ye road,
> you to provide the quarrieing tools.
> To caping 7 roods of your dick 1sh 2d.

When in 1812, the Slaterach ground was to be divided into three separate portions for three tenants, new enclosures were required, according to the following specification:

> a sufficient fence round his lot of the farm with a stone wall of three feet and a half high, with a double feel turff upon the dyke; but where stone cannot be got except at very great expence the fences are to be made in the most substantial manner they can.

With an outgoing tenant came the valuation, and now it was necessary to value the dykes as well as the buildings, and 'Comprisers' were called in. The following comprisement for a mainland farm within the parish is written out in a really beautiful copper-plate hand and if the sum involved is not very great, it has the importance of a job conscientiously undertaken:

A Bill of Comprisement of the Dyke of Barnacarry built by Archd Gray, June

10th 1793

>   To the deficiency of said dyke   £0 9/-
>   To do. of Kail Yard   2/-

We, Neil MacCulloch Dykebuilder at Ardoran, and Angus MacInnes Dykebuilder at Penifure, Sworn Comprisers have viewed and examined the above mentioned Dyke and we find the Deficiency of it to be as above eleven shillings sterling (including the Kail Yard). This we did according to our best skill and judgement as witness our hand this day and date as above mentioned.

Angus X MacInefs   Niel N.M.C. MacCulloch
his mark   his initials

Accounts of 1839 mention stones quarried at 2/11 per rood, and dykes built at 3/- per rood.

In 1857 there was a valuation for the head dykes at Gylen Park;

	£
Head dyke, east, 77 roods @ 6/- per rood	23 2/-
Credit for building head dyke, east	12
Valuation of Head dyke west, 15 roods @ 7/-	5 5/-
20 May 1857	

The head dykes were important, since they divided the cultivated land from the hill grazing. Later, cross dykes partitioned the farmland.

As long as the ground was unfenced, precautions had to be taken to prevent the beasts getting at the growing crops. The new policy of enclosing ground, in time altered the farming pattern, but the change came gradually.

It was the custom, when the crops began to grow, and until harvest, for some, at least, of the family, to take the cattle to graze on the high ground, and ruins of possible sheilings are to be found where they may have sheltered in the summer months. There are many references in the rent books to the 'wintertons' – the main settlement of the households in autumn, winter and spring: 1754 'winterton at Gyline,' 'wintertown of Bailemor.' Besides this, someone was appointed to herd the cattle of a township for the tennants, and the crofters paid him according to the number of their cattle:

1779 – Barnaboc to pay two pecks of meal for herding each cow.
1786 – John MacDougall to herd the Parc, Gylen, for the whole year.
1786 – all the crofters to pay to the tenants of the farm two pecks of meal for herding and watching out for each cow for summer and harvest.

and no doubt there would always be the indiviual cow that needed some 'watching out for'. In spite of precautions, accidents were almost inevitable, and in 1786, 'whatever corn or barley that is destroyed by either cows, sheep or horses, the valued damage to be paid double in stook in harvest.'

There is an account of 1753 'for ye Ardmore Ditch'. It was in the next century however that there was a great programme of draining and ditching in Kerrera, in which every available man took part. The rate of pay varied between 1¹/₂d and 3d an hour, or from 10d to 2/- for an 8 hour day. Twenty-six were employed in 1838 at 'Ditching at Gylen', and these included tenants, sons, brothers and farm servants. The older men managed a few hours, sixteen or so, and some put in a hundred hours.

In the summer of 1840 seventeen men, from Gylen, Ardchoirc, Balliemore, Slaterach and Barr nam boc, worked at 'deepening the Ditch to take the Water off the Peat Moss top of Ardihorck hill.' There is a note: 'Dun McArthur Blasting 6 days full time. All the others wrought about 6 hours each only per day'

Apart from communal efforts, each farm was concerned in improving the ground, and draining off surplus water. April 1850. Lower Gylen: 'They have deepened and straightened the burn, levelled the ground and altered the road so as not to cut up the field, and they have made a little bridge over the burn. They have likewise drained a tract of land that required it; the ground is now all sown, and looks nice.'

Like most of the Hebridean Isles, Kerrera's natural vegetation has great charm, as the seasons go by – a very brief glimpse in the passing:

Wild Angelica	Common skullcap	Halbert-leaved	Trailing St. John's
Hemlock water	Curled dock	orache	wort
dropwort	Ragged robin	Buckshorn plantain	Knotted pearlwort
Fool's watercress	Hedge parsley	Ratstail plaintain	Common cudweed
Brooklime	White deadnettle	Sea arrow-grass	Fairy flax
Water pepper	Heath milkwort	Sea plantain	Grass of Parnassus
Watercrowfoot			Redrattle
Marsh pennywort	Blackspleenwort	Heath grass	
	Sea spleenwort	Crested dogstail	Toad rush
Smooth	Lady Fern	Cocksfoot	Jointed rush
Hawk'sbeard	Sweet Fern	Meadow fescue	Chestnut rush
Corn marigold	Hard Fern	Red fescue	Saltmarsh rush
Wild carrot	and of course	Flote grass	Moor sedge
Marsh willowherb	Bracken	Reed grass	Carnation sedge
Sun spurge			
Dove'sfoot cranesbill			

IV   CROPS AND BEASTS

Oats

Timothy Pont, at the beginning of the eighteenth century, is reputed to have written that Kerrera was 'profitable of corne' and corn may be taken to mean oats.

While it is the ambition of every farmer to do better than making two seeds grow where one grew before, at this time 'the common crop was a very inferior kind of oats, which the inhabitants call small oats… the common return is three seeds, and so light that two bolls of oats only make one of meal.'

This 'small oats', the grey oat (*Avena brevis*) had a double awn, grey husk and small thin kernel; but it had some value in that it could produce a crop where a more useful variety might fail. However, in 1760 the Kerrera rent book has an entry 'Boll white corn' and this heralded the cultivation of a variety which was to supercede the old grey oats and bring increase to the community. This was the white or great oats (*Avena sativa*) also with a double awn, but having a fatter kernel and a greater yield. The superiority of the white oats over the grey was such that in the farm tacks of 1786 came the injunction to 'grow no small oats'. That some mainland farms were still growing both varieties in 1793 is shown by an account of crops on a Kilmore farm, which also shows the difference in price which the two varieties fetched:

> to 3 bolls white (great) oats @ 13/- per boll   £2 [*sic*]
> to 9 bolls grey (small) oats @ 7/- per boll   £3 3/-

Elsewhere it is recorded how the Minister of Kilmore insisted his stipend meal must be of white oats.

A traveller passing through Kerrera in 1738 'saw several patches of oats and barley looking tolerably well' and they were probably grown on 'lazybed' strips scattered between crops of potatoes and flax. In the Outer Isles, where corn is still grown in this way, it is sown by hand from a bucket, refilled from a sack. As the size of the Kerrera corn fields extended when 'the riggs were joined to be sowing oats in the mass' (1798) the sowing sheet was used, hung from the sowers neck leaving both arms free to male the graceful rhythmic sweep as the seed was scattered along a regulated breadth of soil. The crop was cut with scythes or sheared with sickles, and men, women and children were busy at the harvest.

Even in the 1880s much of the actual shearing was done by the women with sickles. A diary of 1881 notes:

> Sept. 1 – women commenced to cut the corn.
>   3 – a good deal of corn cut
>   10 – men at work opening out and setting up corn.

12 – some parts of corn secured.

17 – the rest of the stooks got in.

Children learnt the skill of making the bands to tie the corn sheaves – before the advent of binder twine. Two handfuls of cornstalks were tied at the heads to make a double length to tie round the sheaf, with a special flick of the hand to tuck the ends in tight.

If the oats were to be ground the corn had to be dried; a small quantity for home use could be heated on the girdle over the peat fire before being crushed in the stone hand quern. Larger amounts were dried in the cornkiln or at the mill. A distinction is made between 'grindable corn' and 'horsecorn' – the latter was the small corn which fell through the riddle and was used for the stock.

A successful oat-crop was of great importance to the family, for besides being exchangeable for necessities, and helping towards the rent, it could provide, or eke out, every meal in the home.

> Porridge hot,
> Porridge cold
> Porridge in the drawer
> Nine days old.

The custom of making a large boiling of porridge on a Saturday or Monday to last a week, and pouring it into a wooden drawer in the dresser to settle was fairly wide-spread – certainly it was done in Mull, and for want of definite evidence it can be assumed it was formerly done in some of the Kerrera homes where the peat fire was never let out. And for a very practical reason. Although it was easy, if the fire had been smoored overnight to bring it to useful life in the morning, yet it would take some time from a slow start to boil a pot of porridge in the morning; but it would soon heat up slices cut from the drawer and put in a pan with a little milk. If the cow was dry, the porridge could be taken with ale; there is a special wooden bung with a tap which was used to draw off the ale from the barrel. Squares of porridge were also cut from the drawer to be wrapped and later eaten cold when the man was out on the hill, or building a distant dyke. Once a week there was a fine scouring out of the porridge drawer, sometimes with clean sand, ready for the next week's filling.

A favourite drink, and one most refreshing at the haymaking, was made with a handful of oatmeal stirred at the bottom of a jug of cold water and topped up with buttermilk, or just plain water, with, or without sugar.

Still spoken of with relish are 'Sowers' made from the bran or inner husk of the oat kernel, saved from the milling. These were steeped in a wooden vessel until sour (if a taste on the tongue makes you shiver they are ready) and then strained into a pan. The liquid was thickened over the heat, and made a lovely white white pudding, taken with cream, a sprinkling of sugar or perhaps syrup.

Brose was made by stirring boiling water into a bowl of oatmeal; bread, bannocks and oatcakes made with oatmeal were baked in a pot-oven or on a girdle over the fire, and dried off on the wrought iron toaster.

To cure a sick fowl a ball was made of fresh butter and oatmeal and pushed down its throat. The newly calved cow had a warm drink with a handful of oatmeal stirred into it.

Barley

'In all Kervera the year that the barley does not grow and they cannot pay yr farm barley, the tennants are only chargeable sixteen shillings and eightpence for each undelivered boll', runs a tenants agreement in 1760.

For the barley not to grow, or the crop not to be harvested every few years, was an unfortunately prevalent disaster. Notably bad years were 1740, 1756, 1762, 1782, 1795 and 1799, 1812 and 1816. The failure in 1740 accounted for a famine which resulted in great hardship and death. In later years, when the potato became widely

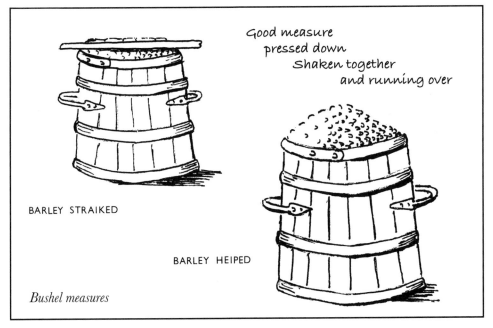

Good measure
pressed down
Shaken together
and running over

BARLEY STRAIKED

BARLEY HEIPED

Bushel measures

cultivated, peoples' lives were not so acutely dependent upon the success of the grain crops.

The barley usually grown was 'bere' (*Hordeum Sativum vulgare*) the ear having four rows of seed. Although it was fairly prolific, the actual grain was lighter, and the yield not so heavy as some varieties which needed better conditions. For in poor ground bere often produced a crop where other strains would have failed to grow, or been flattened by wind and rain, or matured too late when the season was bad.

Normally bere was reckoned to give an increase of from six to ten seeds, but it has been known to produce sixteen-fold on mature ground well dressed with seaware. Probably the Kerrera harvest benefitted from being thus fertilized.

In the rent agreements of the latter half of the eighteenth century it was usually required that about a fifth of the 'farm barley' (rent barley') be 'delivered in harvest kiln drayed' either to the mainland mills or to the Kerrera or mainland change houses, which Dunollie had agreed to supply. Some went to the Minister as part of his stipend. There were two methods of measuring the grain. Fill a bushel measure with as much as it will hold – Biblically speaking 'running over', and this is barley 'heaped' (or 'heipd). Fill the measure and draw a flat straik across the mouth – sometimes a rolling pin was used – and this is barley 'straiked'.

'Sent to the miln before the first of September of the crops of 1722 years – five bolls and three pecks of straiked barley', is noted at Dunollie. A later account book heads one page: 'Accost of Barley Streaked Cropt 1732' and the next 'Accost of Barley Heiped Cropt 1732'. In England there were Innsigns 'Bushel and Straik'.

As mentioned elsewhere, the changehouses at Gylen, Barnabuck and Port Kerrera distilled and brewed producing aquavitae 'whisque' and ale. It came naturally to use the barley grown on the place, the local water and peat to make the drink of the country, and Government interference was much resented when it sought to control distilling. It was the barley crop, when distilled, that brought income, as a letter of June 1780 points out:

> … the distilling is entirely knocked in the head. What to make of the farm barly I know not. It is a disappointment of nearly £100 yearly to me, and the poor tennants, the boll they had to dispose of will get no price for it. There is no such thing as cash – Duncan (his son, of Ardantrive) is squised to the Back bone for it – as I observed to you before, stopping the distilling will ruin this country.

However, the situation was presumably changed in the next decade for Kerrera's barley growers, and they found a new outlet for the crop when a large distillery was opened on the mainland, in Oban.

Oban's distillery was built in 1794 when Oban was a small fishing community. It stands against a cliff rising to 400 feet, and draws from peaty uplands water reputed to be of splendid quality. The old kiln was peat fired, and the whisky a pure Highland malt, and a good self whisky.[1]

Some of Kerrera's barley crop went to supply grain for the maltings, as the following account shows:

Soft barley delivered to the Distillery at Oban.

1819 Feb. 3 from tenants at Barnabuck		6	bolls
do 19 do do	Gylen	16	
do 19 do do	Ardmore	8	
do 27 do do	Ardchoirk	6	
Mar 13 from John MacDougall junr		7	$3^{1}/_{2}$
	at Slatrich	43	$3^{1}/_{2}$

Bere bannocks – barley scones – are still remembered as being made in Kerrera. Barley meal was made by grinding the whole grain after the outer indigestible coat had been removed, but leaving the inner, rich in proteins; thus the meal was probably much more wholesome than modern meal, which, with a desire for apparent 'purity', loses part of the useful food.

Bere bannocks, which are rather dark in colour, are still made in Orkney, and also in Shetland when the barley meal can be got. An old recipe tells how to make them:

Put half a pint of milk into a pan with a pinch of salt and a good nob of butter. When it boils add enough barley meal to make a pliable dough. Turn it out on a floured board, roll out thinly, and make into rounds about the size of a meat plate. Bake on a hot girdle on a rather sharp fire. Turn once.

Another memory is the rich creamy barley pudding, golden pink within, baked in the oven with a crisp shiny dark brown crust – much superior to puddings made from imported grains!

Flax

'In every croft a rig was set apart for the growth of flax; and the women of the early part of the last century were skilled in the details of the various stages in the process of linen manufacture' writes Ian Cormack in his *Island of Mull* (1923).

The growing of flax, and the spinning of its fibres for weaving into linen, was given much encouragement in Scotland in the eighteenth century. In 1727 the Board of Manufacturers offered a premium of 15/- the acre for growing lint; they also allocated £150 for encouraging children to learn to spin lint.

This was reflected in the pages of the Kerrera account books:

1745 – Accott. for lintseed

To the tennants of Gylen	3 pecks
To the weavers there	2 pecks
To Duncan MacLachlan	2 pecks

To Alickna Kaird   a fourth of a peck.

It was reckoned that two and three-quarter pecks of lint seed would sow a quarter of an acre, a middling crop from which would produce 8 stone of lint.

In 1768 came the injunction to the four tenants of Slaterach in their eleven-year tack:

Yr to sow yearly 4 pecks of lintseed. Payment of part of the rent in 'Linnen' continued until 1793.

Garnett noted in 1798 'Flax is cultivated here.'

Linum usitatissimum – the Common Flax. The word 'lint', now obsolete in this sense, was formerly used both for the plant and the fibres which it produced; also obsolete is the 't' in lintseed.

The plant grows two or three feet in height, and the blue flowers, about an inch across open in succession on the stem, so the blueness of the patch is prolonged rather than solid. In the best tissue of the stems are bundles of long fibres; when separated from the outer straw and the inner pith they provide the yarn for linen – flaxen in colour with a silky lustre.

The plant grows well in parts of the Highlands, enjoying a kindly loam, but producing fair yields on sandy or peaty soil. It does, however, exhaust a soil so that successive crops require a change of ground. On the Kerrera farms the strip of flax in the annual rotation of the runrigs would make a nice glint of blue among the other crops.

Cultivation included clodding, i.e. clearing the ground of clods, leaving a fine tilth, sowing broadcast in the spring, weeding in summer and pulling up by the roots by hand in early autumn in dry weather – the growing of this crop involved a good deal of hard work and judgement. Too early pulling meant soft, weak fibre and a poor yield; too late, a dry coarse fibre wanting in spinning quality. A hundred days was considered an average period from seed to harvest, if weather conditions allowed.

Then followed the preparation of the lint for spinning. The pulled plants were tied in bundles, sometimes by a few strands of rushes – and these were steeped in water to soften and partly rot the tissues – a process called 'retting'. Although tradition has not pointed out the 'retting pools' on Kerrera – as it has on Islay, for instance; it is easy to imagine that where its soft water gathers the pools would be ideal for the process.

After a week or two, depending upon the warmth of the water, if the outer straw of the stem broke away readily, the bundles were taken from the pool, untied, and spread out thinly on the grass to dry out and bleach. After they were turned for even drying, the stems were lifted and stored under cover. Then the plants were broken by beating with a wooden spar. Then came the 'scutching' with iron combs, 'heckles' to comb out the woody parts of the stalks leaving the silky glossy fibres for spinning.

Potatoes

'The Kerrera potatoes allso had a promising appearance' in 1798.[2] Potatoes were said to be well established in Lorn by 1767.

A Dunollie account book has an entry in 1734: 'Potatoes 2 pecks', and in 1736 Dunollie was paying his account with the 'Tobacco spinner' in potatoes valued at 6d a peck. He sold 5 pecks between September 13th and October 30th. These would probably have been grown as a garden crop, often the nursery for future field crops.

Potatoes were apparently never paid 'in kind' by the Kerrera tenants and it is not clear when the first were planted in the island. By 1768 their cultivation had become part of the 'services' to Dunollie and the setts of 1780 laid down: 'Any removing tenant is to leave the equale half of his potato ground for the Income tenant in his place but need not give him any ground he has manured but must give him the eqivalent in unmanured ground.'

The old potato beds can still be made out from the shape of the turf moulded in long stripes in many parts of the island, and they show cultivations of the higher ground, particularly near the old road from Balliemore along the hills to Gylen and Ardmore.

A visitor to Mull in 1798 records:

Potatoes grow extremely well here, they are sown in lazybeds by the spade and are the chief substance for three quarters of the year. Before the introduction of this most useful root, for which we are indebted to America, the distresses of the Highlanders, and particularly the Western Isles, were frequently very great. Depending on a little meal, which constituted the chief part of their food, their hopes were frequently blasted, their corn rotted in the ground. This failure of crops through a long continuance of wet weather, happens every third or fourth year; potatoes now prove a comfortable support through the winter when grain and meal fail.[3]

Equally enthusiastic was Duncan MacDougall, tenant of Ardantrive, who wrote from Ireland where he was stationed, to his brother at Dunollie in October 1801:

You have acted very properly as to your potatoes – you should not touch them till their crops are withered, and I beg you to advise my Folks to do the same. The weather here at present would be reckoned delightful in August, no man alive remembers such a season as this. The potato crop is reckoned at double of what

Old Kerrera lazybed workings, still moulding the turf

it was ever known to be. Will you believe me when I tell you I saw three potatoes that grew in a field near town that weigh above three pounds each?

These were the good days. Half a century later there was trouble. 'Potatoes used to pay at least my half year's rent; now they only *assist* in feeding ourselves for two or three months', said the tenant of Slaterach in 1850. He went on 'I have not sold a boll of corn this year, in fact I have been obliged to buy. Stirks sold for little more than half their former value potatoes few or none.' These were the bad years, the years of the Irish potato famine when the disease reduced the heavy crop – the money-makers and life-sustainers of other years – down to a trickle of 'few or none'.

A Dunollie letter to her husband in the Navy records:

At first the potato disease has scarcely proved so bad as was anticipated, but this continued wet is much against those in pits, and of course many have not houses to store them in, particularly as they require to be thoroughly dried and placed in layers. Ours have not gone much, and the pigs and poultry have been fed on the diseased ones after cutting out the affected parts.

About this time a scheme was going ahead to erect a Potato Mill at the Oban Tannery, at the north end of the town, to be run by steam costing 'a very large sum of money.' This was to make potato flour, to try to save the potatoes before they had a chance to rot with the disease. Next spring the situation was worse:

> In consequence of an extremely wet autumn the rot got into the potatoes, and some of your tenents have lost 40 out of 50 barrels... out of 45 carts dug here, 5 were destroyed, and had I not made the men open the pits eight days after they were dug, and aired and dried the whole, putting some up with dry sand and some with lime, our loss would also have been serious.

Urging for a reduction in the tenant's rent, she writes 'it is well to bear in mind the tremendous loss the potatoes have been for the last six years.' Such quotations from the mid-nineteenth century, apart from underlining the real hardship of the times, also show how heavily the community had learnt to lean on the potato crop – on the tuber which was scarcely appreciated a hundred years before.

Kerrera had a high reputation for its potatoes, and especially for the early crops grown on sunny slopes of a farm facing towards Oban; they were in special demand from the town's grocers. *The Farmer's Calender* (1823) remarks about the different varieties of potatoes 'they are endless, and fresh sorts coming every day into notice, till they give way to others in succession'. A Dunollie account book of 1838 notes of potatoes harvested '*Pink eyes* and *Calicos* – 116 barrels. Purple Kind in pit, 40 barrels'.

Cattle

Grazing land was reckoned in 'soums'; a soum was the number of cattle, horses or sheep proportioned to a pasture. The number of beasts to grazing varied in different localities depending upon the quality of the grazing.

On Kerrera one soum was the amount of grazing required by one cow, half a horse or five sheep. Each of the farms was allocated its number of soums. The proportional division between horses, cows and sheep might differ over periods, and soums might be added to, or taken from, crofts which were part of a farm.

A 1768 'Memorandum of the souming and holding of each farm on Kervera' shows the allowance for cows as:

Ardmore	12	Slatterich	40
Gylen	48	Ballemore	60
Barnabuck	28	Ardchoirc	24

Barnabuck croft	6 soums (
Ferry croft	6 soums (whole
Miln croft	8 soums (grazing.
Gylen croft	4 soums (

Allowing for the crofter's cows, the number of cattle grazing on Kerrera at that time was about two hundred and thirty-four.

A writer at the close of the eighteenth century says that 'the Mull cattle are very much esteemed; their flesh is fine grained, juicy and well-tasted. They are easily fattened when removed to the Low country or to the rich pastures of England.[4]

In Colonsay and Oransay the MacNeills were making great efforts to improve the breed:

The breed preferred by John MacNeill is the West Highland or the real ancient pure Hebridian, improved by good management, and by selecting the handsomest pairs as breeders. He is partial to the pure black colour, the long, close and healthy pile of hair. He has gradually increased the size, … because by judicious management of turnips, potatoes grasses and winter housing he can afford to keep a larger stock than the old treatment admitted of. He is, however, by no means an advocate for enlarging the breed rashly in the Hebrides, or going beyond the accommodation the grazier has in his power. He annually rears two hundred calves… They are well fed, carefully housed in winter and bad weather, and have an abundance of succulent food… in February, March and April, when a considerable proportion of young Hebridian stock annually perish from want. After his turnips are finished he gives them potatoes boiled with steam, sometimes mixed with boiled barley.[5]

While John MacNeill was in the forefront of improving the quality of the Highland breed, in 1798 the Highland Cattle Society offered the first premiums for its improvement. Some decades later, in 1830, Ronald Campbell in Ardantrive, competing in the Mid and Netherlorn district won the prize for the best bull. John Stevenson in Balliemore won a silver medal and several first and second prizes for bulls and heifers in the years 1859–63. In later years more prizes were to come Kerrera's way.

Some of the terms written in the old lists of cattle have gone out of present use.

1722 of great cows and three year olds
      of tow year old stots
      of cows now year olds
1729 of tidie cows

of farrow and stirks
of buls tow.

The 'tidie', or more usually written 'tydie' cows were those in calf, or with calf, as
were the 'great cows', differing from the farrow cows; stots were the young cattle
beasts or bullocks.

Apart from the great cattle trysts, which attracted drovers from all over the country
there were local roups. Kerrera buyers attended a 'Sale of Cattle at Roup in Soroba
May 6th 1768.' It is interesting to read how the lots were offered, and the prices they
fetched. The twenty-two 'tidie cows' made a total of £92 odd, and the 22 farrow cows
and 11 stirks £75 odd. The 9 Heifers £17 odd and the one bull sold for £3 14/-.

All the tidie cows were sold as either in calf or with calf and made from £3 to £5
each. The dearest went to Donald MacDonald, smith, Barnabuck, at £5 1/6. John
MacDougall drover in Barnabuck bought a cow and her calf for £4 5/6 and Neil
McLea in Port Kerrera 'a couple and calves' totalling £7 15/6.

Next came the Farrow Cows, and these were all sold as '2 & stirk' at prices from
£6 to £7 15/-. John MacDougall in Barnabuck paid £7 for his three beasts. The
nine heifers were also sold in threes at an average of about £5 15/- each lot.

Another sales list of about this period shows prices:

30 couple Tydie cows @ £9 per couple
20 Dray & 4 yr old Hyfers at £4 each
10 4 year old & 30 3 year old @ £3 10/- each
30 three yr old stots @ £2 15/- each
55 two year olds at £2 5/- each
55 stirks at £1 10/- each
4 bulls at £5 each.
60 goats and bucks at 7/- each.

There was a 'Publick roup upon the lands of Tarbert… upon the 21st May, 1764 of
the Black Cattle and others belonging to the deceased Archibald Campbell of Jura'
at which Alexander McNeill of Oransay bought for his uncle at Dunollie:

41 stots at £3 6/6 each
40 stots at £2 11/- each

the total bill for 'Dunolly and Son, payll as a/c £238 6/6.'

So much depended upon the prices which the cattle made at the trysts, and debts
incurred during the year could only be paid when the money was brought back.
'… he told me to make the payment when convenient which I inform'd him would

be the case when our cattle would be sold – they were so a few days ago, payable at the return of the Drovers from the Dumbarton market, when the money shall be sent to you at the very first opportunity', a correspondent from Appin explains in 1784.

About that time much business seems to have been with the old tryst at Dumbarton; Duncan MacDougall (a younger son of Dunollie) building his new house at Ardantrive, wrote to his brother on 6 November 1783 that he 'expects to have it lodgeable by the time of return from Dumbarton market'.

When stationed in Ireland in 1798 he wrote home: 'I have heard nothing of the August Triste, I am afraid it will be a dull market. I writ Caddleton the number of cows I've to sell, and the kind. He is to come and draw them out according to my description of them'. He went on 'Beef here (Armagh) is pretty reasonable, 3d per pound and mutton 4d to $4^1/2$d; butter is high, meal 14/- to 15/- the boll'.

He wrote again to Dunollie in 1801:

My wife writes you labour'd hard for the sale of my cows, I confess the price is far beyond my expectations. The price you got for your own is a monstrous long one – eight guineas for two yr stots is a nice price.

I don't think you should be very anxious about beasts to winter, at any rate I would rather want a part of the number than buy cattle at such enormous prices, as I think there is little doubt that peace will affect the sale of Black Cattle and every other kind of stock. The Navy and the Army when disbanded wont eat so much meat and pork as they do now.

Meanwhile, John MacNeill was writing from Oransay of the high prices he was getting:

Oransay 12 March 1862

Dear Uncle,

… We have sold our four year stots and my three year olds at what we think *very good* prices, but we are not at liberty to tell out price yet you may judge it was good when we would sell them so early. Jura has sold, and several people in Islay. All here join me in best wishes to all at Dunollie and Ardintrive.

In MacDonald's *General view of Agriculture in the Hebrides*, a report of 1811, he remarks that John MacNeill's management of green crops is particularly good and improves cattle so that his 3 year-old bullocks sell at £10 to £14 compared with the more usual £5 or £6.

Later in the nineteenth century, the five years from 1840, John Clerk, tenant of Balliemore, was selling Black cattle on a large scale. By this time the big cattle boat was running from Port Kerrera to the Main, and in these years he ferried over twelve hundreds beasts, which, at 3d each brought the Ferryman a freight of £15 10/6.

A memory of visiting the Kerrera farms in the past which lingers was the great tumblers of milk that were offered, milk that was really rich cream, often poured from pink and gold fluted jugs. Pats of butter for sale were delivered wrapped in cabbage leaves.

Horses

November 19 1957 – 'The last working horse left Kerrera today as the only farm without a tractor has now bought one' – records a diary.

In her *Highland Folk Ways* Dr. I.F. Grant notes that until the 1930s it was unusual to see a farm tractor at work in the Highlands, and quotes figures for the years 1944– 59 for four Highland counties including Argyll which show an increase of tractors from 882 to 4887, and a decrease of working horses from 11,000 to 1,897.

At the time of writing Kerrera is not horseless; there are three on the island. But the departure of the last working horse because it was replaced by a tractor was an event mirrored on farms throughout the Highlands and Islands in the mid-twentieth century.

The importance of the horse to earlier communities is reflected in the use of the word 'horsegang' as a unit of ploughland. There is an amusing entry by someone in a hurry in a 1747 rent book for Slaterach – 'each horse pays'!

In 1766 the total grazing allocated to horses on the island, excluding Ardantrive, was sixty-seven: 'Ardmore 4, Barnabock 8, Ballemore 16, Gyllen 18 in winter, 12 in summer, Slatterich 12 in winter, 8 in summer, and Ardchoirc 8 in winter and 4 in summer.' The Ferry croft also had a horse. In 1747 the Changehouse keeper at Barr nam boc, John MacDougall, was to have 'the grass of a horse over the whole town'.

A horse was reckoned to eat twice as much as a cow, and required two 'soums'. Sometimes there were special injunctions concerning them:

Slatterich 1779 – souming of cows to be seven cows and a two year old, fifteen sheep including year olds, and two horses; to keep no mears with followers nor keep horses or sheep in place of cows.

A traveller of 1798 remarks that the Mull ponies 'seldom taste oats. These small ponies which are by much the most proper for the country, being a very hardy race, require little or no attention.'

Before the days of wheeled carts, the work of horse and man – or woman – some-times overlapped. The little horses pulled loads on sledges, or wicker carts on runners, or light harrows across the soil, and so did the people themselves. A pair of willow creels was slung across the pony's back; the men and women carried a single creel on their shoulders, filled with seaweed, shell sand, dung or peats.

A small boy wrote rather ruefully to his father – 'the pony fron Kerrera which I told you has been lent us has been sent back to Barnabuck as they require it to bring in the peats.'

An account of 1753 which indicates current prices for somewhat varied types of horses:

To 2 year old horse sold at foard (? Ford) market £4 10/-
Two oyr little mears £5 5/-
Ane old hipd black mear whose followers dyed last season of the fevere £3
Ane oyr little brown mear £2 10/-.

The 'hipd' mare was either hurt in the thigh, or, as seems possible, just wearied.

A Kerrera tenant tells the story of her grandfather, born about 1793, who lived in his retirement with his son at Ardmore. Making the trip to Oban one day, as usual on horseback, he had reason on his way home to call at the Carding Mill to see about some wool which they had sent there. When he came out, the mare had gone. She had carried on to Ardmore, swimming across the Sound to get back to her foal which had been left at home.

Sheep

When the sixteenth century Timothy Pont was concerned, as mentioned, about the 'many foxes on Keareray dangerous for sheep, greater than the ordinary and more bold than on the mainland for killing sheep' the sheep of that time would be rather different from the present breeds, and would be kept for rather different reasons.

Before the massive introduction from the lowlands in the latter part of the eighteenth century of the stronger cheviot and blackfaced breeds, the local sheep were small, with kindly whitish faces, and legs and fleeces varying from white, dun or parti-coloured. If they produced less wool, it was finer in quality, and the flesh sweeter. They were not unlike the Shetland sheep, but they were comparatively delicate and often housed at night in winter.

Each of the farms had its grazing 'soum' for sheep. In 1786 Ardmore's allowance was 30, Barr nam boc, Slaterach and Ardchoirc 60, Balliemore and Gylen 120, with the injunction that 'no sheep to be grazed in place of cows' in some but in others at the rate of '10 sheep or 2 cows'. The cottars, and all the families who shared the different farms, each kept a few sheep mainly for various domestic needs, and for paying the rent in kind, rather than for marketing as nowadays.

The hide itself was valuable, not only for shoes and other articles of clothing, but for many jobs about the farm. Stretched tight across a wooden hoop it made a winnowing sieve when holes were punched with a hot wire to let the grain through. Thongs were cut for joining the two parts of the flail, and used for binding and for

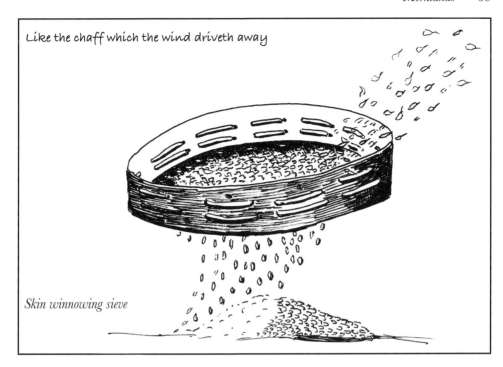

Like the chaff which the wind driveth away

Skin winnowing sieve

making hinges.

'Fatt lambs' or one- or two-year olds were paid as rent; and meat was dried or salted or smoked for the family during the winter scarcity. Mutton fat was melted for tallow, though possibly in Kerrera fish oil was mainly used in the cruisie lamps since it was readily available.

Perhaps most valuable of all was the fleece, which provided wool for spinning into clothes and blankets for the family, and in the latter half of the eighteenth century as part payment of the rent. A blanket was the customary wedding present. Some of the old blankets have ornamental circles embroidered on the woven cloth with wool naturally dyed in beautiful shades of yellows, pinks and browns. There were several weavers in the island, and probably most of the women could spin, either with a spindle, or a spinning wheel.

A 1737 Dunollie inventory includes: '2 small and 2 large spinning wheels; ane old check reel; 3 heckls; 2 pairs cairds; a warping stick and 2 windles, 5 woollen combs'. Also 'a webb undressed black Cloath 24 yd 10/-; 5 yard tartan at 6d per yard; 2 stone lint 14/-; spun woolen yearn 10/-, and woole 4 stone at 4/- per stone.' A hundred years later, the Kerrera tenants were not paying blankets as part of their rent to Dunollie; but Dunollie still needed blankets, and the Kerrera people were still spinning, and probably weaving. There is a 'Memorandum of Expences of woolen Blankets made for Mrs. MacDougall of Dunolly' payable to Mrs. MacDougall, Kerrera.

1838 May 15 For Spinning   10/-
    For Carding   8/-
    For teasing and Babbering   4/-
    For soap   2/-
    For indigo   2/6
    For walking   2/-
               £1 8/6

The indigo would dye the neat blue borders.

Another account, to D. Henderson, possible a mainland weaver:

1838 April 20 To weaving 49yds Blankets $3^1/_2$ per yd 14/$3^1/_2$
          To working one half (?) per yard   2/$0^1/_2$

An 'Account of Tartan Manufactures for Mrs. MacDougall, Dunollie shows:

1837 To Carding Mill   4/6
    To Dying   4/-
    To spinning   6/-
    To Babbering & teasing   4/-
    To soap 1 lb   0/6
    To weaving as p acct 19 yds
       @ 7d per yd   11/1
             £1 10/1

When, in 1958, I wove a similar length of MacDougall tartan at Dunollie, the 13lbs of red, blue, green, drab and white wool cost £9 8/3, and the waulking, done by Hunters of Brora, 1/1 a yard.

Smearing was the process of treating the sheep, and can just be remembered by Kerrera people as being done in their father's time. It was autumn work, just before the tupping season, as a protection against scab and other parasites, with the extra advantage that it was thought to protect the sheep from winter wet and cold.

It is interesting to read that a prospectus circulated in the late 1850s by the proposers of the Oban and Glasgow Railway compared estimates of traffic carried by steamers and sailing vessels round the Mull of Cantyre: Goods, Provisions, wool & Smearing materials 6000 tons. with an assumed estimate of what would pass over the railway: Goods, Provisions, Wool, Smearing materials 5000 tons.

Smearing was on the wane by the end of the 19th century, and practically ceased when it became compulsory by law in 1905 to dip the sheep in chemicals twice a

Smearing bench used on the farm when smearing sheep with butter and tar before the use of chemical dips

year. One farmer who remembers his father smearing says he gave it up because it was not only expensive but very slow work, much slower than shearing. Another remembers her mother's consternation when the smearers came into the house with blackened tarry hands. For the mixture used was generally butter and archangel tar, oil or other grease. The tar was measured into a barrel-half and the warmed butter or grease poured into it, which made it softer to stir. Rather more grease than tar was used; if the tar was too strong, it could burn the sheep's skin and since the grease thinned the treacley mixture, it went further. It took a gallon of tar, and about seventeen pounds of butter to do about twenty-five sheep. In 1753 Kerrera butter was selling at 4d (fresh) and 8d (powdered or salt) the pound. When the price of wool was high and the cost of labour low, smearing was practical, but when these conditions were reversed that it was superceded by a cheaper method.

Since the sheep had to be dry, the work was usually done under cover. In Islay there is a beautiful little 'smearing house', fern-covered, on one of the farms with arrangements for warming the mixture. Special benches were made on the farm, Balliemore had a particularly fine one. Similar to shearing benches, for which they are sometimes used, they were about four feet long, and eighteen inches high, on four legs. The bench top was the typical V-shape, twenty-eight inches at the broad end and ten inches at the narrow, with three rungs across. The worker sat astride the narrow end, with a bowl of the mixture at hand, sometimes clipped to the bench itself. If he was working on the back of the sheep her legs hung down between the rungs. With his forefinger he dipped into the mixture, and shedding the wool smeared the grease along the parting into the skin and the roots of the hair. The 'sheds' were made at one-inch intervals all over the body in a regular sequence. Since it was a slow business, working inch by inch, it was reckoned good if a man did a dozen sheep in one day. Often the work went on late into the October evenings, by the light of cruisie or candle. Smeared fleeces fetched slightly lower prices, but their extra weight usually compensated for this.

In his *History of Highland Dress* Telfer Dunbar quotes a Satirical poem by Lt. Col. Wm Cleland, 1698, describing a body of Highland troops, with an interesting reference to sheep smearing:

> Its marvellous how in such weather
> Ov'r hill and hop they came together;
> How in such stormes they came so farr;
> The reason is, they'r smeared with tar,
> Which cloth defend them heel and neck
> Just as it cloth their sheep protect;
> But lest ye doubt that this is true
> They're just the colour of tar'd wool.

It is said that at first the smearing did not show on the fleece, but when the heat of the body spread it through the wool it compacted it into a coat which conserved the heat.

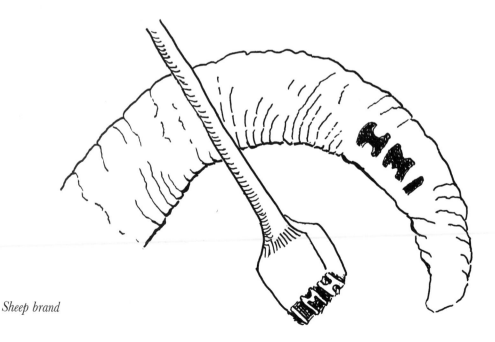

Sheep brand

When dipping became compulsory it was necessary for the farms to make arrangements for dipping baths, draining floors and collecting areas, contained within stone,
wooden, corrugated iron or more recently concrete boundaries. Much ingenuity was
used, but perhaps the most unusual arrangement is at a farm where use is made of
the steading walls.

The sheep are gathered in the steading yard, enclosed by the farmhouse, barns,
stable, cartshed and byre, and two gates. The fank is constructed round the end of
the byre, and part of two sides, so that only the outer boundaries of the pens need be
fenced with wooden spars. The original dipping tank is small, taking only one sheep
at a time, and the dipper stands in a concrete pit alongside.

Each sheep progresses from the yard into a pen against the front wall of the byre;
then she turns the corner into pens running along the end of the building. When she
turns the next corner, round the back of the byre, she is faced with the dipping bath,
and after an involuntary plunge into the disinfectant scrambles up the stepped slope
to the draining floor. When the liquid has dripped off her fleece back into the bath
she earns the freedom of the adjoining field.

SHEEP

And you, O seacoast shall be pastures, cottages for shepherds
and folds for flocks... and they shall lie down at evening.

I will search for my sheep and seek them out; I will
rescue them from all places where they have been
scattered on a day of clouds and thick darkness.

I will feed them in good pastures; there they shall lie down
in good grazing land, and on fat pastures shall they feed.

I will seek the lost, I will bring back the strayed,
bind up the crippled, strengthen the weak.

Is it not enough for you to feed on the good pasture,
that you must tread down with your feet the rest of
your pasture; and to drink clear water, that you must
foul the rest with your feet?

You push with side and shoulder and thrust at all the
weak with your horns, till you have scattered them abroad.

Clipping was done by hand, often on the shearing stools. With the appearance of
electric shears, however, these seem to be going out of use, and the sheep are shorn
on the ground. There is an account of a wool clip in 1839 which compares the average
weights of fleeces from three breeds, and the prices they fetched:

Cheviot, weighing about 5 lb, the fleece sold at 1/- the lb

Leicester, nearer 6 lb at 8d the lb

'Scotch', giving 7 lb of wool at 6d the lb

The older Kerrera rent books, pre-1750 refer to payment of 'wadders'; in the latter half of the century payment of 'Fatt lambs'. Nowadays a man may speak of 'wethers' and write down 'wadders'. A Kerrera farmer might say he had so many 'clippers' at the valuation; but if he was a Skye man, he would only use the word for the men who shear sheep, not for a sheep old enough to be shorn.

When classifying sheep by age and sexes, the nomenclature varies from district to district, and within the district itself. A local farmer helpfully explained terms now locally in use, but not necessarily universally used on Kerrera, for blackface sheep.

By June, an April-born male lamb is either a 'tup' lamb to be kept for breeding, or a wedder lamb it it has been 'cut' for the fattening market. By November the tup lambs are termed 'tup hoggs', and in the following August – after clipping – 'shearling tups'. From November, they may be used for breeding, and progress each season as two-shear, three shear etc. tups. Meanwhile the wedder lamb, often sold off the farm in August becomes a 'wedder hogg' in late Autumn, a 'shearling wedder' next August, then a two-year or three-year wedder.

The ewe lamb by August is called a hogg, usually without the prefix 'ewe'. When, at eighteen months she may be put to the tup she is termed a gimmer. The arrival of her first lamb makes her a milk-ewe; if she fails to lamb, she is an eild ewe. If she lambs, but for a variety of reasons loses it, or fails to suckle it, she is usually termed a 'keb'.

At the 'Valuation', when one of the farms changes hands, there is a factor which adds to a sheep's value, quite apart from the age sex, breed or general quality of a sheep. This is if it is acclimatised to the ground, probably born and bred for some generations, and knows by experience how to make the very best use of the land, according to weather and seasons, and this wisdom can have a survival value.

Part of a Kerrera farm valuation in 1945 went thus:

1. 21 ewes and lambs @ 78/-
2. 40 ewes and lambs @ 52/-
3. 11 ewes and lambs @ 37/-
4. 12 eild ewes   @ 56/-
5. 16 eild ewes   @ 34/-
6. 3 eild ewes   @ 15/-

The above market value prices of the aforegoing sheep as enumerated in their various classes. Plus 5 per cent on prices of items (1) and (4) which are the only two lots of sheep eligible for increment for acclimatisation as regular sheep stock.

There must be many stories relating to the homing instinct of wise old ewes. This is how an Auctioneer with a life experience of local stock put it. If he was farming Balliemore and went to the Mart and bought thirty sheep, fifteen from Appin district in the north and fifteen from Melford district in the south, and settled them at Balliemore, next day he'd expect to find fifteen had wandered up Ardantrive way and the other fifteen down towards Ardchoirc. Or if he was at Slaterach he'd rather buy from farms to the north, or from farms to the south if he was farming Gylen, so that the sea would be the boundary between the sheep and their former pastures.

The Kerrera sheep stock has of course much increased since the days when each man had a few for home use, and the numbers were regulated by the old soumings. One farm soumed at 120 sheep in 1750, was selling off an annual average of 250 in 1850, and about the same in 1950.

V   RENTS AND PAYMENT IN KIND

In general, Kerrera farms have been occupied by tenants who pay rent direct to Dunollie.

However, as in other Highland estates, this depended upon the circumstances of the times. When Dunollie's fortunes were at low ebb after the civil wars, most of the farms were pledged in wadset, an old Scots form of mortgage. In 1654 'Ardintrave was wadsett to Donald Ewing in Bareindroman'.

In 1663 Ballimore and Ardchoich wadsett to John MacLachlan of Kilninver.
1663 Barnabuck wadsett to Donald Oconochir, Surgeon in Lorn.
1669 Contract of woodset betwixt John MacDougall of Dunnolich on the ane pairs and Donald Campbell of Ardintallon on the other pairs for the sex merk-lands of Gylland and the milne thairof.

Early in the eighteenth century Slaterach, Gylen and Ardmore were paying rent directly to Dunollie, but for the Chief's support of the Jacobite cause in the 1715 Rising the estate was forfeit, and only restored when he was pardoned in 1727.

Many Highland farms were tenanted by 'tacksmen', often sons or relatives of the landlord, who paid rent to him, and received rent in turn from their sub-tenants. This was not common practice on Kerrera, since the farms were generally rented by Dunollie directly to his tenants, but a tacksman at the turn of the eighteenth century may be mentioned. This was Captain Duncan MacDougall of Ardantrive (which he rented from the Earl of Breadalbane) fourth son of Alexander of Dunollie, also tacksman of Balliemore and Port Kerrera, and while he paid rent to his father he received rents from the tenants of the little houses on the farm. He combined service in the army – mostly in Ireland – with an intense interest in farming on the island.

Until the nineteenth century, the farms were shared by two to six, or even nine tenants; then by two, three or four tenants, and later the tenancy of each farm was in one name. They paid rent in 'silver', in 'kind' and in 'services', until gradually they took up their option to pay entirely in cash.

Most of the farms had also 'cottars' who had house, garden and grazing, and worked for the tenants labouring the farm.

Such a one was John MacDougall, mentioned elsewhere, of Gylen Croft. In 1786 he 'was to herd the Parc Gylen, for the whole year' – for which the Gylen tenants paid him in 'victual' (grain or meal) and also 'to cast, winn and bring home what peats the dariemaids will require and bring all the whey and butter milk to the point of Kervera' as part of his services to Dunollie for his croft. In 1838, referred to as the 'old man', he was helping with the draining of the Gylen peat moss.

The payment of rent for the occupation of land and dwelling in Kerrera seemed to reach its most complicated form in the latter two-thirds of the eighteenth century. This was a period when land improvement appeared to be receiving more consideration than warfare, so that 'service' on the land took the place of 'service' on the battlefield. It was also the period before money, called 'silver rent' as a form of barter, took over from 'victuals' and other goods in kind. While this period lasted, the Kerrera rents were allocated within the framework of the whole Dunollie estate, which also included some of the farms, mills and inns on the mainland of the parish of Kilmore and Kilbride.

Evidently three aspects were given consideration when the payments were agreed upon. Firstly, the type of commodity a tenant might be in a position to pay. For example, innkeepers paid a proportion of their rent in whisky; farmers in produce; weavers in blankets; ferrymen in boat service. Secondly, the needs of the landlord. And thirdly the requirements of such public services as the inns and the meal mills. Both these latter paid a rent to the landlord, and in their turn were paid by their customers.

On one of the mainland farms, four tenants between them agreed to pay:

> Three stone of meal for the smith; two stone for the plowwright; a stone for the Beddle of the Parish Four stooks of corn for the ferrie at Port Kerrera.

Some of the foodstuffs payable to Dunollie went straight to the inns in the payment of wages, since actual money was little used. In 1753 when Mr. MacKeig rendered his account for 'ye Ardmore ditch' he was paid '4 stone oatmeal; 4 stone barleymeal; $^1/_2$ stone cheese; a wedder: and cash to ye Clachan markett', suggesting that some of the farm rent-produce was ploughed back into improvements on the farm.

Payment in kind included butter, fowls and eggs, sheep, grain, meal and straw, blankets and linen sheeting, and whisky.

The amount of aquavitae or whisky seems to have been limited to a gallon yearly if innkeepers distilled themselves.

> 1715 Alehouse of Gyline pays one gallon of Aquavitae.
> 1754 Neil MacLea pays yearly a gallon of whisque for the liberty of distilling.
> 1754 Barnabock change house is let to John MacCulloch and if he malts any of my farm barley is to pay a gallon of whisque yearly more than his silver rent.

Up till 1715, butter had been paid as part rent, and when the estate was forfeit for Dunollie's part in the Fifteen Rising, the tenants had to make oath to government officials on the amount of rents they were due to pay. Dougall MacDougall of Ardmore being absent, John MacPherson on his behalf:

Makes oath that the said Dougall MacDougall of Ardmore paid yearly ffeu duty to the said John MacDougall (of 'Dunollich') for his lands of Ardmore in the Parish of Kilbryde … one stone of butter at five shillings sterling per stone being the ordinary conversion.

At this time, in Gylen, Ivor McUrchreim, Gilbert McIlichoan, John MacKulloch and Gilbert McChroain each paid one pint of butter, as did the said John MacPherson being 'ane intrant tennant'; Coll MacDougall 'in Gylyne makes oath that he pays yearly for his small possess of said town … and one chappin of butter in the master's option which is the truth as he shall answer to God and cannot write.'

Butter was not included in the Gylen miller's rent, but the four tenants of Slaterach paid, between them, four quarts of butter.

In 1747 Dunollie undertook to supply the inns at Barr nam boc and Port Kerrera with as much butter and cheese as they required. Neither of these items being mentioned in the rent payments of that period, or indeed in later years, presumably he supplied them from his own farm. He also undertook to pay the Barr nam boc changehouse with hens and eggs, and as these were being paid in the rents they probably went straight from the tenants to the changehouse as required.

> 1747 – Slachterach … each tenant pays six fowls and six score eggs.
> 1793 – in lieu of fowls pay 6d for one fowl and one dozen eggs.
> 1800 – six fouls and a score of eggs each, or 1/- for each fowl and score of eggs.

As the century advanced it became increasingly common for the tenants to take up the option of paying in cash rather than in kind. In 1786 the cottars, unlike the farm tenants, paid only 'silver rent' and poultry:

> All Cottars pays for ye house and Gardain 10 sh yearly, two foules and fourty eggs, but if only a house without a gardain, only 5 sh.

Wedders, or 'fatt lambs' were paid in kind; usually on a shared farm each man paid one wedder, but sometimes his share only came to a half, or a quarter. In 1786 the cash value was reckoned at 4/- though 2/6 was acceptable in place of the fatt lamb, but in 1800 the value had risen to 8/-.

The rents were also paid in oats and barley. The oats were paid in grain and in oatmeal.

> 1747 – Slatrach one firlot corn each of the four tenants.
> 1779 – Slatrach 4 pecks white corn or half a boll small oats.
> 1793 – 4 bolls oatmeal.

'Farm barley' as the rent barley was called, was usually paid in larger proportion to the oats, and in two lots.

1760 – Slatrach each tenant to pay 'of barley on (one) boll delivered in harvest and four in winter.

In the 1740s Dunollie undertook to supply annually fifty bolls of 'good sufficient barley' to the two Kerrera changehouses Barr nam boc and Port Kerrera. Some years later Kerrera farm barley was to go to the mainland inns:

1779 – the public house of Kilmore is to have 12 bolls barley yearly from Ardchorik, 4 bolls kilndrayed in harvest, and 8 bolls in winter, for qch he is to pay the milne of Clye 8 pence for each boll of his malt

At the same time the public house at Kilbride was to 'have 22 bolls barley from Ardmore and Barnabuck yearly, 8 bolls kilndrayed in harvest and 14 in winter at 20sh payable at Whitsunday.' But he was to grind his malt and crop at the miln of Oban, paying '8 pence for each boll of malt.'

In 1786 all the Kerrera rent barley was to go direct to the mill:

Clyechombie miln is to have all the farm barley of Kerrera at a guine the boll, Dunollie measure. And is to have 20 bolls at least in harvest, kiln drayed: the rest in winter, 17 pecks to ye boll delivered at the head of Glenfeochan, free, only he is to send to receive it in the tenants kilns, and to pay the one half at whitsunday after receiving it, and the oyr half the lamba after. (Lemmas – August 1).

As noted elsewhere, after all the eighteenth century agreements concerning grain came the note:

1768 – N.B. in all Kervera the year the barley does not grow and cannot pay yr farm barley they only pay 16/8 for each undelivered boll at Whitesunday.

It was laid down that an outgoing tenant must leave half of the straw for the incoming tenant: '1779 – ... to leave the half of yr straw the year of your removal for the Income tennant'. There was also an annual payment of straw for thatching. It is not specified if this must be barley or oat straw; barley straw seems generally considered the better.

1747 – Gylen, each horsegang pays ... one furlett corn, eight shaves of straw.
   Slaterach ... six bolls of drawn straw a fathom in circumference.

(A fathom was measured with outstretched arms).
1748 – six bollets of straw.
1786 – Slaterich 'straw for thatch 32 fathoms of 2 pence each fathom (among the four tenants).

The Barnabuck tenants who had to provide between them the 32 fathoms for thatching the public house had also to make '80 straw ropes alongst with thatch'.

Payment of part of the rent in blankets was mostly only made during the period of fourteen years within the farm tacks of 1754–1760, and 1760–1768. The farms of Gylen, Ardchoirc, Balliemore, Slaterach and Barnabuck produced amongst their tenants, one, two or three pairs of 'blanketts' at 'yr entry' or as 'grassum', grassum being a payment made by a tenant on entering a farm. In the 1760–68 tack they agreed to pay the blankets at 'the end of 3rd year of yr tack'. The blankets were to measure twelve yards-the pair, which suggests that the width of the loom's web made a half breadth of blanket, and two three-yard lengths were joined down the centre, as is often to be seen in the old blankets.

> Gylen 1754 (seven tenants) have taken the farm equally and pay three pair blankett each 12 yds long as part of yr grassome.
> Ardchoirc – 18 yds of a blankett att yr entry
> Slaterach – (four tenants) 'two blanketts att 12 yds each att yr entry.

Ardmore's payment of blankets depended upon whether he distilled: '1754 Ardmore – Neil MacLea pays yearly 12 yds of blankett for the liberty of distilling yearly, and a pair of blanketts wth yr Grassom for your tack.'
    The tenant of the 'Miln of Slatrach' made an annual payment of blankets over a much longer period, from 1747 until 1786. The miller was probably the first tenant to pay blankets, and the mill was apparently worked by Mr. Alexander McIllichonile or his family for most of this period, suggesting the household included spinners and weavers, as was likely.
    At the beginning of the next three tacks, 1768, 1779 and 1786, part of the 'grassum' was paid in 'linnen sheeting,' instead of blankets.

> 1768 – Slaterach – and pay as Grassom 24 yds linnen 600 cloath.
> 1786 – and 10 yds each sheeting linnen for there tack.

Since the clause 'oyr prestations as in Slaterach' was repeated in most of the other Kerrera farm agreements of this period, they also presumably paid their portion of linen sheeting; except the mill, which continued to pay the pair of blankets.

It might be wondered how the laird came to use so many sheets and blankets. By the mid-eighteenth century Alexander MacDougall of Dunollie had fifteen children thirteen who outlived childhood. An account of servants in 1738 suggests there were about seventeen, among them 'two Darrymaids, ye two heards, ye Barnman, Sheepherd, Gardner, House Servant, three spinsters and Dry nurse'. Even though not all would use sheets, the bedding requirements of such an establishment must have been large.

Part of the rent paid as 'services' was work done at, or for Dunollie, and part for the island itself. The agreements stipulated help with hay, the corn harvest, potatoes and peats. Haymaking apparently involved only the cottars on the estate; harvest, potatoes and peats, the tenants.

> 1768 – the Cottars of Kervera to attend the winning of hay at Dunollie (the cottars upon the main the winning of the hay in Soroba.)

Help at harvest, potatoes and peats was distributed proportionately amongst the farms:

> 1768 – Slaterich … to shear the sixth part of the crops of Dunollie yearly.
> … as allso to plant or cover the sixth of what potatoes qch will be planted.
> 1768 – Port Kerrera pays of services in peats, shearing, planting or covering potatoes equal to two horsegangs of Balemore.

It was slightly different for the tenants of Barr nam boc, who ran the ferry to Mull.

> 1768 – all oyr prestations as on Slaterich on each proportionally and equally saving they neither cast or win peats, and sheers in harvest only the half of what the rest of the plaws upon the island does, but in lieu of that does the sea services'.
> 1747 – Slaterich … to cast, foot and stack fourty loads of peats at Dunollich or anywhere else the landlord desireth.

The forty loads were shared between the four tenants and represented a creelful, or possibly two creelfuls slung across a pony's back.

As mentioned elsewhere, in 1786, John MacDougall of Gylen croft had a special job; he was 'to cast winn and bring home what peats the dairie maids will require, and bring all the whey and buttermilk to the point of Kervera'.

Tenants of specific farms had to help with the upkeep or special requirements of the tenants of changehouse and mill.

1760 – Barnabuck changehouse to receive yearly from the tenants there 32 fathoms of straw for thatching the dwelling house and his portion of the kiln, and eighty straw roaps alongst with the thatch.

1779 – Port Kerrera to uphold his portion of the miln dam and thatch his proportion of the mile.

1768 – Slaterich to pay yr proportion of all services to ye milne by land and sea.

In the nineteenth century, when most of the rent was usually paid in money, some of the Kerrera men, women and children came across and joined others (some from Lismore and Mull) in the Dunollie harvest and potato fields for a wage. The standard wages of the time were pitifully low, the men earning about 2/- a day, the pay for the women and children 1/3, 1/-, 10d to 6d a day. The day varied from ten to eight hours, but with a number of workers the jobs took but a few days.

In 1854 five men 'at sitting corn' and five women 'at shearing corn' and 'binding Gaits' (sheaves) with three children 'at making bands' completed the harvest in ten days, by hand, and some of them were only working four to seven days. Leading took the men another four days.

Day labour, mostly done by women for a wage, included gathering stones, clods or brushwood off young grass; spreading dung; cutting or culling weeds; hoeing and singling turnips (kneeling), weeding carrots, spreading molehills in the pastures; 'citting satch'; culling seaweed. In the autumn there was 'cutting and carrying ferns out of the woods for litter' – this was about 9% of the casual labour bill, and what a picturesque sight it must have been! The men forked it into the barn. Then of course there was the potato lifting and in spring 'picking, cutting and planting potatoes' with the practice of picking out the best potatoes for seed and then cutting them, allowing a healthy 'eye' in each portion for planting.

The Kerrera men also came over to join in the wood cutting at Dunollie. In February 1853 there were seven from Slaterach, including the Ground Officer, two from Ardmore, six from the Gylens, three from Ardchoirc, and two each from Balliemore, Port Kerrera and Barnabuck. There were also mainland tenants, the miller and his servant from Glenshellach, Mr. MacIntyre from Dalintart, two MacDougalls from Moleigh, each with a horse and cart, and the miller and his servant from Cleigh with two horses and two carts. Altogether 305 days employment at 2/- a day, but the men with a horse and cart got 4/6 a day. The trees were in demand, not only for their wood, but for their bark, as the following letter shows:

Captain MacDougall   Alexander Barnhill & Co.
of MacDougall R.N.   52 Howard Street
Dunollie, Oban   Glasgow
    25 May 1859

Dear Sir,

We come to renew our respects to you in the prospect of the bark season and will be glad to hear from you with particulars as to the amount cutting and quality in your district this season.

There has been quite an excitement in the leather trade from the war. The natural expectation in such circumstances that higher prices in tanning material should prevail has already been somewhat realized and there has been a good demand for bark lately.

Yours truly,

Alex. Barnhill & Co.

P.S. As we have always special application for larch and other light barks any information about these will be esteemed.

Alan MacDougall, wood valuator estimated the quality of the wood:

Sixteen tons of Oak Bark, sixtyone dozens of oak cabbers, a hundred and fifty strong pantrees, fifty small joists, and eight dozens of boat crooked timbers.

VI FARM GRAITH

'Grath' is a word which comes in Dunollie eighteenth century inventories; Chambers's Scots Dictionary explains the meaning. 'Graith – accoutrements; clothes; furniture equipment; harness for horses; apparatus, tools and machinery'.

Reading part of the inventory of the possessions of Iain Ciar, John MacDougall of Dunollie, at his death in 1737, suggests a prowl among the contents of an antique shop; part amongst the contents of the more interesting type of junk shop; and part moving amongst untidied farm sheds and buildings. It is the latter which may throw some light on farm 'grath' likely to be used on Kerrera at that period.

Among implements for cultivating the ground were '4 spaids; two iron racks; 3 weadocks; flowing and harrowing grath.' An account book of 1715 records the purchase, from Glasgow, of a 'spaid and shovell at 3/6.' Possibly the iron rakes may also have been bought.

The weadock (weedock – a weed-hook for grubbing up weeds) was a most useful all-purpose tool, and probably not unlike the mattock still so universally used for a multitude of jobs in the Holy Land, and the *Croman* used in the Islands for grubbing tatties, breaking clods and as well as weeding.

The usual simple harrow is a square, or triangular wooden frame with cross-bars; embedded in the underside are iron or wooden teeth. This is dragged across the clods with a rope, possibly of heather or horse-hair, and pulled by man or beast. It is still in use in the Outer Isles, with iron teeth.

In his *Code of Agriculture* (1821) Sir John Sinclair wrote of the plough 'the land cannot be cultivated to any considerable extent … without the plough; for it is by means of that implement that the strength of domesticated animals can be most usefully employed in the cultivation of the soil'. Before the middle of the eighteenth century, the plough team consisted of four horses yoked together abreast; later came the improved plough with mouldboards that turned the furrow, and with an easier passage it could be drawn by two horses.

The plough was made mostly of wood, except the coulter and share, which were iron and the most valuable part of the whole implement. In the regulations for a steelbow agreement on a mainland farm within the parish in 1760 is mentioned 'a complete sett of plewing irons weighing 4 stone weight which they are to deliver of the same weight at the removal.' They were also bound to make payment of two stone of meal 'for the plewwright'.

In 1774 Alexander MacNeill of Oransay arranged the purchase of a Rotherham plough for his father-in-law, Alexander MacDougall of Dunollie. This swing plough had been brought into use near Rotherham, Yorkshire in the 1730s, and proved to be very popular in Scotland when it was later introduced there. Those who bought it found it lighter in draught and more efficient than other ploughs. It was among the first to be factory produced.

Mr. Alexander McNeil of Oransay
                                        to Alexander Crichten
    Ordered by Mr. McDougall Dunolly
Oct 14 1774
A Rotherham plew with iron head mounted with
    75 lb of iron and painted   £2 2/6
A spare sock wt 9 lbs @ 5d   3/9
A sett of Barrs mounted and painted   5/-
2 Bridles   10/6
2 crested neats leather Brechams @ 4/9   9/6
2 pair of trace hames mounted with neck straps and breast ropes   4/-
2 pair rope traces with chains   5/-
2 Back bands   4/-
Canvas for packing   1/4
                                                                        £4 6/11

Although Kerrera's farms were cultivated at so many 'horsegangs' it is not easy to guess how much of the cultivation in the eighteenth century was done by horses drawing some form of plough, and how much with the *Cas chrom* (crooked foot) or foot plough, and the hand spade.

The *Cas chrom* was seen in use in Kerrera within living memory, and the iron sock of one recently found stuck in a croft dyke. Like the coulter of the plough, this was the most valuable part of the implement, blacksmith made. The handle was usually part of a naturally curved branch, and the angle near ground level was clamped to a flat piece of wood, with the iron sock fixed to its working point. A wooden peg was stuck in the 'heel' as a foot rest to give leverage to turn the sod which the sock had raised.

Although the *Cas chrom* has nearly gone out of use, the spade and hand-made wooden rakes, with about eight stout wooden teeth, are still the tools for working the many 'lazybeds' cultivated in the Outer islands, particularly the Long Islands (and Ireland), where the small patches among the rocks make a machine impractical. Beautiful crops are grown with the old method of enriching with seaweed or dung, but it is noticeable that plastic handles are replacing the wooden spade handles.

The harvest implements were simple; the inventory mentions: '2 old scythes; 9 shering hooks; a corn fork' the latter possibly made entirely of wood. It is clear that both scythe and shearing hook were used for cutting the corn. At a much later date (1821) Sir James Sinclair compares their merits:

Crops are cut down, by British farmers, either by the sickle, the reaping hook or the scythe. The sickle is light and narrow, and has teeth. The hook is heavy and broad and has a smooth edge. Respecting the superiority between these tools, there was formerly a difference of opinion; but now it is generally admitted that for the operation of what is technically called reaping, those with teeth are preferable to the smooth ones, owing to the time required for sharpening the latter; for those with teeth may be employed for several weeks without being sharpened.

The expence of cutting down by the scythe is less than by the sickle; and in a wet season, corn cut down by the scythe is more easily harvested, or is less apt to heat in the stackyard. It is, however, objected that it does not lay the ears of the corn so regularly as is done by the reaping hook.

He makes another comment about the scythe: 'It may be proper to state that they are variously made up, and are in some places very defectively put together for moving smoothly and with care.' Anyone who still uses the scythe will agree that a well tuned scythe, correctly proportioned to its user, will work very sweetly.

The inventory lists some small tools: '4 sheep siccsers; a pick Axe; a hamer, two hatchetts and 2 ugurs; 2 riddles and two lime boxes.'

Then comes the 'grath' for peat working and transport; 'Two flachter spaides'. Before peats could be cut the surface turf was pared off with the flachter (flaughter, flatter or *Cabar lar*) spade. This has a large handle and a small blade, a two handed implement with a long, broad curved shaft with a wide cross bar at the top and a small metal heart-shaped blade. The shape of the handle is important, for the curve of the shaft makes the action skimming rather than digging, and the spread of the cross handle allows pressure from the chest to give power to the paring off of surface turf. The definition for *flaught* is 'flapping of wings', and certainly the wide cross bar suggests outspread wings. The flachter was also used for paring divots to go beneath the thatching of the cottage roofs.

There are various articles connected with transport and harness; these were the days before wheeled carts, and what could not be dragged or pushed on rough tracks was carried on the back of man or beast. '4 peat slypes; 2 cares; an old wheel barrow; a dung cart with its harness; 6 care saddles with hair and leather gratin; an old sadle and bridle; 3 pair old currans and 4 horse branks; 3 pairs peat creels and 4 pair small ons'.

The peat slype was a form of sledge – the word itself is suggestive, meaning 'to move freely, as a weighty body drawn through mud'. It could be made from the fork of a tree, with rough planks across, and tackle for dragging. The 'carrs' – wicker receptacles, filled with peats, may have been dragged on the slypes.

Horsehair was sometimes used for making ropes or harness. Straw or bents were woven into saddle mats – currans – to protect the horse's back from the wooden pack saddles which carried the creels – these are still in use in Ireland. The saddles themselves were made from a carefully chosen fork of wood. Branks – two wooden cheek pieces with ropes to go round the head, and used for tethering, are still in use in Shetland for tethering cows, as well as horses.

The craft of creel making is still carried on in the Long Island. About eighteen stout willow wands are stuck into holes round the edge of a board, spaced out in the shape of a D, or else they are stuck straight in the ground – six along the straight edge, twelve round the curved sides. Starting at the base, which will in fact be the top of the creel when the work is finished, slender willow wands are interlaced through the uprights until the sides have reached the required height, when the top is drawn in, and the uprights bent across to support a firm base for the creel. Sometimes heather rope replaces some of the horizontal willow interlacings, and this makes a particularly attractive creel.

The straight side makes the back of the creel, to fit comfortably against the back of the person carrying it, or the flanks of the pony, and ease the weight of the load. As is usual in good craftmanship, there are reasons for the methods used to make a creel strong in wear and practical in use. A gap is left in the horizontal lacing some inches below the mouth of the creel and this allows hand-holds at each side. The length of the carrying band, made of heather or straw rope, horsehair, skin, or modern hemp, can be adjusted to suit the wearer by winding it in and out between the uprights. Some creels are made with a separate base, hinged at one side to the bottom of the creel, and fixed with a loop and peg to the other. By removing the peg, the load could be dumped through the open bottom, and save having to remove the creel from shoulders or saddle and tip it upside down. Besides carrying peats, creels were used for many purposes, and a bottom opening was specially handy when emptying dung or seaware.

One of the most helpful innovations to farming was the spoke-wheeled, iron tyred, horse drawn farm cart, only useful when there were roads suitable for their progress. They began to be used in Kerrera near the close of the eighteenth century.

In 1793 Dunollie offered every tenant in Kerrera a loan of twenty shillings to buy a cart, provided he would build a cart shed in which to house it. This was the arrangement; '… tenant who builds a cart house receives its value from yr income tenant and repays the 20 sh they got when they bought ye carts'.

Whatever the earlier cart wheels were like, later they were the most valuable part of the cart. They were beautifully made, and scientifically balanced to take the stresses of the load and the road. One pair in use in North Uist is said to be over a hundred years old, and has outlived a succession of cart bodies.

In 1837 two Oban wheelwrights estimated for building two farm carts, and listed some of the materials they would require for the job.

An estimation & an offer by us Niel and Archd MacCallum wheelwrights.

That is, we undertake & offer to make two pair of cart wheels tuo close carts and the same with trams (shafts) to be completely finished for the sum of three pounds fifteen shillings stg for Captn MacDougall who is to furnish us with wood and iron and all other materials for the completing of the said carts.

Mr. MacDougall accepting this offer will be binding on both parties as witness our hands this 23rd Dec. 1837.

Paid 3rd March 1838

Neill Ferguson

Archd McCallum

Memorandum of Nails etc wanted, full tell

Dunolly 22nd Jany 1838

1 m 2in	oak nails	2lb per m (probably)	3/7
1 m 2½in	do	15 do	3/11
1 m 20lb	palling nails		4/10
1 m 10lb	do	do	2/10
1 m 6do	do		2/3
1 m 4 do	do		2/-
5 c 30 do	do		3/5
	@ 6/9 per m		
			£1 2/7

1 nail hammer; 1 Handsaw; 2 screwed Augers ¾ & 1 inch
4 gal lintseed oil
4 lb red paint for cartwheels made up, about 8d per lb
14 lb blue do   do   do
28 lb brown do
3 lb white lead 4½d per lb
2 paint brushes.

The farming equipment of some of the poorer tenants was meagre, to the bare necessities. In the 1840s one man's possessions were: one box cart with iron axletree, wheels and harness; one half plough and half of graith; one harrow, two spades, four grapes. He was, of course, sharing the farm with other tenants.

It is interesting to compare the farming implements at the time of Iain Ciar's death at Dunollie in 1737 with his great grandson's in a list made exactly a hundred years later.

1 plough (iron) with trees
1 set spare trees (swingle)

1 pr harrows with draught chains
1 wooden roller with frame
2 box carts with wheels and iron axles
2 hay waggons without wheels
2 stone carts (no wheels)
2 pair cart ropes, 2 cart back chains.

Then follows the harness etc.

2 cart saddles & 2 britchens
2 collars, 2 pr hames
2 backbands, almost new;　　2 pr plough chains
1 pr plough lines; 1 leather coupling rein
2 briddles; 1 old cart briddle
2 stable stall neckstraps
1 curry comb & 1 mane comb:　　1 pr scissars
1 dung wheelbarrow (done).

In the barn

1 pair Fanners, 2 flails
1 Bushel OM – a standard bushel wanted;
8 sacks nearly whole; 9 do nearly useless
5 calf skins; 2 lamb skins;
1 beam board and weights
1 grinding stone,
1 meal girnal.

The tools

Quarrie tools – picks, punches or crow bars, mash hammer and shovels
2 dung grapes, 2 dung scrapers, 1 dung dragg
An iron for dragging wood
4 oak barking irons
2 bark scrapers
1 bill hook, 2 hatchetts (2 cutting hatchetts wanting)
1 spade
4 draw hoes (the young gentlemen have one for cockles)
1 clutch hoe
3 iron rakes, 2 patent grass rakes

2 dock irons

1 harp shovel

1 hay knife

2 hayrakes

3 long hay forks

2 syth handles – 2 wanting against haytime

2 short grass syths

12 wooden mole traps

2 beehives

2 wire riddles

1, $^{1}/_{2}$ and 4 inch peck measures

Kerrera steading – Mr and Miss MacRae, 1920

VII BALLIEMORE – TOWNSHIP & FARM

The name Balliemore suggests the biggest township in the island, and in fact it was the largest farm, having six merklands as compared with the five, four and three of the other farms. That being so, perhaps it may be taken as an example in an attempt to turn back the pages on the lives of one of Kerrera's farming communities.

During the troubled years following the burning of Gylen Castle, John MacDougall, 19th of Dunollie, had to wadset most of the Kerrera farms and these included Balliemore.

> In the year 1660 John MacDougald of Dunnollie entered into a Contract … with Mr. John McLauchlan Minister at Soall whereby he disported to the said Mr McLauchlan … the three merks ten shillingland of Ballimore with the ferry therof called Portuinechar with the Croft and pertinents therof redeemable upon payment of three thousand two hundred merks…
>
> … In the year 1663 the said John MacDougald entered into a contract of wadsett with Mr. John McLauchlan Minister at Kilninver, son of the above named (who) paid the further sum of three thousand merks for the six merkland of Ballimore with the ferry called Portnuinechar and also the two merklands of Ardchork redeemable upon payment of six thousand two hundred merks.

These lands were redeemed two generations later by Alexander (23rd) after his father's death in 1737.

> Received from Alexander McDougal of Dunollie the legal rent of six thousand two hundred merks scots money being the wadset money the lay in Ballimore and Ardechork by me … and this Discharge is warrented to be good and valid at all hands by
>
> John MacLachlan.

The Balliemore people, therefore had been tenants of the MacLauchlans since 1660. Even so, in 1715 they were worried that they might become involved in Iain Ciar's (22nd of Dunollie) recruiting when he was trying to raise a force to support the Jacobite claim. So they slipped across to the Island of Seil to tell John MacLachlan of their concern. He wrote thus to Iain Ciar:

> Honoured Sir.
> I met some of the people of Balimore who seem very uneasy and afraid you'll trouble them nor can I persuade them to return home tho' I tell them I am assured you will not molest any person I am concerned in. So for their satisfaction you'll

please to let me have a line of security under your hand which will mightily oblige.

your affect. cousin

Clachan Seil   most humble servant

Oct 21 1715   John McLachlan

P.T.O. I would not give you the trouble herof were it not I can not otherways make the poor fellows return to their work. My humble service to your lady.

As mentioned, Iain Ciar's father, Allan, had married into the MacLachlan family.

For Iain Ciar's part in the 1715 Rising, his lands were forfeit; after they were restored in 1745, and Balliemore was redeemed from wadset, his son Alexander made careful entries in his skin-bound rent book:

Dunollie 1747 Rentall of ye Island of Kervera and my oyr lands as they are sett for this and the following years of this Tack qch is for seven years commencing att this Whitsunday 1747.

Ballemore 6 mksland

	Barley	Silver merks
Dun. MacDougall senior	8	60
Dun. MacDougall youner	4	30
Dugall McDougall	do	30
Dun McLucas	do	30
Don McLauchlane	6	45
John McLauchlane	do	45

Each horse gang pays a two year old wedder a furlett of corn 8 shaves drawn straw 40 loads peats 6 fouls and 6 score eggs and services when called.

Amount	Barley	32 bolls
	Silver	240 merks
	wedders	8
	corn	2 bolls
	straw	64
	peats	320
	eggs	960
	fowls	40

Duncan MacDougall pays yearly for the ferry of Port Kervera 100 mks and a two year old wedder.

Cottars Neil MacArthur who pays for his house and Gardine 3 mks Archd Giles for his house and gardine 3 mks.

The new sett is entered 18 Decr 1760:

Ronald MacDougall   Dun. Lamont
Allen MacDougall   Dun. McIllichoan
Dun. McLucas   Dond. MacLachlane

Kenneth McIlivernoch and Hew MacDougall for ane eight betwixt them
Neil MacLea. The above names persons have taken the farm of Ballemore for the
space of seven years from Whitsunday next.

Silver	15	2/8
32 bolls barley	21	6/8
8 bolls meal	4	8/10²/₃
8 wedders conv		12/-
48 fowls & 48 score	1	4/-
eggs convertable		
64 fathoms of straw for thatching		8/-
2 bolls white corn		13/4
	£44	15/6²/₃

(It was optional whether payment was made in cash or in kind).

They pay all public burthern imposed or to be imposed the half of the manse
money if built during yr tack 48 yds of Blankett at the end of the 3rd year of yr
tack and leave their bigging sufficient.

There is also a 'Memorandum of the Sooming' and holding of each farm in Kerrera:

In 1768 there were sixth tenants, and unlike the previous tack, no split shares
Allan MacDougall, Hew MacDougall senior, Hew MacDougall jun. Dun
McIllichoan,
Dun Lamont and Keneth MacIlivernock,

The rent book reads:

	£	
Silver rent including half cess,	21	10/- (each sixth £3 – 15)
wedders & poultry		
Boll and a half white corn		18/-
48 fathoms straw	7	7/6
6 fatt lambs		12/-
Meal 6 bolls at 8 stone per boll	4	0/-
Barley 24 bolls, 6 delivered in		
harvest and 18 in winter	24	0/-
	£ 51	7/6 [*sic*]

Grassom £12

All oyr prestations as in Slaterich on each sixth.

These were:

> To pay all Publick Burthern imposed or to be imposed on the said farm saving
> the half of the Cess qch is included in the silver rent. They are yearly to lay out
> 600 loads of lime schell sand or of composition of Dung on the ground and to
> leave yr houses Barn and Kiln & Kaill Gardains in sufficient repair and march
> dykes that will be built about any part of their farm. At yr removal to leave the
> half of yr straw likeways at yr removal to cast win and stack 40 loads peats at his
> own expence and as many on mine and to shear the sixth part of the crops of
> Dunollie yearly as allso to plant or cover the sixth part of what potatoes qh will
> allso planted yr to sow 4 pecks lintseed and pay allso the 17 pecks multure with
> knaveship and banochan of yr grindable corns seed and horse corn excepted and
> yr proportion of all services to the miln of Slaterich by sea and land and pay as
> Grassom 24 yards linen 600 Cloath.

Irksome as these details may have been to the families which paid their share, they
certainly shed light on the life of the Balliemore community of those times.

When the next lease became due, Dunollie's fourth son Duncan, became
tacksman of Balliemore. Alexander writes in the rent book:

> 15 March 1779 Dunollie
> Ballemore including the ferry croft – My son Dun. pays silver rent exclusiv of all
> Publick Burthern £40 To pay sixty pecks meal while unlaboured to the miln of
> Slaterich for what is within his enclosure and twenty pecks for what is without it,
> and to uphold his proportion of the Miln and leave the March Dyke betwixt
> Ardentrye and Ballemore sufficient at his removale as allso six Barns and six Byres
> with the Kiln in Ballemore sufficient & the Publick House, kitchen Kiln Barn and
> Byre at Port Kerrera sufficient.

Duncan rented Ardantrive from the Earl of Breadalbane who owned it when the rest
of the island was restored to Dunollie. The Balliemore tenants, during the period
when he was tacksman, paid their rents to him, instead of directly to Dunollie.

With the 'six barns and six byres with the kiln there' were all the little dwelling
houses which made up the cluster of thatched buildings of the township. That Duncan
and his son, Alexander who succeeded him, were responsible for building new houses
is shown in a valuation of the farm before two Campbell brothers from Auchnacraig,
Mull, took over as tenants in 1818.

Comprisement of Houses, Dykes and Ditches on the lands of Ballimore as reported by Archd MacPhail, Licenced Appraiser in Kilbride in Lorn and Archd McLleriach Licensed Appraiser in Ardentinny, Benderloch, on this third day of July eighteen hundred and eighteen years viz.

1st John MacCallum's house
Consisting of four couples, no gavels, valued at twelve pounds sterling. Barn do. of two couples, no gavils, valued at seven pounds five shillings sterling.
Shade do, at one pound fifteen shillings.

2nd Hugh Livingston's house
Consisting of three couples and one gavel, valued at nine pounds ten shillings sterling.
Barn do of two couples, no gavel at six pounds ten shillings.
Shade do. valued at one pound sterling.

3rd Donald MacDonald's house
Consisting of three couples and one gavel valued at twelve pounds fifteen shillings sterling.
Barn do. of two couples no gavel, valued at seven pounds eighteen shillings.
Shade do. one pound three shillings.

4th A Bire of three couples and no gavels eight pound five shillings.

5th A Kiln of two couples and two gavels at four pounds.

The whole of the above biggings are the old houses on the farm.
The following are the Houses built by the late Captain Duncan MacDougall of Ardentrive the Tacksman and his successors viz

1st The large barn consisting of five couples, no gavils and two doors valued at seventeen pounds ten shillings.
2nd John MacDougall's house
Consisting of two couples and no gavel valued at eleven pounds sterling.
3rd Barn do of two couples and one gavil valued at seven pounds. Shade do. at two pounds ten shillings sterling.

If new Houses and Barns shall be required at the dimensions and specifications of the lease we value them as follows viz

Six houses of three couples each and two gavils each valued at twelve pounds sterling each house.

Six barns of two couples each and two gavils each, valued at eight pounds each barn.

The whole of the March dykes, corn dykes and ditches are in sufficient repair in the lands of Balimore.

The new stone dyke built by the deceased Captain MacDougall round Ellarie and the Hay park, at 5/6 per rood – 160 roods.

Ditch connected with the same line at 1/6 per rood – 86 roods.

The dyke of Shernacorach valued at 5/- per rood – 25 roods.

The whole of the above is comprised to our best skill and Judgement and is signed hereby as witness thereof.

Comprisers wages: A. MacPhail charges for three days 10/6 per day. A. McIleriach charges for three days 10/6 per day.

Although the little township of Balliemore had not the bustle of the ferry ports, it was the centre of many converging tracks, and on the route of travellers between the mainland and Mull. Possibly the residents saw the young poet John Keats, heading for Staffa, and his long wet walk down the Ross of Mull. They were well placed for gleaning news from the Post Runner, as he passed by six times each fortnight.

It was said that when the school was at Balliemore it had over fifty pupils at one time, so the sound of children's voices would mingle with the clangour of the smithy and the rattle of the weaver's shuttle, still to be heard in the Outer Isles. John MacLachlan 'weaver in Balmior' has already been mentioned in connection with the '45 Rising, and the family name appears on the rent rolls of the time. There seems, however, no mention on the roll of one John MacCulloch referred to in an account book as 'Tyler in Ballemor' who had evidently made some garments for one of the Dunollie daughters. Nor are the Sinclair family of Blacksmiths on the rent roll.

When plans were drawn up in 1801 for a new road across Kerrera to run between the Barnabuck and Port Kerrera ferries, there is a reference to the smithy: ... 'thence by the old road as far as the meadow below the houses of Ballemore and then to the right through the field and round the barn between the trees and the barn, then take the slope of the hill to the left above the smithy, from there keeping to the left of the old road to the top of the hill in sight of the houses in Slatrich.'

It was Donald Sinclair who in 1757 worked for ninety days at the pier at Barnabuck, and in addition to his pay received 'twelve shillings as Smith work for keeping in repair the quarrie tools'.

Over eighty years later, John Sinclair, smith in Balliemore, worked with seventeen other Kerrera men who were deepening the ditch to take water off the peat moss on Ardchoirc hill. He sent in his account:

1840 June 6 Capt. MacDougall Esqr of Dunolly
    To John Sinclair Smith Kerrera

To 11 jumpers sharpened, 4 steeled and 3 spliced	2/2
To 7 rolled and 2 sharpened	0/5½
To 2 picks sharpd, 2 steld, & 2 spliced	1/5
To one new jumper, 4 lbs of iron @ 4d per lb	2/-
To one pick laid with iorn & steel, one new wedge 3 lb at 4d	2/10

The jumper was used for boring a hole in rock and its diamond point had to be rotated between each blow of the mell to avoid splitting the stone.

The Balliemore smithy was probably a little thatched shed such as can still be found in Ireland, with pear-shaped bellows to blow the forge. With the use of wheel-carts and more complicated farm implements the smith's work increased in its variety, and his accounts show a number of items in need of repair in the township's day to day life.

    1795 – to a shoe for your grey 6d and the rest of his shoes nailed and clinched 3d
        To a pair of shoes cawed at 3d each pair.

By the 1830s the cost of a new shoe had risen to 9d or 10d and removing a horse-shoe cost 4d.

In winter and early spring: 'To 8 shoes frosted 2/-', from time to time was entered on the accounts. The clip at the front of the shoe was drawn down to reduce slipping on icy places; or special nails 'spikes' or 'sharps' were hammered into the shoe to give a better grip. Apart from shoeing, there were other needs connected with the horse and cart. 'Stall chain for a horse; mounting for a cart; new hook in hems & chain'. In 1795 the smith charged 6d for a 'pair of heams mended and 4 cart nails' and another 2d for mending 'the Brichen rings'.

Shoeing a cart wheel with a metal tyre or band was a job that needed two men. A North Uist lady described it:

To heat the bands for a pair of cartwheels took a cartload of peat, so that often a person would arrive with the load of peat when he brought in the wheels. A cartwheel would be laid on the metal circle in the ground, with the centre hub in the hole in the circle. Meanwhile a hot peat fire was made near the circle, and this was spread out so as to take the iron ring and make it red hot. Two men with hooks lifted the ring and laid it over the wheel, and hammered it into place. Then, gradually at first, cold water from pails was sprinkled round the rim to reduce the flames, then more water was splashed to shrink the iron band to the wooden wheel

The length of iron to fit the circumference of the wheel was measured by a 'traveller', which in 1838 the smith made for 4/6. The price of iron influenced the cost of shoeing the wheel:

1837 – 2 wheels shood, 34 lbs at 5d 14/2.

A spell of dry weather could make the wood of the wheel to shrink, causing the tyre to tumble off, entailing a trip to the smithy to have it heated and shrunk on again: 1838 – Cart wheel shooed 2/-.

When the spade, or the *Cas chrom* (foot plough) were the implements used for turning the soil, the blacksmith made the iron sock, or shoe to the foot plough, or 'repeared the spade with plates 1/-'. As the years went on, with the introduction of more complicated ploughs, manufactured by the trade, there were more parts to suffer damage in their rough path through the stones and soil, more parts in need of repair. '1838 – plough chains mended 9d'. The strain of pulling the plough by the two or more horses was eased by the swingletrees, and these wooden bars were mounted at ends and centre to take the chains:

2 new swingletree irons	1/8
A new hasp for a swingletree	
New large centre for a swingletree	
Mounting swingletrees 11 lbs at 5d	4/7
2 swingletrees fitted	0/9

The 'draught chains mended 6d' were attached to the plough by the bridle or 'muzzle'.

1838 – one new muzzle nail for the plough 4d' and in 1858 – 'small musle bolt 1/6'. In 1795 – 'to the sock (share) mended with my iron and coals (peats) $1/2$d'.

1838 – Sock and courter laid, 5 lbs at 6d,	5/6
1864 – Landside put on sock and feather	3/9
Coulter laid high up	1/6
Coulter wedges & chains	1/6

Keeping the harrows in working order also brought jobs for the smith.

1838 – A pair of angle harrows as per contract	8/-
making trees for a new harrow	
New tines for a harrow 9 lbs at 5d,	3/9
3 dozen teeth sharpened	1/-
lengthening harrow chains.	

Then there were the repairs for the small tools:

Toe on grape 1/- Dutch hoe mended with a new mouth; mending a briar knife and whittle knife (was the latter a reaping sickle or a butcher's knife?); hooks and bands far a gate; holdfasts for a rone.
Strap for a boat keel 94 lbs and 33 nails   £1 12/6

Then there were the harvesting tools:

1795 – to a sieth hook at 4d and two do mended at 6d	
3 sieths dressed at 2d each.	
2 sieths clesped at 4d each.	
In 1838 – mounting for Scythes	1/6
1861 – scythes irons mended	0/8
1795 – to a corn fork mended	0/2
1838 – stay for hayrakes	0/9
– 6 hayrakes with iron stays	0/2
– new fork	2/6

An exacting job which sometimes came the smith's way was the sharpening to a chisel or a diamond point the tips of the mill picks used for dressing the grinding surfaces of the millstones. This required such skill that it used to be said the blacksmith never liked to see the miller approaching!

The smith also supplied a variety of domestic needs. Many of the little thatched houses had a swee beside the fireplace, with its hanging chain and hook which allowed a kettle, pot or pan to be raised or lowered or swung aside from the heat. As well as being useful, the swee could give the smith a chance to show his art – many had graceful lines and curves.

1795 – to a crane (swee) mended   0/6

Slaterach had a very solid piece of mechanism whose geared wheels allowed the hanging hook to be wound up or down. Where there was no swee the 'crook' (chain and hook) simply hung from an iron bar across the inside of the chimney.

From the hook hung the 'goblet' or cast iron kettle, and the smith's accounts show: '1837 New Goblet handle 1/6'. He also charge 1/- for 'one new Bool for a kitchen pot' (the curved handle with hooked ends which held the two lugs of the three legged pot).

Perhaps the cooking aid which gave the smith the greatest opportunity to show his decorative skill and imagination was the wrought iron toaster which allowed the bannocks and oatcakes to dry off after being cooked on the iron girdles held over the peat fire. These were adjustable, – the ornamental back could be pushed along runners towards the heat. Again the smith charged 1/- for 'Bread toaster mended' (1837). One of these used at Balliemore has six turned scrolls at the end of the bars; another from Gylen has five thistle heads and corkscrew bars.

Another domestic requirement were the heaters for the box iron: '1839 – new iron heater 2/-'. These wedge shaped heaters were usually made in pairs so that when one was pushed inside the iron, and the door let down, its partner could be heating in the fire ready to be exchanged when the other became too cool to put a proper smoothing on the clothes.

Another item on the smith's account reads: '1840 – one new heater and one mended for the baise' which suggests hot iron was used to heat water in a receptacle. Sometimes heated stones were used for the same purpose, acting as the modern immersion heater.

By this time, 1840, Mr. Nicol Campbell had followed the Campbell brothers of Auchnacraig, Mull, as tenants, and he was followed by Mr. John Clerk. The scene at Balliemore had somewhat changed, for the one rent-paying farming tenant lived in a more modern type of house than the workers he paid.

Mr. Clerk spent £8 in 1840 'rebuilding and altering the site of old dwelling house,' and the new house was built of stone and lime with a slated roof and timber ridge. The walls were harled with arden lime. The partitions were of stone, and floorboards were laid across joists of sleepers, and surrounded by skirtings. There were sash windows, a skylight and a stair of thirteen risers. 'The 'Parlour' had a hearthstone and mantlepiece and there were '91 yards of plaster inside'.

The byre too had been brought up to date – the 'Ruble building itself cost £39 10/9', and its three doors £3. It had 24 cowstakes, trivass boarding partitioning the stable, a stable crib, four feeding boxes and 'Causway' (cobbling or paving); the floor cost over £9.

However in 1845 Mr. Clerk was concerned. As he explained in his letter to Dunollie, the barn

> had become quite ruinous thro' natural decay; in consequence of the severe storms it is now worse than ever, and it is necessary to have something done about it without delay. The expence of building a slated one of the same size will be about £50, if only thatched probably £35 would do. But if instead of either an addition be made to the wall of the byre, stable and cart shade, and a new slated roof put on the expence will be from £60 to £70. The roof of the byre is far from being sufficient, and though it may last my time (he died within five years) it will not last much longer, so that there would be much saved by making one roof cover all the offices.

Mr. Clerk was a very keen farmer, and in a letter to Dunollie of October 1848 he claims

Under my management the farm has not lost its good name. I graze the best cattle of any tenant on the mainland of Argyll and raise oats equal to any, and superior to most Lairds and tenantry.

Writing of the draining which he has already done

I have not an exact amount of the number of roods of draining I have made since I came here, but am safe in saying upwards of 1500, I have not left a single square yard of wet land in my enclosed arable without draining it and bringing it under the plough. I will require to save as much as possible on the draining and lay it out on dyke building, and I will require to lay out a very considerable sum in liming, independent of the Government grant.

His average accounts over five years throw light on how Balliemore was farmed in the mid-nineteenth century.

To Servant's wages 5 servants @ £6 8/-	£32		
Board wages for do @ 3/- a week each	39		
Shearers etc in harvest	2	10	
Seeds viz Oats 12 bolls @ 19/6	11	14	
Rye grass & cliver seed, say	3	10	
Oats for horses, 4 bolls @ 19/6	3	18	
Lime 100 barrels @ 8d	3	10	
Smith and saddlers account etc say	5		
Taxes viz Poors money	1	7/6	
Road money		11/6	
Interest on Capital say £600 @ 5%	30		
	£131	9/- [*sic*]	

By profit from stots purchased as stirks and sold half at Marts
    & the other half at Whity following the average
      for above period 80 @ £2   160

Heifers purchased at Marts and sold at Whity
    following 40 @ £1 10/-   60

Ayrshire cows, say 6 @ £5 each   30

Sheep and lambs @ 7/6 each   46 5/-

Crop of oats average for years 1845, 1846, 46, & 49

96 bolls @ 19/6 par boll	93	12/-
Crop of potatoes 400 barrels @ 2/6	50	
Ryegrass hay sold 400 stones @ 6d	10	
	£449	17/-

When John Clerk died suddenly in 1850, Thomas Stevenson applied for remainder of his lease. Dunollie replied 'I can have no hesitation in letting you the farm of Balliemore as I am perfectly aware with the able assistance of your Father (Mr. John Stevenson) who is one of the most enterprising and best farmers in the District and your own steady and Industrious Habits that all will go well.' Mr. Stevenson was apparently the last of a name famous in Oban. It was he who kept a flock of llamas, which he had bred from imported stock, and pastured with his milk cows in a field in Oban, now the site of the hotel and other buildings opposite the railway station. It is not recorded whether he brought any of the llamas to Kerrera, but is recalled that the scholars were fascinated by his black servant. He died at Balliemore in 1869, and had a large Masonic funeral.

Thomas Stevenson was followed by Mr. A. MacCallum from Lismore, and further additions were made to the Balliemore buildings – 'wrote to Mr. MacIntyre, Lismore for lime for work at Ballemore. Thatching was not at an end, and for the Bailemorbeg byre April 1880 – wrote to Leslie (a Glasgow firm) to send a ton of wheat straw for MacLachlan's byre, and told them to give him notice of delivery'.

Wheat straw sent up from Glasgow, instead of the local straw or rushes being used, was indeed an innovation but even now when re-thatching is done in the Outer Isles, sometimes the straw is ordered from the mainland.

In 1894 Mr. John MacRae and his sister Rebecca, came from Loch Spelve in Mull to Balliemore. They were among farmers who occasionally boarded a lad who could not be supported at home, but who could do simple jobs about the farm.

After Mr. MacRae's death, Miss MacRae carried on into the 1950s – she was a great farmer, and many will remember her tall spare figure, and her hospitality.

VIII   MEAL MILLS

In 1813 the parish of Kilmore and Kilbride had seven cornmills, powered by water. Three of these were on the Dunollie estate, and the remainder on Lerags (Upper Lerags); Glenfeochan (Stronchormay); Lochnell (Strontoiller) and Dunstaffnage (Ardconnel mill). Of the Dunollie mills, one was on Kerrera, one in Glenshellach, Oban, and one at Kilmore, Clychombie or Cleigh. The latter was the last of the little mills to be working.

The first recorded mill on Kerrera was at the south end, as a document dated 1669 shows: 'the sex merkland of Gyllan with the milne thereof'. A paper of 1715 refers to Archibald MacCulloch, miller of Oban and 'Gyleyne'. Meanwhile, lack of evidence, either on paper or landscape, leaves one guessing the actual site of the mill. It seems likely, however, that the building was quite near the shore on the lower reaches of the Usragan burn which drains Glenmore and empties into the sea below and west of Gylen Castle. Thus it could have been approached by boat. Possibly when Mr. MacCulloch removed, it was decided to build a new mill at the north end of the island, and the Gylen mill fell into disuse.

The new mill, below the farm of Slaterach, received its water from the burn draining that lovely loch among the hills and encircled with water lilies, *Lochan na circe* on the map, the Loch of the Water Lilies, also known as *Lochan nan seachd crioch*, the loch of the seven boundaries.

Ruined meal mill beside Slaterach Bay. The mill lade ran past the gable end, turning the big water wheel.

The Mill stands, a picturesque little building, beside the shore, looking across to *Eilean nam Gamhna*, the stirk island or the Shepherd's hat. Existing walls, gabled until 1956, show its size, and until removed in the 1960s the two millstones lay on the ground within.

In 1732, Robert Fraser 'gott when building ye miln of Slaterich £1 10/9 – less the 6d which he had already spent on snuff. The roof was thatched with straw; the tenant of Balliemore was bound 'to thatch his proportion of the miln and uphold his proportion of the mill dam'. The latter is still recognisable, and heaving turf indicates the ruins of the miller's house and barn. When he removed from the mill, he was bound 'to leave all the machinery, whether moving or standing, in repair as if new.'

The machinery of a mill, 'whether moving or standing' is complicated, and when the sluice released the water to turn the buckets of the great wheel, and the moving parts started into action, the building throbbed with the sounds and vibrations of the varied motions. The clappers agitated the grain in the hoppers so that it fell to be ground between the whirling millstones and the resulting meal was urged through sieves by fanners which graded the elements of husk, dust and meal and the latter fell into the waiting sack.

It is difficult to imagine words which more happily bring to mind the rythmn and stir of the mill, than those written by Mr. Donald MacLachlan, hereditary miller of the Romesdale Mill, Loch Snizort, Isle of Skye, some verses of which are here reproduced by his kind permission.

Millstones

Old mill that stands by Snizort Loch, so bare and
weather worn

How oft upon the ocean wide my thoughts would leap
the surging tides

To you where far on Snizort's side
you busy ground the corn.

Still clear I'd see around you, undimmed
by memories haze

The throngs that fast came crowding
to you in bygone days

On land the carts came rumbling
on sea the nut-brown sails

To you old mill on Snizort
they brought the ripened grain.

What changes bring the passing years
that speed so fast away

That now no more we see your wheel turned
by the rushing lade

No more we hear the busy hum,
the throb by night and day

And empty now your hopper stands
where high was piled with grain.

But far away in boyhood years
where memory loves to roam

Will fancy see the running lade
that turns your wheels once more

And hears again the steady beat
and sees the Kiln aglow

While all around the grain comes in
by sea and winding road.

Here when the sluice was lifted
the stream sped on its way

And kept the mill-wheel turning
beneath the brimming lade.

It turned and filled and emptied
in flashing foam and spray

all steady and unfaltering
in sunshine and in rain.

Inside the clapper whirling
was shaking down the grain

that fell between the millstones
like yellow golden hail.

With steady beat, all tireless,
its guidance would not fail

How oft its throb has sounded
through busy night and day.

No well-trimmed lamp was held on high
to shed a clearer glow

As fast the grain came tumbling down
to the waiting sacks below

No steady, bright electric light
the busy scene to show

But by candle's flickering light
when the day's last beams had flown

How high with grain they piled you
Old mill of Snizort Bay

They gathered in your meal room
and at your kiln fire's blaze;

And in the cold' clear moonlight
oft shadows flit and fade

Like forms still lingering round you
like ghosts of other days.

The Romesdale mill in Skye was much larger than the little Slaterach mill; but both stood by the tide line and their trade came by land and by boat.

The miller had to be a man of many skills to keep the mill in sweet running order. At least an annual job, in most mills, was cleaning the dust from the little holes, or sometimes slits, in the metal floor plates which allowed the heat from the kiln fire below to have free passage to dry the grain which was spread out to harden before grinding. According to one of the last of the Slaterach millers there was 'no proper kiln to this mile' and it is not clear whether it originally had one which had got out of repair. Most of the Kerrera farms had their own kilns, so presumably brought their grain kiln dried, as they had to do with the rent barley.

Some of the jobs were only occasional, but needed the help and strength of more men than the mill staff could produce. This was recognised in the farm tacks:

1768 – Slaterich to pay yr proportion of all services to ye milne by sea or land.
1779 – Ardmore (and Barnabuck) miln dues and services to ye milne.

A great event in the life of the mill was the replacement of the millstones. That millstones were cut locally is shown by the circular workings and partial disks of discarded stones left on the surface of flat sandstone exposures at a point on the mainland to the south and east of Kerrera. But by 1851, after the Slaterach mill had ceased working, James Ferguson, the miller of Cleigh, Kilmore, ordered new millstones from two Glasgow firms:

	106 Main Street, Anderstone
	Glasgow Decr 7 1852
Mr. James Ferguson	Bought of John Reid
One Kaimhill Millstone 4 ft 8 in	£5 7/6
	Glasgow 9th Dec 1852
Mr. James Ferguson	Bot of Mathew Muir & Sons
one mill Stone	£4 10/-

These stones were brought up by boat. Hutcheson (whose monument was later erected on the north end of Kerrera) had recently taken over the steamers from George and James Burns, as the scored out names on the bill of transport shows – 'Two mill stones £1 10s. per steamer *Duntroon Castle*'.

The transport overland of such weighty and essential parts of the mill's machinery was quite an occasion. A long stout pole was pushed through the centre hole of the stone so that it could be rolled by squads of men at each end of the pole. If the distance to be covered was long, sometimes their efforts were encouraged by a piper, and pauses were made at any alehouse on the way. The Slaterach mill stands so close to the shore that a high tide would bring a boat near to the building, and the stones had only to be got inside for erection.

In 1851, Dunollie paid Mr. Paterson £1 4/6 for the 'Expences of putting up the Millstone' in the Oban Mill, Glenshellach.

A much more frequent job was dressing the grinding faces of the stones, and this required three men. The lower stone was fixed in place, but the upper had to be levered from its horizontal position with the help of crowbars, then wedges and finally tall blocks to a nearly vertical position leaning against a wall. A smooth spar of wood, with a lick of wet black paint, was rubbed backwards and forwards across the grinding surface, leaving black smudges on the stone. These had all to be picked away with the mill picks. Set in wooden handles, the picks were about nine inches long; usually one was tapered to a point for working the centre of the stone, the other chisel-edged for the outer rim. As the men worked sparks and chips flew as metal hit stone, and they often wore goggles.

The work with paint and pick was repeated until the black smudges were as small as a pin point. and the surface proved and ready. Both stones were thus treated; the upper was then lowered back to its seat of the lower stone. It was an offence for a farmer, by careless winnowing, to leave bits of rubbish metal in the grain – a nail or worse still a coin – and if these damaged the surfaces of the stones the miller could fine him by taking double multure.

Multure was the fixed proportion of the grower's crop that was due to the miller to pay for his work of grinding it into meal, and for the use of the mill. If the miller had an assistant, this man received a lesser proportion, called *knaveship*, and a second assistant would be entitled to his share of *banachan*.

In 1768 the Kerrera tenants were 'to pay to the milne of Slaterich the 17th peck of multure with knaveship and banachan of yr grindable corns, seed and horse corn excepted.' In 1832 'all MacDougall's tenants in Kerrera pay full Moultre on their Oats deducting the seed, ditto in Barley deducting the rent barley and seed. Bailimore – Nicol Campbell pays £2 in full of all dues. The rest of the tenants to pay a stone of meal each markland towards keeping up the machinery of the mile. Ardintrive pays only half of Moultre for what they grind.'

Multure of the Island of Kerrera for Crop 1832

	Multure	Meal for keeping up the Miln	Barley
Gylen	13 stone	8 pecks	1 Boll
Ardichork	4 do	8 do	4 packs
Balimore Crofts	3 do	4 do	8 do
Balimore farm in all	£2		
Ardmore	2 stone	4 do	6 do
Barnabuck	5 do	8 do	3 do

Slaterach	6 do	8 do	2 do
Ferry	2 do		
Ardentrive	$3^1/_2$ do		
	6 bolls 1 peck	$2^1/_2$ bolls	1 boll 13 pecks

Measures then varied locally, but on the Dunollie estate a boll contained 16 pecks, and to pay the miller a 17th peck of grain must be added. The peck contained four leipims, and the multure grain was taken from the filled hopper before it was ground, and thrown into the miller's girnal. To do this the 'leipim' measure was used. This was a double ended flat-bottomed bowl, made of oak staves, metal bound, and by law had to conform to a standard size – as did the hopper. The larger, deeper end, $10^3/_4$ inches in diameter and 3 inches deep was used for an ordinary consignment of grain, and the shallow end, 9 inches across and 2 inches deep, for smaller quantities.

Since the Kerrera tenants were 'thirled' to the Slaterach mill, that is they were bound to support the local mill to ensure it had enough work to keep it going, all their 'grindable' corn (omitting the rent barley) had to be taken to this mill; but the grain which passed through the riddle was 'horse corn' and fed to the stock.

(above) Leipim meal measure, deep side
(right) Leipim meal measure, shallow side

Before the middle of the nineteenth century the custom of 'thirlage' seemed to be breaking down, although each incoming tenant agreed in his lease to 'leave all the machinery, whether moving or standing, in repair as if new' it was reported in 1836 'when I visited the Slaterich mill it was then in wretched order and will now be worse, if that is possible'.

On the other hand the miller in 1841 complained:

I put myself to some trouble and expence in repairing the Mill, and if I saw any prospect of grain being sent I would do more, but it is impossible to make people come to this mill while there is no proper Kiln attached to it.

There was a valuation in 1841 between a change of tenants:

Slatera Mill Kerera
12 July 1841
We the undersigned Duncan MacLucas joiner Oban and John Murray Carding Millar Oban being mutually chosen by Mrs. Donald Lamond the outgoing tenant and John Lamond the incoming tenant to inspect and comprise the differing parts of the aforesaid mill, do find the differing as follows viz:

	£
Water rhone, waterwheel pit, wheel cradle and spindle	3 14/6
Stones, stone cage and hopper	1 13/6
Stone Brig Bearers & etc	3/6
Dwelling house	1 0/-

The Fanners roap and cradle were valued at £4 improvement.
Two years later Mr Murray valued the water wheel:

Sir,
Having examined the water wheel at Slatera Mill, I do find it in such a bad state of repair that it is not fit for work, it being completely done.

So after about a century and a decade of milling the Kerrera grain, it seemed the working days of the Slaterach mill were at an end.

The Millers
Possibly the last miller to work the watermill at Gylen was the Archibald MacCulloch 'miller of Oban and Gylene', whose son acted as runner between Dunollie and Perth after the battle of Sheriffmuir in 1715. Later this family moved to Morvern, where they fostered Ian Ciar's grandson, Patrick.

The first miller at Slaterach, when it was built in 1732, was Alexander McIlichomille, who remained until 1760. He had the house and barn with the grazing for three cows and a horse, or five cows without a horse, and five sheep and two year-old lambs. He had to pay a 'peck of meal for hearding out of each cow he keeps'. He also had the right to the 'fifth load of seaware that was thrown upon the shore betwixt the miln and the march dick of Ballemore.'

For the mill and the croft he paid 120 merks silver rent, eleven bolls and one furlett of meal (valued at 8/- the boll); twelve yards 'blankett'; a two-year old wedder and four dozen 'fouls and 12 eggs with each fowl'.

Mr. McIlichomille was followed by a succession of millers, Donald MacGilvray, Alexander MacIllvray, James Stewart, John MacGilvray and Donald MacCallum. A year after Mr. Fergusson rented the mill in 1805, he died, and his widow's name continued on the rent roll until her son Archibald was old enough to pay the rent himself. He was miller until 1832, and it was he who did the joiner's work at the new school built at Balliemore in 1832.

In 1832 Donald Lamont took on the mill:

May 9th 1832

Sir,

I agree and bind myself to pay you for the miln and croft on the Island of Kerrera £7 sterling and ten bolls of meal, one fat pig 2 dozen fowls and a proportionate number of eggs similar to the rest of the millers.

He died nine years later, leaving his widow Catherine and a growing family. They were given one of the cottar houses rent free at Ardmore, where she remained at least until 1854. Meanwhile Donald's brother John, who had worked with him at the mill, asked to take it on in hopes of keeping 'the widow and orphans from falling on the parish.' Although, by taking on outside work for other island tenants, he succeeded in supporting two of them and helping the others, neither of the Lamonts apparently were skilled millwrights, and the more it fell into disrepair the less custom came to it. In 1843, Angus MacKinnon added the tenancy of the mill croft to his other lands in Slaterach, and there seems no evidence that the mill was worked.

IX   SEA AND LAND HARVEST

Salmon

Timothy Pont, cartographer of Blaeu's early maps of Scotland, is credited with 'noating' that there were 'filches also in the neighbour sea' off Kerrera. From the 'filches' Mr Archibald MacIntyre built up a fine business in the latter part of the nineteenth century onwards.

Born across the Sound, he came to live at Ardmore, and Orasaig Cottage, and moved to Gylen Park in 1893. He kept his boats on the shore in the Sound, near the Cutter rock, and built a fishing hut within the old slate quarry houses. He rented the salmon fishing from the Crown, and fished from mid-March until August. Sometimes the catches were huge, and he piled the fish loose in the boat up to the gunwales, so that it was low in the water as he rowed into Oban – what a sight it must have been! Salmon was cheap then, and much of it was sold locally to a grocer in George Street, but when the railway came to Oban some of the catch went off by train.

He had quite a number of boats, smacks and a schooner, for in the autumn and winter he dealt in herrings and potatoes, and brought the boats to the North or South piers, where some of their cargo was unloaded into carts for the train. Some of his smacks went across to Ireland with potatoes, mostly grown on the island by Mr Livingstone of Lower Gylen. Often they returned with a ballast of black Irish soil; some of this went to the gardens along the Corran in Oban, and some to enrich the prolific garden of Dalintart Hospital.

Mr. MacIntyre's boats were repaired at the old shipyard in Oban, when Argyll Square ran down to the shore – his was the last smack to be mended there before the yard closed. It was a traditional custom on Old New Year's Eve for the MacIntyres to go outside as the clock struck midnight to look at the wind for the year's prophecy for the salmon fishing prospects. If it blew from the southwest, which it usually did, all would be well.

Lobsters

Early in the twentieth century Mr Alexander Leslie became tenant of the houses built a few years before for the quarrymen, beside The Little Horseshoe Bay. By 1910 he had laid the foundations of a lobster trade which was to thrive for over half a century, and make him the biggest lobster trader in the west coast of Scotland. Many of the lobsters were caught in the Firth of Lorn and he held a big stock at Cullipool in the Island of Luing, as well as receiving consignments of up to eight thousand pounds at a time from Mallaig.

In front of his house he built up a fleet of ten or twelve rafts in the bay, mostly floating on light cylinder floats, which could hold a thousand and more pounds of lobsters in their tanks. Here they were fed on fish, but as there was a quick turnover they did not remain in the tanks for long, risking a loss of weight.

The Leslie family regularly supplied the Cunarder 'Queens', and both the *Queen Mary* and the *Queen Elizabeth* would set out on their fortnightly round trips with a consignment of about two thousand pounds of lobsters from The Horseshoe Bay. Almost all their lobsters were bought from the Leslies, and as they insisted that they must be a standard size of about one and a half pounds, a large stock had to be held from which to pick them.

The French required very small lobsters; in fact they would have liked them smaller than it was legal in Britain to trade them.

Constant practice made the family quick in despatching the many orders which came over the telephone, and a consignment would be out of the tanks and shipped down the Sound to catch the evening train from Oban so as to reach London before breakfast next morning.

Thus lobsters from Kerrera supplied the 'Queens', but on one memorable occasion it was the lobster boxes which eased the path of royalty. This was in 1956 when the Queen and the Duke of Edinburgh visited Oban. A freak storm, and torrential rain disrupted plans, and the Royal Yacht vanished from Oban bay. Eventually the Royal party were able to board her pinace from the mainland pier of the Kerrera ferry, where an embarking platform, made of lobster boxes, was hastily assembled over the slippery boulders.

Seaware

Not all shores receive equal shares of the plant refuse of the sea, which may be compared with the annual leaf fall and storm damage of the woods. The 'brook of ware', as it is called in Orkney, brought in by the tides depends upon the strength and direction of the wind, and the season – most of it is brought in by the autumn and winter gales, which may roll it in great piles upon the shores. The seaware is rich in iodine and potash, among other elements, and is appreciated by both cattle and sheep, who judge the time of the low tide which exposes it, and gather to feed.

Fertiliser

The value of seaweed as a fertiliser for the land has long been appreciated, and the tenants use of certain parts of the shore were carefully apportioned:

1786 Barnabuck	is to have the fifth load of seaware thrown in upon the shore betwixt the South and North pier.
Croft of Barnabuck	is to have the seaware betwixt the South pier and the march of Slaterach
Croft Miln of Slaterach	to have the fifth load of seaware that is thrown up the shore betwixt the miln and March Dick of Ballemore.

In a correspondence of 1809 there is a reference to the marks which Ardantrive had previously placed 'where the tenants cut the wrack for manure, and I am informed they are still there.'

In later years, because of the manufacture of kelp which sometimes reduced the supply of seaware available to enrich the land, the position was more carefully set out in the rent agreement for Balliemore and Balliemor beag in 1818:

> They are entitled to the wrack or seaware for the use of the land to the same extent as their predecessors had, but no more, and the crofters upon that farm and the Ferry Croft to have the use of the wrack for their lands as they had formerly, but the proprietor will use his best endeavours to prevent them from hurting or poaching the grounds they come through on carrying away the wrack to their crofts, and he reserves to himself the seaware for making kelp as formerly done by Mr MacDougall, tacksman; likewise seaware to the tenants upon the farm of Slatrach as they were used to get, and no more.

Kelp

The manufacture and trading of kelp in the Hebrides depended largely upon the scarcity of supplies of Barilla imported from Spain. Barilla is a maritime plant rich in soda, and its ash was used in the manufacture of glass, soap, bleaches etc. Supplies were cut off during the Napoleonic wars, and it was discovered that ash from local seaweeds could provide an effective substitute. The word 'tangle' often loosely used, really refers to the thick stems of the large leaved brown *laminaria* weed which were gathered, dried and burnt to brittle resin-like ashes. Button wrack and Lady wrack were mentioned as useful, but a correspondent refers to 'black wrack which is not reckoned to be of much importance and most useful for manure.'

The weed was gathered on the shore at low tide by wading, or from a boat, cutting it from rocks and boulders with a toothed sickle, and dragging it in with long handled hooks. Families joined in carrying it up from the shore in creels upon their backs, or with the help of ponies. Then it was laid out to dry upon the grass or on low broad walls loosely built of water-washed stones from the shore. Since the weed is 75% water it is necessary to dry it before it begins to rot. Often two or three sunny days or drying weather were enough to make it ready for burning in the 'kelp kilns' – at their simplest a trough-like hole in the ground, but more usually built with two foot stone walls, possibly helped with clods, measuring about ten feet long and two feet wide. A fire was started with a few peats, the driest of the tangle was added until there was enough heat to fill the trough with the part dried weed and melt it to a consistency of moist clay, which was stirred with a long pole ending in an iron hook. Great heat was given off, and skill-during the burning produced the best kelp.

The mass cooled to a greyish white lava-like substance, brittle and glassy, which had to be protected from rain until it was ready to bag and await the arrival of the collecting vessel. Little vessels used to call regularly at Oban to collect the kelp and carry it off to the factory at Dumbarton which used it in the manufacture of glass. It is said that one of the armorial windows in the Chancel of St. George's Chapel, Windsor, was made of glass manufactured there. Among the little vessels was the *Margaret and Ann* whose master, Mr Alex. MacDonald delivered a load of kelp from the Oban district in the spring of 1802, and promised Dunollie on the return journey from Greenock to carry 'six chairs and deliver safely at Oban – the dangers of the sea excepted.'

The rival claims of seaware for fertilizing the land or for the manufacture of kelp led to a disagreement between Alexander, who had recently inherited from his father, Duncan MacDougall of Ardantrive, the tenancy of Balliemore, and his uncle at Dunollie.

Dunollie

Dear Sandie,   6 Feby 1809

I am this day informed that you prevented the tennants of Slaterich from cutting seaware upon the shores of Ballymore and islands as usual … if you persist in your resolution let me know in answer by the bearer.

The answer was not immediate, for his wife wrote 'As Sandie has a cold affecting his eyes, he cannot write by candlelight; he begs to say he will write as soon as he can.' When he did, he contended he had full rights over all the seaware of 'Ballymore' and the islands offshore. His uncle replied hoping he 'would follow his father's example of being accommodating and pleasant' and that he would immediately send word to the 'tennants of Slaterich to cut wrack there as usual, so that they may not lose the present spring tides'.

Apparently Alexander could not see his way to do this, for on March 3rd the 'tennants being employed in cutting seaware upon the shores of Ballymore for the purpose of manuring their lands of Slaterich were interrupted and drove off by Alexander and others at his command, pretending he had the sole and only right by virtue of his tack of Ballymore.'

The result was an interdict against Alexander, giving the landlord power to exercise his rights over the seaware, and allowing Alexander only equal rights with the other tenants for cutting sea-ware for use on the land, and not for manufacture. It is clear, however, from later accounts, that the tenants were also employed in collecting seaware for making kelp. During the 1830s there are references to the allowances made to the various tenants on Slaterach and Balliemore for 'seaware' or 'castware' from Balliemore.

Peat

> September 23 1835 – The Lismore men are very anxious to be made an allowance
> of coals as the peats there are quite exhausted. Something will have to be done
> about fuel for Kerrera next year.

The idea of an island's source of peat becoming exhausted must have been very
worrying, and perhaps only somewhat relieved by the knowledge that puffers of one
kind or another were increasingly threading their way among the islands delivering
cargoes of coal. When the tide went out a great concourse of carts surrounded the
boat on the shore and their owners loaded them up with the coal before the tide
floated off the vessel.

The peat mosses were tremendously valuable to the Kerrera people. Peat heated
their homes, boiled the water and cooked the meals. They were used in the farm kilns
to dry the grain, and in the mill to prepare it for crushing. They heated the blacksmith's forge, softened the tar for sheep smearing, were essential to brewing and
distilling, and for burning lime; 'to 120 loads of peat for burning lime' is an entry in
a Dunollie account book of 1762.

It was laid down in the Kerrera agreements that the peat mosses should be worked
in a 'regular' fashion, and care taken to re-lay the turf, sliced with the flachter spade
from the top of the bank, neatly on the ground where previous cuts had been made,
to restore the surface.

> 1779 – Slaterich – to cut your peat mosses regular.
> 1779 – Balemore, Ferry and Public house … hereby empowered to cut win and
> lead peats from any of the most convenient mosses within the Island of Kerrera
> or Island Ganna, meadows excepted, but always taking care to cut the mosses and
> lay the sward.

Winning the peats could be a time of sociable gatherings, enjoyed especially by the
children, when it was a communal family effort – when the sun was shining. But the
peats had also to be made when the seasons were bad, and there was a lot of hard
work involved. Not only had the tenants to provide for their own use, but in the latter
part of the eighteenth century peats figured in the rents and services to Dunollie.

From time to time, when the mosses became filled with lying water drainage was
necessary, and this was sometimes a task which called for the united efforts of the
community.

> June 13 1811 – It being represented by the Tenants of Gylen that they cannot
> make peats this year in the meadow that they used to get them in their own farm,
> they are therefore willing and agree to go immediately and assist the tenants of

Then it becomes fuel for man
He takes a part of it
He kindles a fire and bakes bread
Also he warms himself, and says
Aha, I am warm,
I have seen the fire.

CREEL
SADDLE

HEATHER
ROPE

PEAT
SPADE

Peat

Slaterich, Barnabuck and Ardchoirc to make a proper cut through the peat moss in the muir *Criechlien*, on giving them liberty to cut their peats there this year only. And they engage without delay that is to say before Martimas next to make a proper cut in the meadow upon their farm where they used to cut their peats, so to carry off the water that they may get access to whatever peats may be therein, and this cut to be made in a proper and regular manner and to be used as their peat moss until it is exhausted.

As mentioned elsewhere seventeen men worked at 'deepening the Ditch to take the water off the peat moss top of Ardichorck hill' in 1840. It was becoming apparent that peat supplies were running low, and must be conserved:

1818 Balemore they or their servants are not, or give liberty to cut peats or turfs in any manner or any place but as directed by the proprietor, nor to give away the same, but what is required for the use of the farm.

If Ardantrive ever had a peat moss, it was probably the first farm on the island to exhaust it; but in 1747 it had been granted leave to cut peats on other mosses. As the following correspondence indicates, Alexander MacDougall of Dunollie realised it

might not always be possible to continue this, and wrote to the Earl of Breadalbane
who owned Ardantrive at that time.

> Dunollie 25 July 1770
>
> Dr Sir,
> I have afourded moss leave to the possessor of Ardintryve since the year 1747 I
> do not choice my continueing of it should inferr a servitude yrfore I want from
> Lord Breadbalbane my granting that convenience to them should not be
> construed as such oyrwise must stop the peat and am dr sir
> > your most humble sert
> > Alexander MacDougall

> Taymouth
> 22nd August 1770
>
> To Alexander MacDougall of Dunollie Esq.
> Sir,
> In consequence of your above written letter, I hereby declare that your granting
> moss leave in your property lands to my tenants of Ardintryve for their conven-
> ience shall not infer a servitude however long continuance but that you may and
> are at full liberty to withdraw that favour at pleasure. I am Sir,
> > your humble servant
> > Breadalbane

There was a rumour in 1802 that Lord Breadbalbane was putting Ardantrive up for
sale, and referring to this, a correspondent wrote 'the want of peats is a monstrous
drawback to any person who has no connection with the rest of the island'.

The time was coming when no peat reek would greet visitors to the island. By the
end of the nineteenth century coals were coming by boat from Glasgow and the coast
of Ayr at 'an expence of about thirteen shillings a ton' and gradually the smell of
burning coal, which is as noticeable to people who habitually burn peat, as peat reek
is to those who burn coal, became a normal part of Kerrera life.

Quarries

An interesting feature of Gylen Castle is the variety of the stones with which it is built.
For this it is well placed, standing as it does where exposures of slate and limestone
whinstone, sandstone and shale, as well as conglomerates and breccias full of varied
pebbles, crowd Kerrera's southern coast. It is noticeable, walking along roads in
different parts of the island, that they are tinged with blue grey, or yellowish brown,
depending upon the local rock sources.

Quarries were opened in various parts of the island as the need arose. Had the pier at Barr nam boc, built in the 1750s, been at the south-east end of the island, it would probably have been built of slate, as are the piers of the islands of Seil and Luing, the 'slate islands' to the south.

In the 1793 rent agreement for Slaterach was the clause: 'to leave yr farm houses Barns and Quarrie tools sufficient'. A century later, when Gylen Park was being built, a quarry was opened at the hill in the vein of whinstone which runs eastward to the mainland, through Gallanach to Loch Feochan. The new house was roofed with slates from the quarry at Gylen point.

Some of the Balliemore houses and barns were built of stone quarried near Port Kerrera. This is a special dark whinstone as mentioned in a letter of 1866:

Dear Sir,

Neil Livingstone, Mason, Oban, has got the contract for the new United Presbyterian Church, and has desired me to write to you regarding the dark whin-stone to be found at Port Kerrera. He says it is of excellent quality… and an ornamental building as the Church is intended to be would show the material to advantage. I find the ordinary rate of charge here is 10/per rood. Fifteen roods is the estimate of the job Livingstone has taken, but there will be some freestone used.

The main slate quarrying was in the belt of slate running along the eastern coast of Gylen land, to the point. Quarries were opened both at the point, and by the east shore in the vicinity of *Port an t-Struthain* and the *Sgeiran Dubha*, where the quarrymen built houses of slate. At one time MacDermaids from Crinan worked the quarry. In 1829 the brothers John and Neil Fletcher of Easdale made an offer for working the quarry:

Sir,

We hereby offer you a yearly rent of twenty-five pounds sterling to commence at Marts 1830 for leave to quarry and carry away slates from the point of Gylen in Kerrera on a lease of nine years from Whity next, it being understood that at the above rent we only employ four quarriers, and we oblige ourselves to work the said quarry in a regular and lawful manner and clean away the rubbish so as not to interfere with the operation of the quarry. We also oblige ourselves to commence clearing the quarry at low watermark in Spring tides, and we will set two men to commence clearing on first of April. As we will have to ship the slates at Little Horse-shoe Harbour we will at our own expence erect a quay for that purpose. We will also require three houses which we will erect ourselves; stone and lime and slates, each house to be paid for on our removal on comprisement, but not to exceed £20.

It was not until the beginning of the twentieth century that the row of three houses was built for quarrymen beside The Horseshoe Bay, and when the slate workings were exhausted, or abandoned as impracticable for further working, Mr. Leslie became their tenant and began his lobster trade.

The dark blue-grey slates, contain scattered crystals of iron pyrites – the 'diamonds' of the quarrymen. The operations of making a roofing slate can be divided into three: first, the large blocks are cleaved into smaller blocks. Then a man seats himself on the ground with one such block between his knees, on its edge, and with a hammer and two-inch chisel he gently strikes the chisel into the edge of the block at two or three places along a foliated line of cleavage.

The block is then subdivided into as many slates as there are joints in the piece, to a thickness of two-, three- or four-eights of an inch thick. The third operation consists of dressing each slate to size. A man seats himself beside a pile of slates, and having before him a piece of thin edged iron, about twelve inches by six, fastened into a block of wood, he takes up a slate and holding it horizontally with one edge resting on, and projecting about an inch over, the edge of the iron, he gently chips off with a cleaver the irregularities along all the edges of the slate. The slate is chipped to a uniform length and breadth with the use of a gauge, and is put in a pile according to its size.

X   FERRIES AND CHANGEHOUSES

The history of the Kerrera ferries is immensely interesting. For centuries Kerrera was the stepping stone, the link between the 'Continent' the mainland of Lorn – and Mull and islands beyond. The 'small' ferry crosses the Sound of Kerrera where it narrows from the mainland to what used for long to be called Port Kerrera, and before that Portinmichar. The 'great' ferry made the crossing of the Firth of Lorn from the western coast of Kerrera to the mouth of Loch Don on Mull, on the lands of Auchnacraig at a point more recently known as Grass Point.

The Kerrera–Mull crossing was described as 'one of the wildest and most dangerous ferries in the Western Isles' but it was suggested that 'landing be made (at Kerrera) at all times except when the wind blows strong from the south-east with an ebb tide; or with a flood tide with a strong wind from west-south-west to south – in which case the only places the boat can lay up are at Dunstaffnage in the north and Clachan in the south'

There was a tradition that when Kilmichael was the great cattle market of old a Ferry was established from Mull to the Main, possibly at Barnacarry; but 'since Dumbarton has become the great Mart that has been entirely done away with upwards of sixty years before the established Ferry existed from Mull to Kerrera and from there to the mainland.'

Another traditional ferry for the cattle marts lay between Kerrera and the Main a little south of the present Port Kerrera, between Ardchoirc land and *Port na cuilc* at the mouth of Glenshellach, and so over the hills to Kilmore.

In 1622 there was a 'complaint against Sir John MacDougall (17th) of Dunolly for levying a toll on cattle crossing the ferries from Mull to Lorn'.

Family documents of the eighteenth century recall something of the earlier history of the ferries. One dated 1793 explains:

> The Island of Carvoria otherways Kerrera … is a long stripe of land running betwixt the mainland of Scotland and the Island of Mull and the usual passage to Mull is by embarking on the mainland and landing on the opposite shore of Kerrera called Port Kerrera then crossing the Island and taking boat on the other side and sailing to Mull which ferry has been exclusively possessed by Dunolly and his predecessors beyond all memory of man.

That the ferry for Mull left from Ardmore lands in the south-west of Kerrera is indicated in an agreement of 1663 when John MacDougall 19th of Dunollie entered into a contract of wadset with 'John McDowall vc Allan alias MacDougall in Ballamoir' for 'All and Haill the two merk land of Ardmoir with the priviledge of the ferry of the same'. (It was this Ardmore's son who, as an old man, presented his Bible to

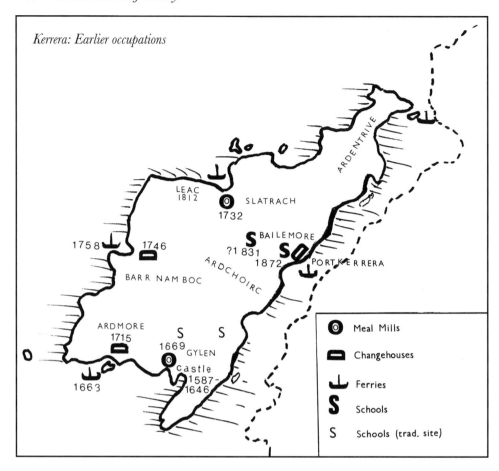

Kerrera: Earlier occupations

LEAC 1812
SLATRACH
1732
1758
1746
BAILEMORE
?1 831
1872
ARDCHOIRC
PORT KERRERA
BARR NAM BOC
ARDMORE 1715
S   S
1669 GYLEN
Castle
1587-1646
1663

Meal Mills
Changehouses
Ferries
S   Schools
S   Schools (trad. site)

Dunollie's young grandson in 1728.)

When these lands were redeemed two generations later by Alexander 23rd of Dunollie in 1750 the ferry was still running from Ardmore, although Slaterach in the north was also used. But some years later (the document continues)

> ... it was found eligible to remove the ferry between the Island of Mull and the Island of Kerrera from the lands of Ardmoir to the farm of Barnabuck being a more centrical situation and this remove was aproven by the Commissioners of Supply and proper Quays built for ferrying horses and Cattle.

Alexander, applying to the Commission for some help from the Roads and Highways assessments in 1760 to improve the landing place, describes the situation in picturesque language:

> The Ferry of Kerrera to Mull having for a long tract of years backward yea past

memory been used to be keept alternately for three months at Slattrach and three moneths at Ardmore which lye about two miles distance from one another, the proprietor being sensible how troublesome and uncertain this method proved to the leidges passing that way sought to remedy this inconvenience and for ease of the leidges several years ago fixed the ferrying place at Barnabuck being not only the centre betwixt the two aforesaid old ferrying ports but also a much shorter and safer run to Mull than either, as is known by the whole people.

At this new ferrying place there is a small creek betwixt rocks which at present is extremely rough and foull where boats cannot safely be moored or drawn up in a storm. But that by Blasting of these rocks and cleaning the bottom the same could at the expence of about fourteen pounds sterling be made a safe place for mooring and drawing up a boat. The doing of this would tend to a real advantage of the Country and whole leidges.

The Quay had already been built, as the workmen's receipt shows:

Dunollie 23rd October 1758

Then received by me Hector Maclean blaster and quarier from Alexander MacDougall of Dunolly the sum of three pounds fifteen shillings as payment of ninty days work performed by me at the pier of Barnabock at ten pence per day as allso Received by me Donald Sinclair smith in Kervera the sum of two pounds five shillings as payment for ninty days work performed by me at the above pier at the rate of sixpence per day allso twelve shillings as smith work for keeping in repair the Quarrie tools as allso received by me Angus MacInish fifteen shillings sterling as payment for thirty days wrought by me at the above pier at the rate of sixpence per day as witness our usual mark place and date as above written.

Hector H M L Maclean
Donald X Sinclair
Angus A M I MacInish

In connection with building the pier there is a further account:

Powder 16 lbs @ 1/4 per pound
Steel 7 lbs 11 oz @ 6d per pound
Iron 3 stone 11 oz @ 6d per pound.

The Barnabuck to Auchnacraig ferry was in use for rather more than a century; after which it became redundant since the traffic was making ever increasing use of the new steamers making direct passages between Oban and Mull. Even before the arrival of the steamers, from time to time disputes arose, mainly because Dunollie

The old pier at Barr nam boc, built c. 1756 for the ferry to Auchnacraig

contended he could not maintain the expence of boats and men for a ferry service for the public if the ferry was bypassed by other routes.

In 1793 he applied for redress regarding encroachment made upon his ferries in the Island of Kerrera – 'which petition … had been remitted to the Lorn District, but had fallen bye and could not be found'. In it he claimed that the and his predecessors had held exclusive rights of ferrying passengers and all kinds of cattle from 'the Continent to the Island of Kerrera, and from thence to Mull without interruption till within these few years past that some of the villagers of Oban (which has risen to some consequence and population) had taken it upon them to ferry passengers &c from thence directly to Mull, by which means the two established ferries were much injured'. He hoped their honours would consider it 'as a hardship upon him to lye under the expence of supporting two men and two boats at Port Kerrera and four men and three boats for the ferry to Mull, when almost the whole emoluments arising therefrom were carried away by the inhabitants of Oban'. That although he had 'every desire to promote the convenience of the public yet it could not be expected to do it at so material a loss'. He asked that if he was not to have the exclusive ferrying rights if he might withdraw his boats.

The Justices of the Peace and Commissioners of Supply for the District of Mull were consulted, and their prophetic reply is of interest in view of the present Oban to Mull car ferry service. They expressed the 'Opinion that the establishment of a Passage Boat from Oban to Mull is a matter connected with the progressive improvement of the Country, and necessary to an easy and convenient communication between the Island and the Countries about it; but at the same time they are of the opinion that the great and small ferries to Mull by Barnabuck cannot be dispensed with'. Curiously enough, the problem apparently found some sort of solution by accepting the recommendation to raise the fares of saddle horses to 2/6.

Another problem raised in 1817 was mainly caused by 'the introduction of sheep stock into Mull which took place some years ago and has afforded much additional employment at the ferry of Auchnacraig transporting them on their way to market'.

Dunollie explained the established ferry route:

Although Barnabuck is the landing place for passengers and baggage from Mull, a little to the westward at the landing place at Ardmore there is an enclosure for confining the cattle and sheep that arrive from Mull until they are driven off. The custom is and has been to drive the cattle … to the north end of the island … and swim them across to the mainland. But as sheep cannot, like black cattle, swim from Kerrera to the Continent they pass from the fank by the public road to Port Kerrera and be then carried across by the boats for a reasonable freight to the mainland where a quay is made and fanks to receive them until they are driven off.

This, however, is not the practise of the Ferrymen of Achnacraig, for without landing at Kerrera the sheep that come to their ferry they proceed round the north end of that island and land them on the farm of Dunolly, sometimes in one place and sometimes in another, and these animals after being landed escape in great numbers from their Keepers and traverse the Farm trampling and destroying corn, grass and plantations, doing material damage before they are driven to the public way, besides which Port Kerrera is disappointed of freight.

Apart from the regular traffic, there was the great seasonal movement of the drovers with black cattle heading for the trysts. Cattle provided one of the few sources of income in the Highlands. It was estimated that at the peak of the droving two thousand cattle annually were moved from the islands of Tiree, Coll and parts of the Morvern mainland to join beasts in Mull and cross by way of Kerrera to the mainland,[1] through Glenfeochan and Midmuir among the hills on their way to the trysts at Dumbarton, Crieff, Falkirk and the South.

From Auchnacraig the cattle were landed at Barnabuck or gathered in the fanks at Ardmore. It was then the custom to drive them to the north end of the island 'through part of the farm of Ardentrive to a small bay where the sea is narrow betwixt it and the mainland where they remain until some particular time of the tide when the Drovers swim their cattle over to the main and land them upon the Dunolly grounds and drive them to the road that goes to Glenshellach'.

The tidal island where the Sound narrows is marked on older maps *Rhu cruidh* or Cow point. Ardantrive, or *Aird an t-snaimh* means the point at which cattle swam across to the mainland. In spite of its long usage, this method of getting the island cattle to the mainland had its disadvantages.

'I well know', writes a correspondent, 'from my frequent attendances *stoning* cattle to the point the inconvenience both to the landowners and the dealers' (but no mention of the cattle's convenience).

Dunollie himself had 'no concern whatever with the ferrying of the droves of black cattle from Kerrera, beyond sending a boat from Port Kerrera to attend the cattle swimming to the Main land here, and the possesser of the farm of Ardentrive is bound to send another boat for the same purpose'.

Ardantrive complained in 1818 'respecting the droves of cattle that come from the adjacent islands through Kerrera … the droves lie upon the grass days without compensation'. Across the Sound 'Dunollie has had occasion to complain of the droves committing waste upon his land, and I have seen his servants collected to keep the droves from his cornland, and frequently employed for hours upon this business, and to protect his corns he has within these few years built a stone wall from the place where the cattle land to his march'.

By 1823, on all sides opinion was rising against this route. A cattle owner in the Island of Coll 'seemed to think making the cattle swim from Kerrera to the mainland very injurious, and made a plea for a good boat at Port Kerrera to carry the cattle … if there was, every horn of mine should come South by that route in preference to any other'.

Dunollie wrote to Maclaine of Lochbuy, chairman of the Mull District Council and offered to maintain a boat at Port Kerrera 'sufficient for the purpose of Ferrying the Cattle and sheep of the Island of Mull to the Mainland and to improve the Boating place at Port Kerrera, providing the practise of Floating cattle from the point of Ardintrave to Dunollie be discontinued.' Lochbuy, awaiting his meeting's views, asked meanwhile 'so as to be more fully master of this business I would wish to know from you what description of boat you propose having as also what per head may be required as ferry money'.

The meeting agreed 'that an arrangement of this kind would be for the general advantage of the Island of Mull – but hesitated on the grounds that it might involve a question of the Earl of Breadalbane's rights to 'preserve the practise of Floating

Cattle from Ardintrave' – as superior to that farm – 'it was only our delicacy with regard to his Lordship's share that made us not at once close with you'.

Since no objection was made from that quarter, in 1824 the Mull cattle owners agreed to relinquish their right by usage to float cattle across from the north point of Kerrera to Dunollie if: 'A good sufficient boat of not less than 22 foot keel be provided, the crew to consist of four men when any black cattle or sheep were to be ferried'.

In the nineteenth century Duncan MacDougall, a tacksman from Gallanach (one of the family is credited with being the first to introduce gold quartz crushing machinery to the goldfields of South Australia) carried on a boatyard at Port Kerrera, building sailing boats and dinghies as well as doing repair work. He was able to build the cattle boats on the spot, and Dunollie usually supplied the wood, as entries over the years show:

March 1853 Wood supplied from Dunollie to Kerrera tenants – Two large trees for a pair of oars for the large ferryboat at Barnabuck. Two ditto for large ferryboat at Port Kerrera. Two small trees for a pair of oars for small ferryboat at Port Kerrera; two ditto for Barnabuck.

In 1861 Dunollie supplied 'eighty feet of sawn elm and sixty feet of sawn larch for the Port Kerrera ferryboat'.

An 1872 diary records:

Nov. 11 went through the woods here with the old Boat builder to mark trees for a new ferryboat.
Nov. 15 – wood sent down to ferry for boat
Nov. 28 went to ferry and found boat had been commenced.

There is a valuation of the ferryboats in 1847: 'The large boat – £24; the middle size do – £3 10/- and the small size do £1 10/-. Keel for large boat 12/-.'

The cattle boats, in succession, have been large, broad and pitched black. The bottom had a thick covering of birch brushwood as a protection against the hooves of nervous herded cattle and horses. Rings fitted along the inside of the gunwale secured the cattle. The boat could usually take four cows or eight yearlings or about fifty sheep, though old lists of fares suggest the sailing boats took more beasts at a time. About the middle of the twentieth century motor power took over the task of towing the cattleboat.

Freight charges for men and beasts fixed in 1767 remained in use (saddle horses excepted) until 1813, when an increase was allowed. These included:

For a single cow – 2/6

For every head of black cattle in a Lot consisting of four or more – 1/2

For a single horse other than a saddlehorse – 2/6

For every horse in a Lot consisting of three or more, other than a saddlehorse, not including sucking foals   – 1/6

For a saddlehorse and his rider – 3/-

For every parcel of sheep under ten in number – 2/6

For every clad score of ewes – 5/-

For every clad score of wedders – 6/-

For a single foot passenger – 1/6

For every person attending one, two or three cows or horses not saddlehorses, or on a lot of sheep under twenty-one in number, – 6d

The Kerrera residents had a special arrangement with the ferryman at Port Kerrera, and there is an 1840s list of ferrymoney paid by the tenants of Kerrera to Mr. Duncan MacDougall, ferryman in corn and meal:

Name of tenant	Place of abode	No. of stooks:	of corn meal
Allan MacDougall	Slatrich	2 stooks 8 skis	1 stone
Archd MacDougall	do	2 do, 8 sheaves	1 do
Angus MacKinnon	do	do do	do
Hugh MacLachlan	Ardmore	8 stooks	4 pecks
Donald MacInnes	Barnabuck	2 stooks	1 peck
Allan MacDougall	do	do	do
Allen MacGregor	do	4 stooks	4 pecks
John MacCallum	West Gylen	2 stooks	1 peck
Alex MacCallum	do	do	1 peck
Alex Cameron	Winterton of Gylen	4 stooks	2 pecks
John MacCulloch	Park of Gylen	4 stooks	1 peck
Angus MacDougall	Ardchoick	2 stooks	1 peck
Mall Livingston	do	do	do
John Clerk	Balemore Park	(paper torn, illegible)	
Mall Livingston	Balemore croft		

Although in the 1820s it had been agreed by the cattle-owners of Mull and beyond to give up swimming their cattle from Ardantrive to the Main if a suitable boat was provided at Port Kerrera, the new route apparently found little favour with the cattle drovers or dealers, who took every chance to make a passage direct from Auchnacraig to the mainland, usually on Dunollie farmland so that crop damage continued as before. As in the case of the sheep, although the law granted an interdict preventing deviation from the from the established route, the practice continued.

The Achnacraig ferryman, in reply to a complaint in August 1850 wrote 'We have no hold on the dealers, They will go where they please, <u>and from the Quay at my door by other boats than the ferry boats</u>. And if I do not take my chance I will have nothing to do. Sheep, cattle and horses were shipped close to this ferry lately rather than go through Kerrera and <u>not</u> ferry by me. Hundreds of cattle and sheep go past us both, and they offer me an occasional chance only if I run them to the mainland.'

In a final bid for the ferries a compromise was sought. The two proprietors, Dunollie and Campbell of Possil, Mull, made a joint petition in 1833 to the Commissioners:

> That your petitioners are most anxious that their ferries should be so regulated as to give satisfaction to the public … suggest the following regulations for the Auchnacraig and Kerrera ferries:
> 1. Sheep, Cattle and other Bestial are to be ferried from Auchnacraig to Barnabuck or the usual landing places in Kerrera and thence driven across that island by the public road or Muir to Port Kerrera (except in the events after-mentioned) and ferried from thence to the main.
> 2. But in the event of stormy weather and that they cannot with safety land on Kerrera the Auchnacraig ferrymen shall be permitted to land sheep cattle and other bestial on any part of the mainland they can fetch, making a suitable remu-neration to the Kerrera ferry.
> 3. In case of a push to catch a market, they shall have the same liberty, but shall be bound to make a suitable remuneration to the Kerrera ferry in that event also.
> 4. Passengers shall be allowed to hire a Boat to convey themselves and luggage from Auchnacraig to any part of the main without making any remuneration to the Kerrera ferrymen.

Later it was agreed that suitable remuneration was to be half ferry dues.

When, in 1823, Lord Breadalbane had been approached concerning the discon-tinuation of floating the cattle from Ardantrive to the mainland, his factor in replying had made a prophecy:

> Steam navigation is now so generally and so advantageously used, that I should think in a few years an arrangement will be effected for employing a Steam Boat for some days before each South Country Cattle market, for the purpose of towing across the cattle boats direct from Mull to the mainland, thereby avoiding the necessity of cattle passing thro' the island of Kerrera altogether which would undoutedly be the best mode for all parties and the only one in my opinion that would prevent some from taking the Ardantrive ferry.

He was quite right, of course. If the appearance of a boat powered by steam in the Sound of Mull in 1818 caused amazement and its advantages were soon realised and made use of. Even if the forecast of a steamer towing a line of cattleboats across the Firth of Lorn was never realised, the increasing use of steamers to carry the cattle meant the decrease of beasts passing through Kerrera, until eventually none were ferried between Auchnacraig and Barnabuck. A high monument was erected on Kerrera to the memory of Alexander Hutcheson (died 1880), pioneer of steamship communication in the Hebrides, and it stands overlooking the narrows at Ardantrive where by long use and wont the cattle had swum to the Main.

Years before the railway reached Oban the organisers for the 'proposed Highland lines of railway' circulated pamphlets prophesying its advantages. One of these (1846) underlines that 'the means of conveying livestock from the Highlands to the Low country are … exceedingly tedious and inconvenient. The drove cannot be driven a greater distance than ten to fifteen miles a day. It is also very expensive for the stock and those in charge of it have to be fed daily … and there are losses from deaths or other accidents on the road; the condition of the stock deteriorates through the length and fatigues of the long journey.' They go on to say that island cattle, where practical, are made to swim across the ferries, and in other places are conveyed in boats

Cattle boats from Kerrera loading at the mainland pier, c. 1935

constructed for the purpose; but admit that 'this disadvantage cannot be remedied by railway communication.'

However, in 1870 (before the railway arrived) Mr. Thomas Corson founded his Auction Mart in Oban, and gradually the long treks to the Kilmichael, Dumbarton, Crieff and Falkirk trysts gave place to the shorter journey through to Oban. Although the Kerrera ferries ceased to carry animals from Mull and beyond to the mainland, Kerrera's own stock has to be brought across the water, as well as beasts which have been bought at the mainland sales for the island's farms. So at Sale seasons the big cattleboat at the Kerrera ferry makes many trips across the Sound.

On a calm October morning in 1973 the fine Slaterach herd of Highland cattle were ferried across to the mainland in readiness for Corson's autumn cattle sale in Oban the following Monday. As the two boats approached the pier, with skilful timing the leading launch turned aside, casting off the cattleboat which continued under its own momentum, steered by the tiller, and drew alongside the jetty.

The final group of cattle, the beautiful tawny bull, his two cows and followers, were driven down the slipway to barricades which penned them alongside the boat. The leading cow, with a rope around her head, was drawn towards the edge of the boat, and pushed from behind, her foreleg was lifted to ease her in; then she was tied

Highlanders leaving Kerrera for the mainland mart, 1973

to a ring near the bow. The second cow was tied to a ring on the opposite side, trimming the balance of the boat, then followed the bull, finally the young beasts.

Nervous beasts react in different ways, – some take to the water – and the Highlanders, with their grand sweep of horns could present an extra problem with even a turn of the head, to the combined efforts of farmers and ferrymen working in the confined space. But these beasts took their departure steadily, and when the cattle-boat was towed across the Sound to the mainland they were joined by a previous lot waiting their arrival in the shed. Then they made their way slowly up the old drove road up the hill to the glen where the rough grazing was divided into parks for cattle awaiting the mart. When the cattle changed hands a few days later, the Slaterach bull went for eight hundred guineas – which would doubtless have astonished earlier generations.

Although the days of the cattle-swim are long past, Kerrera continues, in miniature, the old system of cattle ferrying and cattle droving, as dog and man follow the herd winding through the glen.

Although the passage of man and beast between the mainland and Mull must have crossed Kerrera for centuries before there was a regular mail service, curiously enough it was the mails which remained loyal to the Kerrera route for some years after the men, beasts and cargo had abandoned it for the direct Oban to Mull steamers.

'Because', as was stated in a correspondence to the Postmaster General in 1856, 'while the steamboats have altogether deprived the ferries of the source of profit arising from the transport of passengers they are at the same time perfectly unsuitable for the conveyance of mail, owing to the uncertainty of their voyages, the time of arrival of the South mail at Oban or Port Kerrera, and their not plying during some of the winter months.'

From small beginnings in the eighteenth century, improvement in postal communication had spread through Scotland until in 1897 Queen Victoria, celebrating her Diamond Jubilee desired that every house in Britain should receive its mail delivered to the door.

After the mid-eighteenth century the Mull postal service began to take shape, and for the first hundred years or so all the mail for Mull, Iona, Coll and Tiree from the mainland was carried across Kerrera and ferried from Barnabuck to Auchnacraig. Then, for a decade or two, a sailing smack conveyed the mail directly from Auchnacraig to Oban, by-passing Kerrera. As soon as the railway reached Oban in 1881 a regular daily steamer carried passengers and mail between Oban and Mull, and although steam has been overtaken by progress, the route has continued to the present.

A *Town and Country Almanack* of 1798 – (most respectfully inscribed 'to the Lord

Provost of Edinburgh') – gives a fair indication of conditions for postal delivery in the Lorn district about the close of the eighteenth century. It lists 'the roads through Scotland' and these include

> no 17 – from Stirling, Down, Callender, Lochernhead, Tyndrum, Kingshouse
>   Inn, to Fort William.
> no 18 – Tyndrum, Dalmally to Inveraray.
> no 19 – Dalmally to Buna.

There was at the time no road to Oban, and Bonawe was of some importance in the network of mail distribution. The *Almanack* lists the Post Towns, of which there were about one hundred and sixty in Scotland, and these include Bunaw (this time with a 'w'), Oban and Auchnacraig.

The *Almanack* also mentions that the mail for Bunaw, Appin, Oban and Auchnacraig (among other places) left Edinburgh at eight in the evening every Monday, Thursday and Saturday, the charges for letters being 6d to Bonaw, Appin and Oban, and 7d to Auchnacraig, Fort William and Strontian. When the mail reached Bonawe, part of it crossed Loch Etive for Appin and north, and part was carried to Oban, some to continue across Kerrera to Mull.

Post Offices, or 'receiving' houses were increasing in Mull, and by 1801 mail went from Tobermory to Croig on the north coast of Mull, where a small packet carried it once a week to the islands of Coll and Tiree.[2]

The General Post Office, Scotland, made some contribution to ferries which carried mail, and in 1823, in answer to a petition for an increase for the Kerrera ferries, the Postmaster General, somewhat grudgingly sanctioned it:

> The future pay for the conveyance of the mails across the long ferry (Barnabuck – Auchnacraig) will be thirty-six pounds per annum, and for the little ferry (Port Kerrera-mainland) will be five pounds per annum to commence from 6th October last.
>
> His Lordship desires me to request you to be so good as to impress on the persons employed on this service our hope that this instance of consideration will have a proper effect on stimulating their exertions to maintain a regular communication.
>
> If we should be able hereafter to revert to three pafsages weekly, of course this extra allowance will cease.[3]

Doubtless such sentiments had little appeal to the crews who conveyed the mail across 'one of the wildest ferries in the Western Isles', or to a public who were urgently pressing for a daily mail-service. The sum was apportioned between the boatmen at the three ferry points of departure, Auchnacraig, Barr nam boc and Port Kerrera, and as far as Kerrera was concerned was dispensed by the Oban Postmistress, as an account shows:

> 1834 June 10th – Colin MacCowan, proportion of Post Office allowance for Barnabuck ferry, received from Miss Rankin £3.
> 1836 May – Allan MacDougall, Barnabuck Ferry; cash from Miss Rankin for Post £4 10/-.

From time to time the ferrymen also received an allowance for a new sail: '1833 – Colin MacCowan, by allowance for sail £1' and the following summer Allan MacDougall and Peter MacCulloch received a similar amount for the same purpose.

There was another petition in 1856 for an increase in the allowance. After explaining the loss of passenger support due to the steamers, it goes on:

> For the purpose of transporting the mail across these ferries two boats have to be kept on each side, Auchnacraig, Mull, and Barnabuck, Kerrera, a row boat for calm and a sailing boat for stormy weather, and to maintain their crews, that in the most moderate weather two men are required for the management of the boat, and when the weather is in the least unfavourable four men are always necessary, and are often in stormy weather occupied the whole day in transporting the mail and returning home.[4]

In 1864 the Mull people were pressing for a six day post direct to Oban. So keen were they that:

> All classes in the Island of Mull have contributed to a fund to indemnify the Post Office against loss so great was their desire to get the present very defective communication improved. Captain Campbell of Possil, Captain Campbell of Aros and Mr. Greenhill of Glenforsa have become personally bound to the Post Office that the additional communication should pay for itself and the Revenue sustain no loss.

Since it involved the loss of his 'rights of ferryage' at Barnabuck, Dunollie's views were sought. His answer was forthright:

> Dunolly
> Dear Sirs,   August 31st 1864
> I observe your recommendation to communicate with the Post Office, but I have already done so. Their object is to increase the Revenue, mine to get rid of the

Ferry with as little expense as possible, particularly now, as the mails are to be sent daily, with less pay, at all events not sufficient to remunerate the tenant at Barnabuck Ferry, but the Mull Trustees guarantee the Post Office to perform their part, which is impossible in winter without a steamer.

As the new Road Act authorizes the Proprietor of a Ferry to resign a Ferry <u>if it does not pay</u> I am disposed to give Possil and Co the benefit of their new arrangement, provided they satisfy my tenant by taking his boats and gear, which I presume can be affected by a petition from me to the Road Trustees at their meeting in October.

He had already consulted with the tenant when the scheme was broached, with the result:

Barnabuck 18 April
Sir,   1864
As tenant of the ferry at Barnabuck I am prepared to give up my right to the ferry at Whitsunday next (old style) on my being released from all my obligations as tenant, and on condition that everything belonging to the ferry such as the two ferry boats and all their appurtances shall be taken off my hands at valuation by competent persons mutually chosen.

I am Sir, your most obedt servant
Angus MacKinnon.

So the long use and wont for the 'mail crossing two ferries and an Island route' on its travels between the Main and the Island of Mull came to an end. With the object of running a six-day service between Mull and Oban, a special smack was built for the Auchnacraig ferrymen to make the direct passage. A writer in the 'Oban Times of 1867 suggests gloomy forecasts were not entirely unfounded:

We are still thrumming away at the good old tune of a post three times a week. We heard of a committee appointed to get a daily mail, it seems to have gone missing … it seems her Majesties Government can only afford a small skiff for the conveyance of mails to this unimportant island of eight thousand.

A certain amount of criticism of the uncertainty because of the weather, and the infrequency and the irregularity of the arrival of the mail – which, it was suggested, compared unfavourably with Calum Posta's regular journeys of previous decades – continued until the spring of 1882. By this time the railway had reached Oban, and with it the beginning of a daily steamer service between Oban and Mull which carried the mails.

Aptly named, the Paddle steamer *Pioneer* began the new service and route. From her berth at Tobermory she called at Salen, Lochaline (on the Morvern mainland) and Craigenure on her passage down the Sound of Mull as she headed for Oban. She was succeeded in about 1894 by the paddle steamer *Carabineer*. About 1908 the sturdy little motor vessel *Lochinvar* began the mail run which she held for over half a century, winning the affection of all who knew her, until M.V. *Lochearn* relieved her in 1961, soon to be followed by the much larger car ferry, R.M.S. *Columba*.

The Post Runners

Until 1840, when Rowland Hill changed the system, mail was not charged by weight, but by the distance it was carried, and since it was literally 'carried' by the post-runners, the mileage really meant something. It was not unusual to expect a man to carry mail twenty to thirty miles a day, possibly three times a week, for a weekly wage of five or six shillings. Much of the travelling across country was done at night, for their times had to fit the links with the arrival and departure of the mail coaches.

In the early days the amount of mail was light, and the Post Office allowed 4/- for the post bag which carried the letters. The bag for the Iona and Ross of Mull mail, carried between Bunessan and Pennygael was said to be only twelve inches square. But the weight of the mail increased in the nineteenth century, and it became more than even the strong highland runners could manage, and gradually horses or ponies were needed to carry it.

By 1830 a horse was needed to carry the mail on the Tyndrum–Dalmally road, and by 1830 the Bonawe – Oban mail, which included that for Mull, was up to forty or fifty pounds, and the runner's pay was nearly doubled so that he could keep a horse to carry it.[5] This of course increased the postal charges, as the services of blacksmiths and saddlers were needed as well as food sufficient to allow the horses to keep the required steady miles per hour over the distance.

Among locally well known runners was Calum Posta, or Malcolm the Post, who carried the mail between Tobermory on Mull and Oban on the mainland for forty years from 1820.[6] Even for those days his record was impressive; in these it makes epic reading, not only because of his long service, but also because of his character, and his mileage. His travels, it is reckoned, would have taken him five and a half times round the world had his duty not kept him to his mail route.

For twenty-five years he did the Tobermory–Oban–Tobermory round on foot, apart from his two ferry crossings, and for the following twenty years when his route was between Tobermory and the Auchnacraig ferry on Mull he had a horse. Starting with the mail at Tobermory he passed through Salen, where his home was, through Glen Clachaig, up the thousand foot shoulder and down to the head of Loch Scridian, where he was met by the Bunessan–Pennygael runner from the Ross of Mull. With this usually light addition to his load he carried on through Glenmore to

Lochdonhead, branching right down the road to Auchnacraig Post Office and ferry. Here, perhaps, he may have spent the night before crossing by ferry to Barr nam boc. His route across Kerrera took him within sight of the school, then near Balliemore farm, and stories have been handed down of how the scholars enjoyed watching out for him – sometimes he would be carrying something of recognizeable interest, such as a horse collar. After crossing the small ferry to the mainland he took the hill road to the Oban Post Office in Shore Street, where Mrs. Bayne, followed by Miss Rankin, was Postmistress. Here the letters would be laid against the window panes, address outwards, to be called for by the recipients when the word went round.

Usually it was the recipient who paid the freight charge although this might also depend upon the circumstances of the writer and the receiver, but in 1840 when the Penny Post came in, letters had to be prepaid by the sender with an adhesive stamp. Surely Calum must have been intrigued when he first saw a letter embellished with the portrait of Queen Victoria – the original 'Black Penny' stamp.

After collecting the incoming mail in Oban, he set off on the long journey back, making the double trip three times each fortnight. When he retired in the mid 1860s he was a much loved man. Hardly ever seen without his mail bags, on duty or off, he had the confidence of everyone along his route. Many was the 'oblidgement' he did for them, and apart from his duties he was often entrusted with quite large sums of money to deliver.

Until 1879, Kerrera did not have its own Post Office, and the mail route which crossed the island lay between the post offices of Oban and Auchnacraig in Mull.

The early post offices received and despatched the incoming and outgoing mail, but in general the letters remained with them until collected by the recipients, some-times, as in the case of letters at Bunessan for the Island of Iona, a matter of weeks. There were no sales of stamps or postal orders, and the postmaster or mistress had to find money for rent, fuel, candles etc. There was a rise in salaries in 1793, when Oban's postmaster received £15 a year instead of £6. The Auchnacraig salary was raised from £5 to £8 at the same time. About the close of the century Oban's postal revenue was £200; Auchnacraig rather over £100.[7] Even by 1830 the work was not full time, and Miss Rankin, postmistress at Shore Street, Oban, also ran a school for girls.

In 1879 the G.P.O. agreed to provide Kerrera with its own post office, as the following letter indicates:

General Post Office
Edinburgh 12th Novr 1879

Colonel MacDougall
Dunollie, Oban.
Sir,
With reference to your communication of the 16th July last, I beg to inform you

that it has been decided to establish a sub-Post Office in the Island of Kerrera, with a post to and from Oban by Ferry Boat <u>three times a week</u>, and it is hoped this accommodation will be satisfactory to the inhabitants on the Island.

I may add that the revenue from the correspondence for Kerrera is not sufficient to warrens the expence of a daily post.

I am, Sir

Your obedient servant

A.M. Cunningham

Surveyor General

This welcome announcement had the G.P.O.'s printed heading but was otherwise written by hand on paper of a delicate pink. It had not, however, the gilt edges of the letter which announced a rise in the ferrying allowance for the mail in 1823.

So the ferryhouse at Port Kerrera took on yet another public service. For many years it had been a changehouse, inn or publichouse, brewing its ale, distilling its whisky. For a period it had run a thriving boatbuilding business, and now it was to be Post Office.

Usually it fell to the Ferryman's wife to be postmistress, and whatever the original arrangements were, latterly the 'Post Office' was a large cupboard in the house, and if any household possession was mislaid it was usually discovered 'on top of the Post Office'. The red letterbox is attached to a post outside.

Kerrera
letterbox

As cold water to a thirsty soul
So is good news from a far country

When correspondence increased, Kerrera received a daily service, the Post Office van arriving from Oban at the mainland slip and exchanging the bags between boat and van. After the incoming mail was ferried across and sorted, the delivery round began. The Kerrera round hardly compares with the great mileages of the old post runners; nor does it compare with modern urban rounds carried out by fleets of red motor vans. There is no road which covers the whole route. In calm weather the delivery to the north is usually made by boat; failing this it entails a tramp through bogland, the double journey taking up to an hour and a half.

Starting off again from the ferryhouse the route is by the schoolhouse, Balliemore, then across the old road to Ardchoirc, down to the shore road past The Horseshoe to Upper Gylen and Gylen Park. Then by the short cut past the Castle to Lower Gylen, Orasaig and Ardmore; finally across bogland to Barr nam boc, joining the road, and then down to Slaterach, and finally back to the Post Office.

At one time there was always a cup of tea for the postman at Ardmore. Mr. Kay, who farmed the Croft, used to talk of his cow and tell stories of Effie-the-cat, who once greeted him on his return from Oban by leading him to the bread bin, and proudly displaying her new-born family.

Naturally the postman was in a position to gather up the news and disperse it as he went his rounds:

November 1900 – On Monday morning the postman told the parents that measles had broken out at Ballemore farm … so only four children turned up.

Generally the mails were carried on foot, and when all the houses were occupied this took about five hours. During a period when the mail arrived at the ferry in the afternoon, winter darkness fell long before the delivery was finished, and the Post Office supplied a very small lamp fueled with colza oil, but this was hardly adequate for the hazards likely to be met on the route.

Sometimes a pony was used, or a motorbicycle for parts of the round, for at times the quantity of mail was quite considerable. There is a nice story about one such vehicle. One of the Islanders had a new motor bicycle sent in parts by post. As eleven pounds was the maximum weight allowed at that time, quite a quantity of parcels passed through the Post Office before the delivery was completed. Finally assembled, the machine went beautifully. Eventually its owner decided to sell it, and it was finally bought by the Post Office and in its turn helped to deliver quite a number of parcels before it went into retirement.

In 1939 a telephone kiosk was erected below the Post Office, and apart from its obvious convenience it made a useful shelter. One lady went to retrieve her messages, and when she turned round to come out, found her way barred by the billy-goat, Lavender Flower by name. Unable to attract help, she telephoned to the Oban

exchange and asked them to telephone back to the Kerrera Post Office on the cliff
above her, to ask them to send someone to come to her aid.

'We embarked' writes Dr. Samuel Johnson 'in a boat in which the seat provided for
our accommodation was a heap of rough brushwood'. A.M. Faichney in his most
valuable *Oban and the District Around* (1902) adds: 'They crossed from Grass Point, Mull,
in the ferry boat to Barnamboc in Kerrera, walked across the island, and again made
use of the second ferry boat to take them over to the mainland'. This, as Mr. Faichney
knew, was the established ferry route at that time. Dunollie was concerned that it was
running at a loss because it was often by-passed by boats making a direct passage
between Mull and the mainland, and wished to close it.

Both Johnson's and Boswell's descriptions suggest that Lochbuie persuaded the
Auchnacraig ferryman to make the direct passage, and so save a somewhat portly
passenger the Kerrera gradients. Boswell records 'We bid adieu to Lochbuie and to
our kind conductor Sir Allan Maclean on the shore of Mull, and got into the ferryboat, the bottom of which was strewed with branches of trees or bushes upon which
we sat. We saw the old Castle of Duart at a distance while we sailed… We landed at
Oban having had a good day and fine passage'. He omits reference to Kerrera, and
goes on 'Sir Allan had given us a card to introduce us to the Laird of MacDougall.
But as we understood from his way of speaking, whether rightly or not, that the Laird
would not be very willing to entertain us, we did not go to his castle, though very near.'

Dunollie was not approached, and had no opportunity to show his willingness or
otherwise to offer hospitality but Lochbuie may have felt that bypassing his established ferries might be a tactless approach to seeking his welcome. Another traveller
was the French scientist, B. Faujas Saint-Fond, who had crossed Kerrera, and was
returning from Mull in the autumn of 1784. He records: 'at length in the evening of
th October … a bark having come into Achnacregs with a cargo of beeves which was
to return on the morrow, we resolved to embrace the opportunity of a passage in her,
We accordingly embarked at six next morning, not for Oban, but for the Isle of
Kerrera, where we landed at eight.'[8]

The poet John Keats wanted to make the trip to Staffa in 1818. He had the chance
of a boat going there direct from Oban, but as this would have cost him seven guineas
he decided to walk across Kerrera and take the ferry to Mull. Days of bad weather
and incessant rain on his long walks through the Ross of Mull brought on the severe
chill which undermined his health, and on his return he spent six days in Oban until
the fever left him.

Travellers by the ferries could get refreshment at the inns. At Port Kerrera 'the
accommodation at the inn or clachan which stood within a stone's cast from the ferry
was of the most limited description'. At Auchnacraig, on the Mull side of the
Barnabuck ferry 'the accommodation for ourselves tolerable, but those for our horses

very bad indeed. The stable was a little low hut, with a floor of mud, without any divisions or stalls. We could procure no oats for their food, nor straw for their bedding, but after a considerable dispute between Mr. Walls and the woman who acted as hostler, whether it was proper to give 'the food of Christians to horses' we got them each a mess of oatmeal.'[9]

Among the ferry passengers were students, local born and brought up, but making the long journey to college or university. An account of the travels of a young man from Morvern heading for his entrance into College in Glasgow gives an idea of what such a journey entailed.

> On Monday morning Sandy MacIntyre, with two horses, was ferried across to Mull from Ardnamurchan. My father and I followed, and we got the ferry at Auchnacraig, near Duart that night, where we had to remain for a couple of nights, the weather being too stormy to proceed. We next crossed to Kerrera, rode to the next ferry, and arrived in Oban in the course of the afternoon, Sandy accompanying us on foot. A pair of saddlebags on each of our horses carried all our baggage.
>
> At Oban we sent for the "English" smith to shoe our horses … Then by Taynuilt, Port Sonachan, Inverary, Arrochar … and so to Glasgow, having been ten days on the journey.[10]

A Mull lady recalls that her great grandmother, and her two brothers, made the much longer journey to school and university in Aberdeen. They came home once a year, and returning after their holidays rode to Auchnacraig, taking their horses in the flat-bottomed ferryboat across to Barnabuck. Then they rode across Kerrera, where the horses swum the Sound from Port Kerrera to the mainland.

Three inns, Publichouses, Alehouses or Changehouses are recorded on Kerrera, and they were all easily accessible to the ferry traffic. As Ardmore was the older ferry to Mull, the records suggest that there was an alehouse at Gylen or Ardmore long before there was one at Barnabuck. Possibly the inn at Portninmachar, which was the old name for Port Kerrera (now the Ferryhouse) may have had the longest useage.

References to the Gylen Changehouse are mainly in connection with the rent paid, and distilling.

> 1715 – the alehouse of Gylene paid yearly one gallon of aquavitae or 12 merks…
> Gyllen Changehouse crops 1737: Of Aquavitae 2 gallons and 3 pints. By malt 2 bolls and 10 pecks.
> 1737 – Hew MacColl in Gylen Changehouse
> 1743 Duncan MacCulloch – Changekeeper at the Changehouse of Gylene,

1747 Duncan MacCulloch Ardmore, Changehouse Gylen for being allowed to malt and distil pays 20 merks yearly and is not to retain either leper or greater quantity of spirits within the Island of Kerrera under penaltie of 20 pounds Scots for each fault.

At Barnabuck the Changehouse was among a cluster of little houses in the township, built from materials at hand, nestling into the background, and needing constant repair or rebuilding.

Mr. John MacDougall, from Mull, took the tenancy of the Barnabuck Changehouse in 1746, but a new house was built by John MacMartin in 1749 at a cost of £3 10/-. In the tack of 1752 the new Changekeeper was to leave 'the houses and biggins in as good and sufficient condition at his removal therefrom as at his entry.' By 1786 the tenant was to leave 'the house worth seven pounds ten shillings in timber thatch and stone, and the oyr small houses annexted to the publick houfe sufficient as also the gardain dick.' But the removing tenant was likely to be recompensed for buildings which he had improved during his tenancy, unless he was considered to have had the full use of their value. 'Any amelioration he does on the buildings he is to have two thirds if he continues seven years; if fourteen one third; if twenty-one no compraisement.'

It was not, however, until 1810 that any Changekeeper stayed even the fourteen years. When Mr. Allan MacDougall took the tenancy in 1810 he remained until 1845, and possibly later. He was known as 'Allan Public' to avoid confusion with another at Barnabuck known as 'Allen Mor.'

The Changekeeper had 'the grass of seven soums, to wit three cows, ten sheep and a horse'. He paid two pecks of meal for the herding of each cow, and the other tenants had to supply him with straw and straw ropes for thatching the Inn and his share of the Kiln.

When, in 1747, John MacDougall took on the Changehouse which may have been the first of the Barnabuck inns, Dunollie agreed to supply him with certain provisions. These included fifty bolls of 'good and sufficient bear, sixteen bolls to be delivered in harvest, consisting of five firlots to the boll, and thirty-four bolls of the same deliverable in winter consisting of seventeen pecks to the boll'.

Provision was made for the all too prevalent bad seasons; the tenant was not to 'insist against Dunollie for delivery of said bear' but Dunollie 'obliged himself and his tennants in Ardmore, Barnabuck, Gaolin and Ardchoirk not to sell their farm bear until the Changekeeper shall compleatly receive the said quantity of fifty bolls.'

The Changekeeper was to pay eight pounds Scots for each of the fifty bolls, in equal proportions, one half payable at the 25th December and the 'oyr half at Whitesun day' – giving Whitsunday its original spelling, and regarding Christmas day as a reasonable day to ask for payment!

In 1748 Dunollie agreed to provide the Changekeeper with all the cheese he required at 3/6 the stone, and his butter at 7/- the stone; and all the meal he required at 10 merks the boll. The following account indicates the consumption of cheese and butter during spring, summer and autumn at the Changehouse.

Alexander MacDougall (who took on the Inn when John MacDougall left after one year for Dunach) in Barnabuck his account of Cheefe and butter:

1748	May 23	to cheese a stone	3/6
	June 8	to cheese 1 stone	3/6
	Aug 8	to cheese 4 stone	14/-
		to a stone of butter	7/-
	Sept 18	to a stone of cheese	3/6
	Oct 26	to 5 stone cheese	17/6
		to butter 1 stone	7/-

In 1752 Dunollie 'likewise obliges to sell and deliver five dozen kain fouls and a score of eggs to each foul' for which the Changekeepr was to pay 'four shillings sterling for each of the said five dozen fouls [*sic*] and a score of eggs to each fowl [*sic*].'

At Barnabuck a window at the back is pointed out as where formerly drinks were handed out to customers sitting on the bench outside.

During the nineteenth century the one-floored thatched inns were replaced by slate-roofed two storey houses, some details of which are given for Port Kerrera. In 1748 John MacMartin built the Ferry house and Milk house, probably replacing older houses, for the sum of £4 11/8, and Duncan MacDougall, tacksman of Gallanach Beg 'has taken a seven year tack of Portninachar commencing at Whitesunday 1747 … and is to get fifty bols of bear att eight pound the bol'. As well as 'victual' (grain) he was to get all the butter and cheese he required from Dunollie, and from the accounts it seems that the arrangements for the inn at Port Kerrera were much the same as for the inn at Barnabuck at this period. A tack of 1781 laid down 'whatever malt is made by the Innkeeper at Port Kerrera shall be grinded at the Mill of Slaterach and pay for the same at the rate of half a peck of malt for each boll of malt grinded'.

In 1779 the buildings consisted of the Publichouse, kitchen, barn, byre and kiln, and in 1818 the house, kitchen barn and 'bire' were valued as 'sufficient' but a new kiln was wanted.

During the tenancy of the MacGregor family, in 1843 a new house was professionally built, of two stories, and with a slated roof of slates from the quarry on the little island of Belnahua which lies north of Lunga off the west coast of Luing; the quarry is long since 'wrought out'. The stairs were to be of red pine; the flooring properly tongued and grooved; the ceiling of the big room on the left of the entrance to be 'lathed and plastered' and the walls to be plastered. The windows were to be sashed.

The passenger route between the mainland and Mull was from Port Kerrera across the island to Barr nam boc and doubtless the track was fairly rough. A committee, of which Patrick MacDougall of Dunollie was convenor, met on March 31 1801 to:

> examine the line of road from Port Kerrera to Barnabuck and are of the opinion that the best and easiest line is to proceed from the quay by the foot of the hill immediately below the Publick house then by the gullet at the west end of the house till it joins the old road at the burn, thence by the old road as far as the meadow below the Houses of Ballimore and then to the right through the field and round the barn between the trees and the barn then take the slope up the hill to the left above the smithy from thence keeping to the left of the old road to the top of the hill in sight of the houses of Slatrach and from thence keeping to the left as the ground is marked out to the height above Barnabuck keeping generally to the left of the old road by the brow of the hill from this height the road slopes across the upper part of the field striking over the gullet to the right from that direction as pointed out.

Twenty-three years later the 'Committee of the Road Trustees of the District of Lorn' met in April 1824 to report on the new line of road proposed to be made from Oban by the shore to Port Kerrera to Barnabuck. In giving their general approval to a survey made in 1922 they made the following observations:

> The small croft at the (mainland) landing place will be injured by the cattle when landed from Kerrera, but to prevent this as much as possible they recommend an enclosure sufficient to prevent the cattle from straying, as they may be landed at different times, and if required by the proprietor they recommend a fence on the upper side of the road for about two or three hundred years from the landing place…
>
> They also consider the line of road which passes through Kerrera the best that could be drawn, and though it passes through a great portion of arable land they consider it an improvement… should the arable land through which it passes be enclosed, which the committee consider as necessary as the inclosures recommended betwixt Kerrera and Oban… They likewise approve the proposed communication from Port Kerrera to Gallanach by the shore a little above high watermark, and when finished recommend the road leading up the hill from Port Kerrera to be shut up.

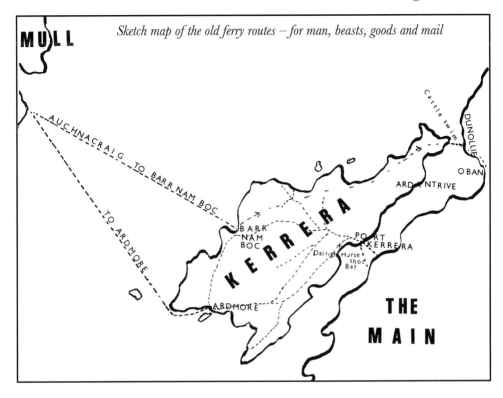

Sketch map of the old ferry routes – for man, beasts, goods and mail

By 1832 the new routes were open. Among the men who worked on the new Kerrera road were the tenants of Ardchoirc farm, Malcolm Livingstone and Angus MacDougall.

> Dec 5 1831 – half of road to Barnabuck
>   200 roods @ 3/6

for which they each received £17 10/- with small later additions, probably for repairs.

In connection with the new route, and also because of the decision about this time to ferry the black cattle from Mull by boat from Port Kerrera, instead of using the traditional swim across to Dunollie, repairs and an addition were needed to the landing slip at Port Kerrera. Estimates for the work were sought, and that of Mr. Campbell was accepted for £78 8/-. It is interesting to compare this with the bill for the building of the pier at Barr nam boc in 1758 (£7 7/-).

Specification for the work to be done by Mr. Campbell included:

> present slip to be taken down from the turn and a new addition built 15 feet broad
> and carried out in a straight direction so that a boat can load at the outer extremity

of it at low water spring tides. The height of the outer extremity to be four feet from the foundations, and carried with a regular slope to join and correspond with the upper part of the slip. The whole of the stones to be regularily laid lengthwise through the thickness of the walls. The top of the slip to be coped with stones set on edge, and the outer corners to be secured with iron bars running six feet each way, two inches broad and half an inch thick, and fixed with iron bolts set six inches into each stone.

Four iron rings to be placed on the top of the slip and fixed into large stones where answerable, and the whole to be done in a substantial and workmanlike manner.

XI SCHOOLS

John Knox's ideal was for a school in every Scottish parish. Half a century after his death in 1572, Parliament passed an Act declaring 'every plough- or husband-land according to its worth should be taxed for the maintenance of parish schools'.[1] A law of 1696 decreed that a schoolmaster and school should be appointed for every parish, and that assessments be made from the heritors and tenants for the master's salary to be enforced by the Presbyteries. By the 1730s the Church had achieved over a hundred Parish schools; and although by 1750 there were nearly two hundred parishes without schools this was remedied by the close of the century.

Education, or the lack of it, had long been the concern of the Presbytery of Kilmore, and they 'lamented the desolate state of several parishes within its bounds with respect to the education of youth for want of proper schools … not withstanding the good and even laudable Acts of Parliament'. In 1749 they called a meeting of elders, heritors and heads of families, which decided to appoint a parochial school to be settled in the most convenient place in Kilmore. Alexander MacDougall of Dunollie spoke of his desire for a school in Kerrera, and it was agreed that the legal stint from the Island's 'ploughlands' should go towards providing learning for its bairns.

In the larger parishes, such as Kilmore and Kilbride, many children lived too far from the parochial school for them to be able to attend it, even in the days when they walked many miles to receive their education. In such cases it was very often the Society in Scotland for Propagating Christian Knowledge who appointed school-masters and partly financed an extra school where it was needed. This society was not a Presbyterian foundation, but in Scotland it worked with the General Assembly of the Church of Scotland, and the Presbyteries. Whatever the immediate outcome of the meeting held in 1749, this Society made arrangements for a schoolmaster to be appointed in Kerrera, and in 1757 Dunollie received the following letter:

To Alexander McDougald of McDougald Esq of Dunollie
Dear Sir,
In great haste I have pleasure to inform you by this the Society have appointed a school(master) in Kerrera and £5 stg. in sellery.
Mr. John MacDougal your nominee is fixed on for master of it. But before he has any right to his benefice he must be firstly qualified to the Govt.
Secondly he must be examin'd and attested by the Presbytery of Lorn as to his sufficiency and moral character, and 3rdly the Pbty must ascertain that a school house is provided for him (if its an empty barn its enough).
After he has taught for some time, let the Pbty order his school to be examin'd; let them next examine himself in March or April next, and transmit me a

certificate of his being qualified as a Catechist in that Island and I will procure him at least an addition of 40sh pr. an. from the Committee.

His sellery commences from the date of his taking up school, and as I have assisted in a school for Benderloch your schoolmaster is entirely your own. The Bursars from the publick collections are to be named by the respective Synods ...

your most sincerely affectionate

Canongate Edin   oblig'd & obedient sert

June 25th 1757   John Warden

P.S. Excuse the hurry wt wh I am obliged to write this and pardon me to put you in mind, that the continuance and increase of the sellery to your schoolmaster depends on the schools being properly attended and the greater number of scholars he has the better it will be for your people and the schoolmaster himself; and the greater satisfaction it will give here. I know your influence will not be wanting.

The S.P.C.K., writing in 1803, were not satisfied with the way things had been going, and set out their requirements:

We require all Candidates for employment in our service to come to Edinburgh and be examined by two of our Ecclesiastical members, and it is not till after they are sustained by them that they are put upon our list – and of that list the Candidates are appointed to the Schools as vacancies occur; but before a school-master is sent to a school, we require that an attestation shall be transmitted by two clergymen founded on their own observation that the accommodations are ready for his reception.

These are a comfortable dwelling house, a schoolroom of sufficient size furnished with tables, forms and glass windows, a kail yard, and provision for a cow in summer and winter – and that the tenants shall be bound to drive his fuel gratis. In Kerrera's case, the 4 pound must be paid regularly, and fuel provided by you.

So in the latter half of the eighteenth century Kilmore had its Parochial school, and Kerrera its S.P.C.K. school partly financed by the heritors and the Kerrera tenants; The rent book records:

1760 Ardmore – John and Donald MacLea they pay no publick burthern of Cess of Tythes saving the schole master's sellery and interest of manse money till ye manse is built… they pay the half of it.

Later entries, into the first two decades of the next century range from 'schollmasters sellerie' to the more brief 'school and straw – 6/- and 4/-'.

In general the path of these early country schools seems to have been very rough. Whether the Society's 'if its an empty barn its enough' was taken too literally, certainly the 'comfortable dwelling houses' and suitable school rooms were slow to materialize, and in Kerrera conditions were apparently no better.

Tradition suggests at least two buildings which were used as early schools, the sites still marked by ruined walls. Both are on the high ground near the old tracks across the hills, and would not then have been so isolated as they seem now. There is a lack of information about these early buildings. Most description of Argyllshire schools of the period dwell upon their delapidation; in spite of this, some fine highland types emerged from homes and schools described as 'very insufficient'.

… Even the buildings specially erected for the purpose were as poor and comfortless as could be imagined. Their walls were of turf or rough undressed stone, through the crevices of which the wind whistled … their windows were irregular without glass; in many cases there were no benches.

Of another Argyllshire school it was reported:

A small building on the side of a hill, little attempt to level the floor, a fire in the centre and a hole in the roof for the smoke to escape, windows broken, and the roof seems to be falling in.

In winter 'every boy is supposed to bring two peats from home to fuel the fire, but on summer days the pupils were allowed to learn their lessons in a nearby field.'

Whoever succeeded Kerrera's first school master, Alexander McLuglash was teacher from about 1789 until 1803 when thoroughly discouraged by the conditions of his employment he 'took up his abode in the village of Oban' to be succeeded by a Hugh MacDougall, of the beautiful copperplate handwriting. There is mention in the rent book of 1807 of 'the school at Balliemore' and this may have been on the site where the school was built or repaired in 1831.

In 1811 Mr. Malcolm MacIntyre was appointed schoolmaster and began the long family teaching connection with the island which was to last, father to son, for nearly ninety years. When there was no dwelling house for the teacher, country school masters often lodged with local families and in 1817 Mr. MacInytre was lodging with John MacDougall, junior, one of the three tenants at Slaterach who had built their own houses when the land was partitioned into three holdings in 1812.

To Pat. MacDougall of MacDougall
Dunollie 12 July 1817

Sir,

You'll give John MacDougall in Slaterich credit for Seven pounds sterling that I am due him for boarding, which I will sustain to you in paying my salary as Schoolmar in Kerrera.

I am Sir,

    Your mt obt & Hule Sert

     Mm MacIntyre

It appears to be in 1815 that the Kerrera school became a Parochial school:

At Oban the 12th day of April 1815 a meeting of the Heritors of the Parish of Kilbride was held … Malcolm MacIntyre late Schoolmaster of Kerrera was elected to fill the said office of Parochial Schoolmaster of the Island of Kerrera in the United Parish of Kilmore and Kilbride… The meeting having taken into consideration the School dues for the Island of Kerrera determined that the following dues should in future be charged:

For English Reading	2/6 per quarter
For Reading & Writing	3/- per quarter
For Arithmetic	4/- per quarter

When, in 1884 there was a rise in fees, there were protests from some of the parents of children attending the Kilmore school, addressed to the schoolmaster, Mr. Burton:

Sir, I got your account, and it is impossible for me to pay such High Fees. I would do my utmost the way it was, but I cannot pay it now.

Dear Sir, I have to tell you that I am not able to pay such high fees for school, they are too high for the like of me and if you will not make it less I am no able to do it because they are the double of what they used to be.

Sir, I think the fees of my children is to dear in fact I am not hardly able to pay it all at this time on the account of short days and [?] weather and I would feel oblight to you if you reduse it a lettle.

Dear Sir, I feel it impossible hereafter to pay the school fees for my daughter. If they were what they used to be I might with a struggle manage. I should feel much indebted to you if you would speak in my behalf to the members of the School board. In doing so you would much oblige.

Living so near the poverty line, there must surely have been much relief when school fees were abolished for the younger children in 1889 and for all by 1891.

The heritors and Minister of the Parishes of Kilmore and Kilbride met in 1829 'to fix the salaries of the parochial schoolmasters'. Since the average price of a chalder of oatmeal for all Scotland for the twenty-five years preceding 1826 was £17 2/2¼, the meeting considered they were now to determine in terms of the 'Act 43d Geo. III Cap 54' the salaries of the schoolmasters. It was resolved that the schoolmaster of Kilmore should have for his salary 'ane chalder and a half – which at the above named average amount £25 13/3 sterling, which sum will be paid yearly to the schoolmaster by the heritors in the rates of their valued rent…'

It was resolved that there be three parochial schoolmasters in the parish of Kilbride, one at Kilbride, one at Oban and one at Kerrera, and that the schoolmaster at Kilbride shall have £21 7/9 the same to the schoolmaster in Kerrera and £8 13/3 sterling to the schoolmaster in Oban, 'being the amount of three chalders of meal for the salaries of the parochial schoolmasters at Kilbride'.

In 1831 there is an account for building or rebuilding the schoolhouse beside the road between Baillemore farm and Baillemor Beg by two men from Slaterach: Archibald Fergusson, retirng from Slaterach Mill, and Angus MacKinnon farming tenant.

I, Angus MacKinnon bind myself to thatch the Kerrera Schoolhouse, point it outside with lime, plaster the ins de and do the floor with clay for one pound and fifteen shillings.

I, Archibald Fergusson bind myself to finish the doors windows and seats, you supplying the wood, for one pound ten shillings.

In 1848 the heritors held a meeting within the (old) Caledonian Hotel for the purpose of considering the state of the schools in the parish –

the meeting taking into view the present very unsatisfactory state of school accom-modation within the Parish and the necessity of having it remedied and a proper arrangement come to as to the school stent to be levied upon the whole.

They therefore propose to substitute the following general arrangement for the present one:

1. That the maximum assessment of three chalders of oatmeal be laid upon the united Parish and allocated in terms of law on each heritor for the purpose of raising the necessary fund for the payment of the schoolmasters required within it.

2. That there should be only two schoolmasters, one to be established in a centrical point of the mainland part of the parish with two thirds of the whole

salary, and another Schoolmaster for the Island of Kerrera, with the remaining third as his salary.

3. That a proper School and Schoolmaster's House be erected at such centrical point as may hereafter be fixed on and obtained at the expence of all the heritors of the united Parish, such expence being levied according to the real rent.

After thirty-five years as schoolmaster of Kerrera, Malcolm MacIntyre had died two years before, and meanwhile his son Peter had continued as teacher.

The Presbytery of Lorn applied to the Commissioners of Supply, who met at Inverary on September 25th 1848 and directed the Clerk to insert an advertisement in the Glasgow Herald and North British Advertiser calling a meeting for the purpose of electing a schoolmaster 'for the said Parish of Kerrera'. There were two candidates 'viz Peter MacIntyre who has taught the school of Kerrera since the death of his Father the late teacher, and Duncan MacDougall schoolmaster in the parish of Delavich'. Peter MacIntyre was unanimously elected 'if found qualified for the office' and the meeting 'remitted him to the Presbytery of Lorn for examination'.

And at Kilninver the 30th day of November 1848 the Presbytery of Lorn met and was constituted:

Compeared Mr. Peter MacIntyre and produced a Certified Extract minute of the proceedings of the Commissioners of Supply for the County of Argyll dated Inverary 31st October 1848, bearing the said Commissioners had appointed *dune devolute* the said Mr. Peter MacIntyre to be Schoolmaster in the Island of Kerrera, also Certificates of character and Qualifications for Schoolmaster, together with a certificate of Qualification to Government, and craved to be examined as to his fitness for said Office.

Whereupon the Presbytery having caused the said Extract and Certificates to be read to them, proceeded to examine them and take trial of his proficiency in the several branches usually taught and necessary to be taught in the school of Kerrera, and being fully satisfied with the same, they required him to sign in their presence the Confession of Faith and Formula of the Church of Scotland... found and do hereby find him qualified, and did and hereby do declare him legal School master in Kerrera and entitled to the salary and School wages attached to that Office.

He was to adorn this office with honour for half a century and more.

In a letter to John MacDougall of Dunollie his wife wrote:

I went with the boys yesterday to witness the examination of the Kerrera school by our Minister, and really think the children did the schoolmaster much credit.

Peter MacIntyre,
schoolmaster for
fifty-four years

He told me that the children were so irregular in their attendance that much could not be expected of them; I therefore promised a few prizes for the most regular attendance and the best scholars.

They were very clean and tidy, and really surprised us all by their quickness in arithmetic, the sums were no sooner given out than they were done, and in almost every instance correctly. I was surprised that none of the parents were there.

Mr. Campbell (the Minister) has received a parcel of valuable books from the Highland Society, I think, which are to be competed for next month at Kilbride by all the neighbouring schools. I think the Kerrera arithmetic class stand a very fair chance of carrying off a prize or two in that department.

Mr. MacIntyre, the schoolmaster, later wrote to Dunollie concerning the prizes offered for attendance and merit, and enclosed the findings of Mr. Campbell and two other clergy men who examined the school: 'they express themselves highly satisfied with the progress made by the children, and consider that there is a marked improvement in the school work which they attribute in great measure to the emulation excited by the distribution of prizes.'

A list drawn up about 1860 shows there were twenty-three children on the Island 'from five years and upwards': Duncan and Janet Cowan from Ardmore, and Anne, John, Margaret Dugald and Mary Cowan from Upper Gylen; Mary, John, Janet and Anne Livingstone from Lower Gylen, James, Mary and Catherine Stevenson from Gylen Park – at that time Mr. John Stevenson rented it as well as Balliemore farm. From Balliemore Croft Malcolm Campbell, and John, Neil, Archie and Donald Connel, and newcomers from Barnabuck Colina Love, and Alexander, Anne and Hugh Campbell.

By this time, however, the school accommodation was referred to as 'a thatched house not in good condition' and the teacher's house just across the road as a 'small thatched house very insufficient'. Mr. McIntyre complained – vigorously, and in November of 1861 the heritors gave him the somewhat grudging answer:

> The Schoolmaster of Kerrera Mr. Peter McIntyre is granted £10 by the heritors for putting his house and Schoolhouse in repair, and is not to demand any further sum for the like purpose for two years from this date, but reserving to himself any legal right he may have.

The proportions payable by each of the heritors to make up the £10 was carefully worked out. Dunollie's share was £2 15/6, Lochnell, Breadalbane and Glenfeochan a pound or so, Dunstaffnage, Gallanach, Sonnachan, Lerags, Dunach and Soroba a few shillings. These nine heritors also paid their proportions of the salaries payable to their schoolmasters, increased from the terms of the Act of 1803 by the Act of 1861. The Kilmore schoolmaster received an annual salary of £35 1/-, instead of £30, and Mr. McIntyre in Kerrera received £24 instead of £21 7/-.

By 1864 the state of his little buildings were bad. On examination it was found 'The schoolhouse roof requires repairs, being dangerous to keep a school within untill such time as that is done to it. The dwelling house is in bad state, the whole roof being in a decayed state also the back wall is bulging out and is only hinging and standing and requires a thorough repair.'

Meanwhile the heritors had built a new school and schoolhouse at Kilmore in about 1862, and when Mr. McIntyre lodged another complaint about the Kerrera school the Minister of the parish, the Rev. D. Campbell called a meeting 'stating its object from the pulpit of Kilmore Church' to be held on February 2nd 1864. The findings of the meeting were not encouraging:

With reference to the schools in the mainland portion of the parish and the Island of Kerrera find in respect that the heritors of the united Parish have already built a school and schoolhouse for the parish they are not called upon to build another for the same parish and as the numbers of scholars attending the school in Kerrera are so small and as the school and schoolhouse are not the property of the heritors the meeting decline being at further expence in the matter of accommodation for the Kerrera teacher.

Although repairs were done, and Mr. MacIntyre's house rethatched, it was in the next decade that Dunollie replaced the old buildings with new ones. It was reported in the *Oban Times 1872:*

> Colonel Charles McDougall of Dunollie has contracted with Messrs. McDougall and MacColl, builders, Oban, for the erection of a new teacher's house on the site of the present dwelling, which will be removed off the ground to make room for its successor.

The building began in June and 'was expected to be finished in the autumn.' By this time the school had come into the care of the School board of Kilmore and Kilbride, set up in 1872, and it agreed to grant Mr. Peter McIntyre £3 as lodging money during the time the residence was in the course of erection.

The new house (now privately occupied) had a slated roof, a kitchen, a 'room' and a small bedroom off the room where Mr. MacIntyre's mother slept. She died about 1881, and three years later he married Christina MacGregor. 'Kirsty' had kept him waiting for years; she was head Nannie with the MacDougalls of Soroba (and Battlefields, near Bath) and would not leave her charges until she considered the youngest baby – of six – old enough to be trusted to other hands.

Kirsty kept the schoolhouse garden full of flowers and fruit – it is still remembered – and had a beautiful scarlet tropaeolum growing up the wall of the cottage. She was a fine baker, and famous for her potato scones and barley scones – bere bannocks. The children came to her for lessons in sewing and knitting.

In 1894 H. Walker, Painter & Decorator Oban rendered his account: 'Mr McIntyre Schr, Kerrera – Size tinting and painting, as per estimate £3'.

The new school, built in 1872, was on an entirely different site, near the Ferryhouse, and overlooking the Sound of Kerrera. Above the entrance is a commemorative plaque:

In memory
A.J. MacDougall of MacDougall
Born August 23 1827
Died August 26 1867

The 1872 church and school, with the teacher's house on the right. Beyond is the Ferryhouse and the Sound of Kerrera

Alexander, 26th of Dunollie, had been engaged for seven years; six weeks after the marriage he died of pneumonia. His widow, who went blind, decided to provide a building on Kerrera which would serve the island as both Kirk and school. A contemporary diary recounts the choosing of the site and the progress of the building, still in use. The diarist, Colonel Charles MacDougall, Alexander's brother, and 27th of Dunollie, had the help of his sister Louisa, who procured the site for the present St. John's school in Oban, and had its welfare so much at heart.

> 1872   Feb 13   Went with Louisa to fix site of school.
>
> March 30   Met Mr. Sims at Ferry at half past eleven to mark out ground for school.
>
> April 27   Freestone for school being unloaded
>
> May 30   Paid MacDougall and MacColl on account for school in Kerrera.
>
> June 10   School walls nearly at full height.
>
> August 7   Went with Annie (Alexander's widow) to the new school.

The new school was a substantial slate-roofed building, and Mr. MacIntyre taught in it for twenty-eight years until he retired in 1900. He had a high standard and himself wrote beautiful letters in a hand which remained steady even in his latter years. His weekly entries in the school log followed a regular pattern; typical is the entry date December 6th 1895:

Attendance irregular this week, chiefly owing to the stormy state of the weather, which retards the progress of the school. Bible and other lessens given according to time table. School opened and closed with prayer at the usual times.

Irregular attendances were his constant worry. Although these were sometimes due to his pupils being kept at home to help with farm work, it was often the 'boisterous state of the weather' the 'rain and storm which consequently marred the progress of the school'. The subjects he taught included Bible study, arithmetic, spelling, dictation, grammar, parsing, reading, writing, copying, slate writing, composition, geography and history. Among the books he used were Chamber's *Expressive and Fluent Readers* and Robertson's *English Grammar*.

In an entry of 1898 he logs that 'special drill given in grammar, dictation and composition'. Even now, former pupils especially recall his grammar lessons, his teaching of decimals and fractions, and the speedy answers required from his scholars during the mental arithmetic sessions. As a member of the Educational Institute of Scotland and an office bearer in the local branch, he had to attend meetings in Oban – as such log entries indicate:

21 Feb. 1896: Mr. MacIntyre (Headmaster) was away from home on important business on Tuesday, but school was kept on Saturday.

According to the log, school was always kept on Saturday when he had business during the week.

In his latter years 'Schoolie' as he was called, was an impressive figure, with snow-white hair and side whiskers. He usually wore a long frock coat, in the back pocket of which he was said to have kept a tawse. When he came to teach in the new school building he found something there which the old school at Balliemore with its clay floor did not possess. This was a loose floor board, which when lifted gave access to a space below the building. This was a great aid to discipline, and years later elderly farmers recounted how as boys they were put down the hole as punishment.

In the light summer evenings he used to like to walk over to the Ferryhouse and sit on the bench outside, taking his snuff and discussing the day's news with the Postmistress. In 1895 his Jubilee was honoured, and the testimonial circulated to advertise the proposal indicates his career in an earlier scholastic climate.

… The school on Kerrera … was for a very long time the principle school in the parish of Kilbride, and had at one time more than fifty pupils on its roll. On the passing of the Educational Act the school was placed under the School Board of Kilbride, and since 1875 has been annually inspected by H.M. Inspectors who hold a very high opinion of Mr MacIntyre's conscientiousness as a teacher. He is

Kerrera School prizegiving, 1899. Mr and Mrs MacIntyre and scholars.
Standing: Dugald Cowan, Neil Cowan (Gylen). Middle: Alex MacKenzie (Burnabuck), Jessie
MacInnes, Mary Ann Cowan (Gylen), Mr and Mrs MacIntyre, Barbara and Jessie MacIntyre
(Orasaig and Gylen Park), Jean Cowan (Gylen). Front: Johnnie MacInnes (Ferryhouse), Hugh
MacInnes (Ferryhouse), Joanne MacKenzie

not only one of the very first parochial teachers still remaining, but one of the
oldest members of the E.I.S., his name being on the first Roll in 1847. The Lorn
Branch was founded in the same year, and in 1853 Mr MacIntyre became treas-
urer, and has held office ever since. In 1891 he acted as President of the Branch
and made local arrangements for the Conferance on Secondary education which
the Institute held in Oban that year, and which did so much for the course of the
Secondary Education in this district …

The 'Testimonial' was followed by an invitation to a 'Conversazione to be held in
the High School, Oban' (Rockfield Building). A neat little programme printed in blue
with the delicate flourishes beloved by Victorian printers had a photograph of the
grand old man on the cover. Among the songs was *Cruachan Beann* fresh from winning

the open song competition at the 1896 Mod, and there were selections on the pipes by Mr John McColl, of Oban, a notable player in the piping world for many decades. No doubt two of the speeches 'An Educational Retrospect' followed by 'An Educational Forecast' would make interesting hearing. Then followed the presentation, from a grateful community, of a Clan tartan plaid and a silver brooch, together with a purse of golden sovereigns.

His last entry in the Kerrera school log was on May 25 1900, when he wrote 'Mr MacIntyre who taught Kerrera Public School for fifty-four years and twenty-five of which under Government inspection is retiring on Monday 28 May 1900. School opened and closed with prayer at the usual hour'.

A few years later, his successor, Miss Rodger recorded in the book: Feb.5 1904 'The School was closed on Wednesday as it was the funeral of Mr Peter MacIntyre late schoolmaster.'

With Mr. MacIntyre's retirement in view at the turn of the century, it had been decided that he and his wife, Kirsty, should continue to live in what later became known as 'the Old School House'; a new teacher's house was built by the School Board near to the new school. The foundation stone was laid in the autumn of 1901 by the young Chief Alexander whilst on his honeymoon. Kirsty, Mrs MacIntyre had been Nannie to his bride, Colina, when she was a baby at Soroba.

Under the foundation stone was placed in a jar the coins of the realm, copies of the *Oban Times*, *Glasgow Herald* and other papers, names of members of the School Board, the Contractor and his workmen, the Teacher Miss Rodger, together with verses she had written specially for the occasion.

The new century brought a new generation of teachers – ladies who gave long years of their best to the Kerrera school against a background of changing educational ideas. On 1900 May 28 – 'This day I, Margaret Rodger, Certificated teacher began duty in this school – and there were present four boys and four girls.' Until the new teacher's house was completed she lodged at Balliemore farm and at the Ferryhouse. The children had been used to being 'drilled' mentally, reciting tables and mental arithmetic, passages from the Scripture learnt by rote, the questions and answers of the Shorter Catechism. Miss Rodger introduced drill for their bodies: 'have given drill and singing lessons each day'.

Sewing lessons continued, but an entry in November 1900 remarks 'the knitting was started on Wed. as it is almost impossible to sew on these dark days'. The kindergarten began to sew maps and time was given for drawing – the children drew on their slates, or practised on the blackboard; but on Jan. 10 1902 'received a dozen boards for free arm drawing' – and later, drawing books, brushes and copybooks.

Encouragement was given to wider reading. She introduced the *Laureate Poetry Book* to the school, and the School Board recommended that Scott's *Lord of the Isles*, *Alice in Wonderland* and *The Pilgrim's Progress* be used as reading books.

Then the school received a very practical gift, and in this connection Mary Cameron writes in her *Childhood Days on St. Kilda*: 'There was am oak-bookcase filled with books … most of them part of the library which the beneficent Coats family had bestowed upon St. Kilda among other places.' Kerrera was among the 'other places' as the Log records: '1906 Oct. 20 – Mr James Coats, Ferguslie, Paisley, sent book-case and books' and, later, 'Library books labelled and catalogued, and given out on Thursdays. All are delighted.'

Miss Rodger used part of two summer vacations to attend classes at the Marine Biological Association at Millport; her enthusiasm resulted in:

> 1904 July – A new feature in the school this year was the Botany class, and great eagerness was shown by all in the work… one little girl alone exhibiting and knowing as many as 302 of the Island's wild flowers. They are mounted and named by their popular names.

On Nov. 25 1910 Miss Rodger received a letter from the Clerk 'informing me that Miss Nimmo was appointed teacher of Kerrera and would begin duty on the 28th the day I was expected to take charge of Kilmore school'.

So 'I, Isabella Grant Nimoo, certificated teacher' began with seven children. Her sister married Mr Alexander Leslie, who began the thriving lobster business at The Little Horseshoe Bay, and in due course her young nephews and nieces became pupils in the school. She had an excellent understanding of children, and continued to foster their natural interest in the wild life around them.

The school had many friends and visitors who gave books, offered prizes, or left money for the Church:

> Nov. 29 – A lamp has been bought with the 3/- which has left for Church funds by Mrs C.
>
> 1914 Sept. 18 – Miss L left 1/- for anything that might be required for the Church.

Every thing was carefully logged, and money seemed more elastic in those days!

Miss Nimmo guided the school through the First World War, when news came from time to time of the loss on active service of some of the island's former pupils. In June of 1918 a speaker visited the school and 'advised the children what they could do to help to win the war'. They had, in fact, made considerable efforts; in 1916 the junior boys began knitting socks, and next spring all the children gave the socks, gloves, mitts and scarves they had made to the 'Soldiers Comforts' collection. It is interesting to note that of eight prizes awarded in knitting and darning, six were won by boys.

At the summer prizegiving in 1916 'most of the prizes were given in money, of which a considerable amount was handed over to the Red Cross funds.' They were also contributing to other war efforts, and it was reported in the Press in 1917 'Pupils of the Kerrera school have done splendid work in contributing and collecting sphagnum moss for our wounded'.

The depot for collecting eggs from the West Highlands and Islands, including the West Coast lighthouses, was in the tiny six-sided Dunollie Old Lodge, (now no more) at the foot of the hill approaching Oban from the North. Eggs were needed for the wounded in hospitals, and response to appeals brought in over a hundred thousand. These were carefully rubbed all over with butter, packed and transported by whatever means possible (including collections made by the old *Hesperus*, lighthouse ship under the late Captain Budge) to the Dunollie Lodge. Here they were checked and despatched to the different hospitals as required. A slogan asked everyone (and many more then kept hens) to 'Give an Egg a Week' and it was the school children who so often kept the collections going.

There was also a sphagnum moss depot in Oban at Raasay Lodge (later the Youth Hostel) in World War I, and at the Manor House in World War II. Of the many species of sphagnum, some had greater powers of absorption, and these were carefully collected, cleaned by relays of volunteers, dried and put into cotton bags and sent off as hospital dressings for war wounds; it was considered they had healing properties. The quality of the Kerrera moss was highly regarded.

Over the years the school was regularly inspected by Educational Inspectors, who found it a 'very happy little school, characterised by an excellent tone … the children are frank and alert, and seem eager to do well. Their oral response is good, and they are willing to think… The ordinary subjects are supplement by a fine variety of practical and recreational activities (this was 1917), all admirably fitted to compensate for the isolation of the place'. It might be added that the children's good manners, commonsense and helpfulness were appreciated far beyond the school buildings.

A photograph of 1899 shows the girls in the long sleeved dresses and light pinafores typical of the period, and all the children barefoot. At that time most of the children wore boots in winter and none in summer, and on occasions carried them round their necks till needed. Locally, Easter Monday was reckoned as the customary day for boots to be left off for the summer, not to be worn again till late autumn. The boots were stout, tacketed and calf length, and usually kept out the wet. They were, however, an expensive item of clothing. A Lismore family counted on selling enough whelks to buy the children's boots, each autumn, but those who could not afford them came to school without.

By the time of World War I, 'having no boots' was given as a reason for absence from school, and this happened more frequently in World War II, when coupons as well as money were needed to procure footwear. Several times a girl was marked as 'off two days because she had no boots'; a brother and sister 'off two months as no boots'; a family absent because boots were wet; a boy off 'because his boots are too small, he has sore feet.' One problem was solved, when a family couldn't come 'because they've no wellingtons and the hills are boggy,' by the teacher, who visited the Women's Voluntary Service depot in Oban, and achieved some suitable boots.

Lack of boots was not the only reason for absence from school. Weather naturally affected attendances, especially for those children who had to cross over from Gallanach and other nearby areas of the mainland. Wild seas sometimes prevented a morning crossing; or if a storm rose later in the day, children were occasionally storm-stayed overnight on the island. Two sisters prided themselves on taking an oar between them across the ferry.

A report in 1917 recorded 'visited the school and found attendance bad, and never will be better as long as the children have to cross the ferry in winter.' Even the island children sometimes arrived drenched, and had to be sent home early or sit by the stove to dry off. It was the custom of each child to bring a glass bottle filled with tea, and these were set beside the stove to keep warm. On occasions, if the stove was very hot there would be explosions as the corks popped, or even a whole bottle burst.

In the weeks of short daylight some of the children were allowed off earlier to reach more distant homes before dark. During World War II instructions were received, that, to comply with black-out regulations, school would not open until 10 am between November 3rd and March 3rd.

Often a child might be needed at home, sometimes in the house to look after younger children, more often to help outside. As a report puts it 'Attendances only fair during harvest', and that could also apply at the potato lifting and planting, and sheep dipping. When he was pressed, the ferryman might want his son to help with the boat, and children were sometimes needed as herds taking stock to and from Corson's Mart in Oban. 'Two older girls absent today, showing a bull at the Highland Cattle Show in Oban' – and this was followed by a picture in the *Oban Times* of one of the girls proudly holding the bull which had won the championship.

In the October of 1900 'Four children were absent because of the feeing market in Oban' – where employer met employee, and farm servants were hired for six months or a year and later a cart fetched their belongings in a wooden trunk. One small boy 'was off school all day without proper reason' but as this was frowned upon many and varied were the 'proper reasons'. 'March 18th, the ... were absent yesterday; their excuse is that yesterday was St. Patrick's Day'. In the spring of 1897 little Jeanie MacIntyre Cowan walked over from Gylen to start her school career; but in the autumn the old schoolmaster records in the log: 'Jean McI. Cowan has not returned to school owing to her youth and distance'.

The main school vacations were in the summer and at Christmas. The summer holiday began about the end of July and lasted into the second week in September. Possibly about the second decade in the century it changed to the present earlier dates, and lasted longer. The Christmas holiday began a day or two before Christmas, ending a day or two after the New Year's entry. Even in the old schoolmaster's time, at the end of the last century Christmas was celebrated with a party for the school. These parties are still spoken of by former pupils as being the highlights of the year. One vividly recalls how Mr. Hugh Cameron, head gardener at Dunollie for nearly fifty years, used to come over and set up a Christmas tree in the corner of the school. Each year there was a special surprise, and she remembers a moss-lined tank full of presents which had to be fished for with a hooked line. Another looks back sixty-five years to remember her sister's joy at receiving a little workbasket as her gift.

Sometimes the school was invited to a Christmas party at Gallanach, or at Dunollie, with what seemed to small children a huge glittering Christmas tree with the rich scent of pine needles and burning candles. Even at the Christmas Eve parties at Dunollie in the 1950s and 60s this nostalgic smell was not ousted by the more fashionable artificial alternatives. A 'reliable person' was always detailed to stand by with a bucket of water and a sponge on the end of a long bamboo.

A guest at such a party early in the century writes:

I do remember very clearly an innovation. In the hall, each guest was given a label with a string attached; the strings led all over the house to a hidden present at the other end. It might be in the attics or the coal cellar, and tremendous unravellings took place when strings got crossed and countercrossed, as they were designed to do. It became quite hilarious performance when three strings got crossed and had to be sorted out.

In 1907 the scholars had the thrill of watching a magic lantern in their own school. One Old New Years Day, Mr. Neil Munro of Oban sent a launch to bring the children in to see the Poultry Show, and probably the island had entered exhibits. In 1909 they were invited to the Gallanach Silver Wedding celebration. Occasionally there were unexpected holidays: 'school closed on Thursday and Friday to allow the walls to be whitewashed. The man who got the order neglected to do it during the holidays' – and that was in 1902! In 1903 – 28 May. 'Monday was given as a holiday as there was a sale of Ardmore Farm'.

There is a dignified account of 'Visit of young heiress to the school to meet the tenants. Cake and wine were handed round to the grownup people, and cake and sweets to the children, and a half holiday was granted to the school'. But one of the young pupils of the day recalls more than half a century later how she was so terrified by the sight of the 'young heiress' (aged three months) that she covered her face with her hands and refused to risk another look at the baby. To this day she remembers her parents shocked disgust, and the 'clapping' they gave her in their embarrassment.

Much enjoyed were the annual ploughing matches held in rotation on the island farms, and the scholars were granted a half holiday:

> 1896 Feb 28 – no school on Thursday afternoon, there being a ploughing match at Barnabuck.
> 1897 March 12 – no school on Friday afternoon, ploughing match at Ballimore Croft.

By 1820 the holiday was less assured:

> March 5 – perfect attendance, except John … who was out on Thurs. as he was required to take something to his uncle at the ploughing match. As the ploughing match was held on the island I gave no dinner interval and closed the school at 2 pm.

From time to time a new holiday featured in the calendar:

> 1905 26 May – Friday given as a holiday as it was observed in Oban as Victoria Day.
> 1907 7 Aug. – Scholars granted a holiday to attend Mod.

> 1898 8 July: Monday and Tuesday given as holidays after the examinations.

This two-day break in the term which ended July 29th was surely well earned, by both teacher and pupils. The examination by the Inspector sometimes accompanied by a member of the School Board must have been a strain, requiring much preparation and concentration on the day. The report reads: 'This school is taught with Mr. MacIntyre's usual earnestness and ability, and makes a very satisfactory appearance in the examination.'

Prizegiving followed later. Apparently initiated by the Dunollie family in 1852, over the years, many people, Islanders and others, have offered prizes for various subjects as well as for attendance; more recently, a cup for sports. In 1898 there was 'also a prize for the best sewer.' Later this prize came from Gallanach, and was earnestly prepared for:

> 1911 July 28: As Mrs. Patten MacDougall is going to judge the sewing on Thursday I allowed the senior children to sew all day Tuesday and Wednesday afternoon to get their seams finished.

In 1920 Miss Bruce of the Highland Home Industries – she was a household word in that connection – was staying at Gallanach, and Lady Patten MacDougall invited her to judge the handwork for the prizegiving. She had this to say: 'I have often judged sewing and knitting in the Islands and other parts of the Highlands, but I have never seen better work, considering the age of the children.'

Recreational activities 'were carried out with gusto and success' and the children's interest in their natural surroundings was infectious. 'The children watched with eagerness the development of a tadpole into a frog…' and before term ended 'tadpoles taken back to the burn – most of them had their four legs… We put peas and beans into water to observe the first phase of growth'. 'The children are observing the changing of a caterpillar into a moth [*sic*].'

Accounts of nature walks make peaceful reading as the Nations recovered from the conflicts of the First World War:

16 May 1919: On Wednesday we went for a ramble up the burnside in quest of nests and eggs. We saw a few nests, some old, some being made, and some with eggs in them. We saw the yellowhammer, wren and moss cheeper's nests with eggs in them and we found old nests of the thrush (song) and the blackbird. On the way we picked up a few flowers such as celendine, daisy, marsh marigold, violet, may flower, cress, lady's mantle, primrose, bugloss, Orchis and sphagnum moss. We also saw the elm, elder and oak trees.

We didn't return till 1 o'clock as Mary MacInnes lost her boot on the way, and we spent some time looking for it. (moss cheeper – meadow pipit)

On another day there was a ramble along the seashore, where 'the children observed the different rocks, the layers of clay, sand and gravel left by the tide, as well as the different kinds of seaweed'. Later generations were absorbed in visiting a pond, and finding caddie grubs, nymphs, dragonflies, diving beetles, newts and whirlygigs. One morning the children from Ardantrive arrived with news of a stranded octopus so during playtime the whole school went over to see it. They put it in the sea, and watched it swim away. Great was the school's joy when one autumn the cotoneaster berries near the building were visited by two of those colourful birds, the waxwings.

Over its generations, on the whole, the school has not been Gaelic speaking. In its early days, the S.P.C.K. who produced the teacher, discouraged Gaelic speaking in school, just as presently the young scholar in Shetland must be careful only to speak English in the classroom, reserving his native tongue for the home.

By the time Gaelic was allowed, or encouraged, much harm had been done for parents began to feel that to speak English rather than the natural tongue might help their children to advance in the world. Many alive today feel bitter at the active discouragement of Gaelic in the schools in the past; many wish they had had it as a second language. One lady, however, made the point that although they were not allowed to speak Gaelic in school, she felt the extra effort of having to learn lessons in what was virtually a foreign language perhaps made her learn the subject more thoroughly. She personally did not regret it, but then Gaelic was the language of her home, so she never lost it.

Both Gaelic and English reading were taught in the schools in the parish of Kilbride in the nineteenth century, but 'not a word of gaelic was taught or spoken in the Kerrera school' in the early years of the twentieth century writes a scholar of that time who was later to become Bard at the 1962 National Mod.

The first children's concert of the Mod was held in Oban in 1905, and in 1907 the 'scholars were granted a holiday to attend Mod. Jessie Isabella MacIntyre was there all day, and at evening concert' – she had previously been awarded a prize at school for 'dilegance in music'. In 1901 incomers to the island sent a girl to be admitted 'who although nearly eight has never been to school and cannot speak a word of English'.

However, from 1948 until 1966, the scholars had the benefit of an enthusiastic Gaelic-speaking teacher and member of *An Comunn Ghaidhleach* in Miss Miles from Mull, later Mrs. Leslie. Taught by her, some of the scholars entered the local Mod competitions in 1959, and brought home prizes for Solo and Duet singing, Reading for Native Speakers (a family from Tiree) and also for Learners and Recitation. Their tiny choir of seven was the sole entry that year for the Junior Rural Choir Competition, but they were awarded the first prize of £3.

There is an account of how the Choir's prize money went towards the purchase of a second-hand piano at a local auction sale to replace the one bought by public subscription in 1907. After being ferried across to the slip it was carried by three men 'up the steps and into the school in the light of a parafin lamp'.

The children again did well in 1962 when the National Mod returned to Oban – its birthplace in 1892 – and they received unexpected encouragement from the winner of the Bardic crown, Mr. Angus MacInnes. His father had run the Kerrera ferry, and his mother the Post Office from about 1892. After winning the Crown, Mr. MacInnes sent a donation to his old school to be used for prizes for Gaelic. He later remarked 'I had no Gaelic lessons from anybody, I was entirely self taught. Perhaps some junior might therefore be encouraged to "go and do likewise"'.

Apart from the credit the children were gaining for their school at the Mod, they also gave great pleasure at the Christmas Eve parties at Dunollie. During the carol singing it became a custom for them, as an unaccompanied choir, to sing Mary MacDonald's (1817 – 1890) beautiful hymn *Leanabh an Aigh* 'Child in the Manger' sung to the tune 'Bunessan', her home village in Mull:

> Leanabh an aigh
> An leanabh aig Mairi
> A rugadh'san stabull

Righ nan Dull
Thainig do'n fhasach

Dh'fhulang nar n-aite
Is sona do'n aireamh
Bhitheas dha dluth.

Iriosal, striochdach
Thainig an Ti so
Is deacair dhomh innseadh
Meud a chliu
Prionnsa na Sithe
Rugadh mar chiochran
Ann an staid iosal
Is gun mhuirn.

Neartaich ar dochas
Meudaigh ar n-eolas
Cum sinn 'nad roid 'nad roidean
Direach dluth
Le oladh'nar lochrain
Mar ris na h-oighean
A'seinn ann an gloir
An orain uir.

XII CHURCHES

As part of a group of islands which include Iona and Lismore, where St. Columba and St. Moluag sowed early seeds of Christianity, it is tempting to look for visible signs of early Christian worship on Kerrera. However, until research discovers something more tangible than the suggestion that traces of building at the north end of the island at Rudh'a Bhearnaig may have had ecclesiastical origins, the first known building for public worship had its foundations laid in April 1872.

The first Service was held on Sunday September 1st, 1872, which, as a contemporary diary records was 'a very fine day; wind from the north. Went to new school in Kerrera where Service was performed for the first time by Mr. McKercher and a Mr. Stewart. A large assemblage of people of the Island and others.'

A few days later, the *Oban Times* reported:

> A meeting of a very interesting character took place last Sunday in Kerrera. A very neat and unique little building has been in course of erection… To Mrs. MacDougall of Dunollie it owes its origin out of regard for the memory of her late beloved husband Captain Alexander John MacDougall who died five years ago at the age of forty. She has erected this elegant structure for the two fold purpose of school and place of worship. The opening service was conducted in English by the Rev. P. Stewart M.A., of Gilmerton, Edinburgh.
>
> The Rev. P. MacKerchar presided and gave a very earnest and impressive address in Gaelic.

A fortnight later the Service of Holy Communion was celebrated.

So this little Church-and-school was the newest addition to the churches being built about this time in the parish of Kilmore and Kilbride, in the Presbytery of Lorn, in the Synod of Argyll. According to the 1794 Statistical Account, the united parish was seven miles long and six broad, including the Island of Kerrera. Kilmore was the seat of the Presbytery.

Before the Kerrera people had their own church on the island they had to cross to the mainland on Sundays and make the long trek to the church at Kilbride, or the more distant Kilmore. It was a day's outing, the men dressed in their Sunday blacks – it is remembered the women carried a sprig of rosemary or southernwood (Apple reenie) with their clean linen handkerchifs – they left their farms and cottar houses to gather at the ferry. Here the number was such that the big cattleboat had to be used for the crossing. Then began the long trek up the hill leading into Glenshellach (some found it more comfortable to carry their boots round the neck until they neared the church) over by *Loch na gleann bheathrach* and down past the farm of Cologin into the glen of Kilbride.

The church of Kilbride, now ruined, was built about 1740 by the site of a much older church, and was in use until 1876. In the 1794 Statistical Account it is described as 'of lesser size than Kilmore, being 40 feet in length and 16 in breadth. Its walls are not sufficient, and the seats are equally bad. It stands greatly in need of repairs, and has no churchyard, but it is proposed to have one soon. Indeed, a few excepted, the Kirks in the West Highlands are in a miserable condition compared with those in many other country parishes in Scotland. But as improvements of all kinds are everywhere going on rapidly we hope the churches in this part of the county will soon come in for their share.' So wrote the parish Minister and as far as the churchyard was concerned hopes were realised and in coming years many of the Kerrera families had names carved on the gravestones.

The Minister, the Rev. Patrick MacDonald, went on:

… the whole parish observe the rites of the established Church, excepting two or three families who are of the Episcopal persuasion; there is only a single family of the Secession … The people of this parish have been, since the present imcumbants admission, as regular on the whole as any on the West coast, Indeed he has observed that not only within his own parish, but within the bounds of the Presbytery in general there has been since his first acquaintance with them, a very

Ruined church and burial ground at Kilbride (mainland) showing track across the hills used by the Kerrera worshippers after they crossed the Sound

remarkable change for the better, in one very important part of duty, namely in their attendance on, and decent behaviour at public worship, and at all religious ordinces. Most of them are docile, and fond of instruction, and few people less subject to divisions. The inhabitants in general are rational in their religion; sober, with very few exceptions, laborious and industrious. The gentlemen are well bred, polite, discreet and hospital.

Mrs. Grant of Laggan, in her *Letters from the Mountains* describes her attendance, in the spring of 1773, at a service in the old Church of Kilmore. The services, for a period were held alternately at the churches of Kilmore and Kilbride, and the Kerrera people were used to walking the extra miles to Kilmore. Mrs. Grant wrote: 'People here cross ferries and ride great distances in bad weather not only to hear sermon but also to converse together and hear all the news of friends at home and abroad'. She describes the 'grandmothers' in the congregation, by whose dignity and poise she was much struck:

Stately, erect and self satisfied without a trace of languor or coldness of age, they march up the area with gaudy-coloured plaids fastened about their breasts with a silver brooch like the full moon in size and shape. They have lively blue eyes, and a fair fresh complexion, and on each cheek depends a silver lock. Round their heads is tied the very plain white kerchief.

In the Second Statistical Account the parish Minister, the Rev. Dugald N. Campbell, claims that 'the attendance in both these churches is usually good, considering most of the population is scattered over a wide area of country. The average number of Communicants is about 200. There are fifteen Dissenters, either Baptists or Independants.'

In each of the two churches, Kilmore and Kilbride, Divine Service was performed on alternate Sundays, sometimes in Gaelic and generally in English. The November Communion was held at Kilmore, the May Communion (at one period it was June or July) held in Kilbride Church. Communion Sabbaths were in those days in some respects a 'holy fair'; crowds attended from Oban, Kerrera and the surrounding district

> Here to keep the hallowed tryst,
> This calm sacramental Sabbath,
> Far among the hills with Christ.[1]

There were so many communicants that at Kilbride the Minister sometimes had the Table outside the Kirk, on the piece of ground which is now family burial ground, and the people sat on the hillside opposite. The horses which brought worshippers were put in the little nearby garden, and occasionally their owners had to leave the service to quell trouble amongst them.

The Church was entered by the west door, and the Minister came from the little vestry and ascended the pulpit by eight steps. A gallery ran round the upper walls, entered from the east side. It was remembered as an 'inspiring sight to see those in the gallery rise from their seats and proceed slowly and with great dignity towards the Tables.' The Communion was served simultaneously in Gaelic and English. 'In singing, the line was repeated, and the cadences of *Martyrdom*, *Tallis* and *Dumfermline* being repeated over and over again as the members reverently took their places at the Tables, after the "fencing" which was intended as a reality and performed with unction.' Communion tokens were in use, and wooden ladles, with long handles were stretched along the pews to collect the offerings.[2]

In 1843 consideration was given to building a new church at a point between the parish churches of Kilmore and Kilbride, to serve a united congregation. By the time this was actually done (1876) Kerrera had its own place of worship. About this time, however, there was a petition to 'the Reverand the Presbytery of Lorn' to annexe the people of Kerrera to the Church at Oban' This was the Chapel of Ease built in 1821, which held over five hundred; services were held in Gaelic and English. It was pointed out that with the new coast road to Oban 'a very great majority of the inhabitants of the Island are at the present moment regular sitters and form a portion of the present congregation of the Oban Church'.

For long the Kerrera people were parishioners of that famous minister, the Rev. Patrick MacDonald. Inducted to the charge in 1757, he died in office in his 96th year, after sixty-seven years of service in the parish, and father of the Church of Scotland. He was a colourful figure, tall and broad, with expressive face and dark piercing eyes. A distinguished player on the pipes and violin, he also composed. He published what is thought to be the first collection of Gaelic music, which included reels, country dances and bagpipe tunes, some of which his brother Joseph had collected in their native Sutherland.

Mr. MacDonald was something of a wag, and many stories are attached to him and his trusted man, Paul MacPhail the beadle. Paul, a short man of shrewd and ready wit, is usually given the roll of besting his master; be the stories true or legendary, their telling gives a flavour of the times. One such story is linked with the old inn below the Church at Kilbride. Here people gathered after the service to talk or take refreshment, while the horses were being prepared. Before the service started it was Paul's duty to make arrangements at the Inn for the Minister's dinner, after which he went up and slipped into the back of the Church. One warm Sunday he woke during the sermon to hear the Minister ask the rhetorical question 'And what has Paul to say about this?'. Paul jerked up and answered: 'Paul says, "They say down there you can't have any more till you've paid for the last lot".

Many years after this, in 1840 there arose the question of closing this inn, and the Minister, the Rev. Dugald Campbell was asked for his views. He wrote in reply:

Kilmore Manse
15 June 1840

My dear Sir,

As you asked my opinion in regard to the expediency of withdrawing the public house at Kilbride, I have no hesitation in saying that though opposed to having publichouses in general in a country, under present circumstances I do not see how the one at Kilbride could be dispensed with.

There being no vestry, children brought to the Church for Baptism are obliged to be kept in the public house during the time of the service, and for the same reason, that is the want of a vestry, in rainy bad weather I am often obliged to go in there to put off my wet things. I must again repeat that I disaprove highly of the very great number of public houses in Oban, and in this country in general, and would rejoice to see many of the licences withdrawn. But in addition to the reasons I have already given rendering it expedient to retain the house at Kilbride, I am happy to say that the present occupiers are most respectable people and keep a very regular orderly house.

He adds a postscript: ' I should like to see a good stable added to the public house at Kilbride.'

Sheltering babies awaiting baptism and acting as minister's changing room may seem a novel reason for rendering it expedient to retain a publichouse, but it seems as if his point about the want of a vestry was taken when repairs were made to the Kirk a few years later, and a vestry added.

Another traditional story about Paul baiting the Minister took place at the Manse. One winter Paul was affronted when the Minister failed to give him a customary portion of the Manse pig which had been salted down to tide over the lean season. Determined to put this right, he went down to the cellar and sprinkled a few grains of rice on the surface of the salty brew. When these were swollen and floating, he went to the Minister with a long face and said 'Come and see the terrible thing that has happened.' Leading him down to the depths of the murky cellar, he pointed to the vat and said darkly 'maggots'. The Minister, disgusted, told him to throw the whole lot out; so Paul, as he had planned, was able to have the pig for himself.

One thing, according to the records, was true – the state of the cellar. After an inspection of the Manse in 1800 by the Presbytery and Heritors, they recorded 'a cellar contiguous is dark and damp with bad earthen floor'. Although this might have been said of many cellars of the time, their report on the rest of the building was equally depressing.

When Mr, MacDonald first came to the parish it had no Manse. Its erection in 1760 was foreshadowed in the Kerrera rent agreements of 1748 which stipulated the tenants were to 'pay half the manse money if built during your tack.' The cost of building was shared among all the heritors of the parish, and their tenants. Of this first manse, which cost £130 sterling, it was written thirty years later in the First Statistical Account 'it is very slight and insufficient; it underwent some repairs not long ago, but it can never be made a good house'. It was not, however, replaced during the long life of Mr. MacDonald.

The new manse was built in 1828, at a cost of £1000, and remained 'sufficient' until the time came when there was to be no Minister resident in Kilmore.

On October 14, 1952, the Moderator of the Presbytery of Lorn presided in the little Kerrera Church for the election of a new Minister to the charge of Kilmore and Kilbride. When the Islanders recorded their votes probably they scarcely realised that the man chosen was to be the last Minister before the charge became united with the Oban Old Parish Church.

For when the Rev. Iain Carmichael, who has been referred to as the 'Churchill of the Church, the West, and the Presbytery' retired, Kerrera, Kilmore and the Oban Old Parish Church came under the charge of the Rev. John MacLeod from Lewis. Mr. Carmichael preached the last sermon before the charges were joined on Sunday 25 September 1967, in the Church of Kilmore, nine years short of its centenary. He based his sermon on the symbol of the Church of Scotland – the Burning Bush – 'Behold the bush burns with fire and the bush is not consumed'.

At a time such as this, when the congregation is about to experience changes, it is inevitable that not a-few should have misgivings as to what the future holds for their fellowship which has endured in some form or other in this area for more than four centuries

I have thus taken our text as a corrective against Christian despondency. Looking back over the history of the Church, observing how it has surmounted all kinds of trials and dangers, how it has maintained its identify through the many revolutionary changes of time, you behold the bush that burns with fire and yet the bush is not consumed.

The very flame which might at first suggest its destruction is its very life. You may consider that the flame stands for the spirit of God – or that the flame is the flash which follows the impact of God's truth on the hard material world; but however you regard it, you must understand that this flame cannot destroy the Church, although it may help to purify it.'[3]

This historic service, from which part of the sermon has been quoted, and Mr. Carmichael's retirement, ended the long line of Ministers who had served the generations of parishioners who worshipped in the now ruined churches of Kilmore and Kilbride, and in the closing quarter of the nineteenth century in the combined church of Kilmore and Kilbride, and the combined church and school in Kerrera.

To find the link between Kerrera's acres and Church finances means delving far back into history, for, biblically speaking, Abraham started it: 'And Abram gave him a tenth of everything – that is to the King of Salem, who was also the Priest of God most High.' More dramatically, Jacob, after his dream of a ladder to heaven tried to bargain with God in return 'for all that Thou shalt give me I will surely give the tenth unto Thee.'

Among the twelve tribes of Israel the Levites were set aside for the service of God, and laws were made ensuring the payment of tithes (tenths) to them. They received the tithes as representing God, from the other tribes; they themselves were allocated no land. The tribes brought them a tenth of their increase, firstlings of flocks and herds, first fruits of grain, wine, oil and honey and of all the produce of the field: 'And they brought in abundantly of the tithe of every thing, and laid them in heaps'. And the Priest said 'Since they began to bring the contributions into the house of the Lord we have eaten and had enough, and have plenty left …'

The Rev. Patrick MacDonald scarcely found himself in a position to echo the words of the High Priest. Nevertheless, it was this system of some thousands of years before Christ that was influencing Kerrera's merklands to add their quota to the Minister's stipend under the Scottish word – 'Teinds'.

A pair of balances in his hands...
A measure of wheat for a penny
And three measures of barley for a penny

4 Lippies - 1 peck
4 pecks - 1 firlot
4 firlots - 1 boll
16 bolls - 1 Chalder

Teinds

Prior to 1629 there was a charge on the produce of the crops and beasts on the land, a tenth part of which was due to the Church; originally this was collected in kind, and the tenth sheaf of all grain crops had to be set aside in the field.

There was a land valuation in the seventeenth century which fixed a rent to be paid annually, partly in measures of meal and partly in money, payable, not to the Levites, nor to the Priest, but to the Established Minister of the Parish. In 1629 the Subcommissioners of the Presbytery valued the Parish of Kilbride, and the document they authorised specified in detail the

> Lands underwritten pertaining to the persons afterspecified ... the lands and Yle of Corivory or Kerraray the Lands of the tua Dunnoleyches Sorobay Glenshellach Gallanyches and Colgyne with parts pendicles and pertinents therof pertaining to Johne McDougal of Dunnoleych knyt of parsonage and great taynd the number of fourescoir tuw bolles thrie firboles meal and for the vicarage brokes and small teyndes of the semen sum of an hundreth and fyve pundes money.

To understand the complications of payment of the Minister's stipend it is as well to know something of the meal measures then in use, the local measuring system, and the importance of the 'Friars Prices'.

The Meal Measures

The boll was an old Scottish dry measure, 'not exceeding six bushels'. The chalder was a measure of grain 'nearly eight quarters'. Payments were made in Lippies, Pecks, Firlots and Bolls, and Chalders.

The stone weight was also in use, but it varied locally and also in period how many stone were reckoned to the boll. Before an augmentation was made to the Minister's stipend in 1792 nine stone were reckoned to the boll, but after that augmentation eight stone went to his boll of meal.

Barley was weighed up by the Inveraray or Winchester measure, or else by the Linlithgow measure. A note from an Inveraray official in 1814 explained the position:

> The meal is at eight stone.
>
> The Bear is Inveraray measure, which is one and five/eights peck more than the Linlithgow boll. You can calculate accordingly the price of that boll which is the price of one peck and five/eights less than the Inveraray Boll price.

The difference between the Inveraray and the Linlithgow calculations were to prove a sore trial to the Rev. Patrick MacDonald, particularly when, in his nineties, he didn't immediately realise they changed from using the Inveraray measure to the Linlithgow.

The Friars Prices

These were the prices of grain legally fixed for the year in each county. The livelihood of the population, let alone the Minister, was affected by their fluctuations.

Between the years 1808 and 1821 the price of oatmeal varied between 18/6 and 28/6 per boll, allowing eight stone to the boll.

The bear (barley) in these years had a minimum of 30/- and a maximum of 42/, but depending upon whether the Linlithgow measure was used, or the Inveraray with its extra one and five/eights pecks, there was also a difference in the quantity sold at the price.

The Stipend

When the Rev. Patrick MacDonald accepted the charge in 1757, the stipend was

sixty bolls of oatmeal and thirtynine pounds seven shillings and ninepence halfpenny together with a competent glebe.

At the ordinary conversion of £100 Scots to the chalder,

60 boll of meal (9 stone to boll) is in sterling	£31	5/-
the money stipend	39	7/9$^{1}/_{2}$
From which deduct Communion Elements	5	0/-
Total of ye present stipend	£65	12/9$^{1}/_{2}$

The Heritors, paying their proportion towards the total stipend due to the Minister, conducted the business in the usual mixture of money and goods in kind. The Minister rendered careful, if complicated accounts:

1789 Feb. 20th

Mr. Patrick MacDonald to MacDougall of Dunollie

To five sheep at 8 t, per piece	£2	
To cash from Archd Gray on my acct	2	1/-
5 bolls oats at 16th per boll	4	
To 3 stone Butter	1	16/-
To 9 stone Cheese	2	5/-
	£12	2/0

Contra Cr.

By tythes, Augmentation of Stipend)	11	16/11
& Vicarage due to Mr. MacDonald)		
Ballance due to MacDougall	0	11/1

The above being the stated Account for the year 1788 on the 20th Febry 1789 settled between

Alex. MacDougall

Pat. McDonald

The following year 'six barrells of potatoes' and 'four bolls seed oat large measure' were part of the barter.

As the century wore on, Mr. MacDonald found the cost of living had risen well above his stipend, and about 1796 he asked for an augmentation, four additional chalders of meal and one pound and sixpence halfpenny in money. This request came before the Court, who agreed to the augmentation. (It was remarked at the time 'every augmentation just now is allowed, for the court seems very favourable to the clergy'.)

The gist of the Court's decision was:

George R. ... forasmuch as it is shown to us by our lovite Mr. Patrick MacDonald Minister of the Gospel of Kilmore and Kilbride in the Presbytery of Lorn ... that the united Parishes of Kilmore and Kilbride are a very great charge containing about two thousand and thirtysix inhabitants and of considerable extent being in length seven miles and in breadth six miles and provisions and every other article of Life are very dear in these united parishes ... notwithstanding whereof he is but very meanly provided for in his stipend the same being only sixty bolls of meal and thirtynine pounds in money and five pounds sterling for Communion Elements is by no means sufficient for a Minister in these Parishes ... They therefore recommend that augmentation be made ... the money at Whitsunday and Martimas... and the victual betwixt Yule and Candlemas after the separation of the crop from the ground.

The Heritors were responsible for providing the Church and Manse, as well as for the Minister's stipend. In 1797 there were ten heretors, or owners of land in the parish, and according to the recent augmentation they were assessed for meal and money for the Minister's stipend:

Estate of	MEAL				MONEY	
	boll	fir	peck	lip	£	s/d
Dunollie	17		2	3	18	0/11^{1}/$_{4}$
Lochnell	21	2	1	3^{1}/$_{2}$	7	18/9^{1}/$_{2}$
Dunstaffnage	2	3	1	0^{1}/$_{4}$	8	2/2
Combie	3	–	–	–	1	12/-
Glenfeochan	3	1	1	3	5	19/3
Gallanich	16	–	–	2^{1}/$_{4}$	4	8/6^{1}/$_{2}$
Soroba	1	3	1	1	3	4/8^{3}/$_{4}$
Lerags	15	1	1	1^{1}/$_{4}$	3	2/0^{1}/$_{4}$
Duke of Argyll	14	–	–	3^{1}/$_{4}$	1	17/3
E. of Breadalbane	–	2	3	13	–	14/4^{1}/$_{2}$

Kerrera's share of the Dunollie stent is beautifully written out in copperplate writing by Mr. Hugh MacDougall, the Kerrera 'Schollmaster' in the first decade of the nine-teenth century. He explains… 'agreeable to your order I have examined the whole of the Tennants of Kerrera Concerning the Stent money and oatmeal paid by them yearly to the Minister of Kilmore which is as stated.'

	marks land				Bolls & Stone	£	s
Gylen	4 @ 3/- and 2 stones meal per mark –				1		12/-
Ardmore	6 @ 2/6 & 2	do	do		1		10/-
Barnabock	4 @ 3/- & 2	do	do		1		12/-
Slatrach	4 @ 3/- & 3	do	do		1 – 4		12/-
Balimore	8 @ 2/1 & 1½	do	do		1 – 4		16/8
Ardchoik	4 @ 2/6 &	2	do		1		10/-
					7	£3	12/8

Bolls meal	7	
Money	£3 12/8	

Kerrera meal was usually paid direct to the Minister, though sometimes it was convenient to arrange by barter for a Kilmore tenant to deliver to the Manse the quantity due, as this receipt shows:

> Manse 2nd Feb. Candlemas 1811
> Received by the hands of Peter McArthur, Tennant in Molieg one boll and two firlots Teind meal being ordered as he says in name of Balliemore in Kerrera as the proportion of that town of the teinds payable by them to me as Minister of the Parishes of Kilmore and Kilbride, and for last year 1810.
> Sustained by Patk MacDonald Minr.

However seemingly all was not well, for in January of the following year Mr. MacDonald wrote to Dunollie:

> The Manse, Kilmore
> … As you are pleased to say that for my convenience you would, if I liked inclined arrange with your tennants to pay me immediately in part, and that you settle the balance at Candlemas … accordingly I, on this express condition, agree to take part of the appointed stipend (the Molieg part) in Meal – but it must only be of great or white oats – we will receive no other, as formerly they were in use of palming on us small or mixed oats.

A few months later he wrote 'As I did, at your proposal agree to take once more from your tennants the proportion formerly in use to be paid by them – I must herein aquaint you of the Deficiencies of payment by some of yr tennants, particularly those in Kerrera – assuring you that I will have no more to do with their partial, broken, unfair payments – but have recourse to you. It is left to you Sir, to settle with me about these deficiencies.'

In 1925 there came a change in the system by which the payment of the Minister's stipend depended upon the price of grain which was fixed annually. The Church of Scotland (Property and Endowment) Act made provision that the money payment be stabilised in every parish at a level of existing grain prices at a chosen date. The payment was to be a fixed charge on the land, and the heritors were relieved of their legal obligation towards Church buildings.

XIII   COMMUNITY

The Kerrera folk were known as pullets – the Kerrera Pullets – such district names were customary, though the origin may have been forgotten. Occupants of the farms also had nicknames, as the Gaelic jingle shows:

> Feannagan na Goillean
> Faolleanan Ardachoirc
> Fitheac dhuth Bhailmhor
> Oragan na Slatarich
> Croman luchaidh Tigh a phuirt
> Ardcaran Ardentrive
> Ceacan Chutach Barnaboc
> Iagan na Feundan.[1]

And so the picture builds up of the bird life on the island – the crows of Gylen, gulls at Ardchoirc, ravens at Balliemore, the mouse-hawks – kestrels – hovering over the Ferryhouse and lapwings peesweeping the flat lands of Ardantrive.

Another jingle, a *phuirt a beul* tells of the remarkable three hind toes of the cock which was in Kerrera:

> An Coileach a bha'n Cearara.
>
> Bha tri-casan deiridh air a'choileach a bha'n Cearara,
> Bha tri-casan deiridh air a'choileach a bha'n Cearare,
> Bha tri-casan deiridh air a'choileach a bha'n Cearara,
> Tri casan-deiridh agus ceither casan dearg air.
>
> Tha tri, tri, tri, tri, tri, casan dearg air,
> Tha tri, tri, tri, tri, tri, casan dearg air,
> Tha tri, tri, tri, tri, tri casan dearg air,
> Tha tri casan-deiridh agus ceithir casan dearg air.
>
> There were three hind toes on the cock which was in Kerrera
> Three hind toes and four red toes.

Three toes or four, many a Kerrera floor must have swung to the beat as the dancers were accompanied by this rousing music of the mouth.

Mrs. Hilda Leslie, for so many years schoolteacher on Kerrera, also gives another version:

An Coileach a bha'n Cearara.

Bha tri puind geire anns a'choileach a bha'n Cearara,
Bha tri puind geire anns a'choileach a bha'n Cearera,
Bha tri puind geire anns a'choileach a bha'n Cearara,
Bha cirean a bha loinneil air a'choileach a bha'n Cearara.

Bha spuirean a bha greimeil aire a'choileach a bha'n Cearara,
Bha gairdeanan fade air a'chaillich rinn a mhabadh;
Chaidh puinnd ann an coinneal dheth 's chaidh roinnean dheth gu armadh,
Is thum fad na bonnaich anns a'choire 'san robin 'n eanraich.

The Cock which was in Kerrera

There were three pounds of suet on the cock which was in Kerrera,
There were three pounds of suet on the cock which was in Kerrera,
There were three pounds of suet on the cock which was in Kerrera,
A comb which was elegant had the cock which was in Kerrera.

Strong spurs had the cock which was in Kerrera,
Long arms had the old woman who killed him;
A pound was used as a candle, and some was used for greasing,
And they dipped their bannocks in the pot which held the soup.

It was the Barnabuck folk, aided by some from Ardchoirc, who were in trouble on that July day of 1764. This was before the tax on that most precious commodity, salt, was repealed (1825).

The incident is recorded in 'the Petition and Complaint of Duncan MacVicar, Collector, and Alexander Campbell, Comptroller of His Majestie's Customs at Oban, to the Honble the Justices of the Peace for the Shire of Argyle' in which he

Humbly Sheweth… that Allan Cameron, Commander of the King's Boat at Oban, being on a cruise upon the 6th day of July 1764 betwixt the Continent and the Island of Mull, he spied a small boat making for the Island of Kerrera, to which boat he gave chase, and soon arrived at the Harbour of Barnabuck in said Island, where the foresaid boat had put to shore, and landed several bags of foreign salt containing ten bushels which had not paid his Majestie's duties, and was landed without a Warrant and the presence of an Officer of the Revenue in terms of law. Of which salt, the said Allan Cameron made a Seizure, and ordered the crew of his Boat to put the same on board of His Majestie's Boat in order to transport the same to His Majestie's Warehouse at Oban.

That as the said Allan Cameron and his men were about to put the foresaid quantity of foreign salt seized by them on board the King's Boat, Duncan and John MacCullich, Duncan Roy McPhail, Changekeeper, Hugh MacDougall and John MacDougall his son, all in Barnabuck, John MacPherson in Ardchoirk and Mary Gray spouse to Charles McCullich in Barnabuck, assembled together in a Riotous and tumultuous manner upon the said 6th day of July 1764 and forcibly carried off and deforced the said Allan Cameron and his crew of the foresaid quantity of foreign salt seized by them in contempt of the Laws and Acts of Parliament in that behalf made.

The sequel was that 'the Justices find them all guilty art and part in landing and conveying the Salt mentioned in the Petition, and carrying the same from the shore and opposing the same Allan Cameron and his crew in the exercise of their duty therefore the said Justices fined and amerciated each of the foresaid persons complained upon the sum of Ten Shillings Sterl.'

However, this was not the end of the matter. The Petitioner, satisfied that the sentence given was not within the terms of the law, since the sum should have been not less than double the duty payable, which in this case for the ten bushels would be £6 13/4, and it was again referred to the Justices of the Peace sitting at Kilmore, who referred it to the Quarter Sessions held at Inveraray. Sentence was passed that each of the accused (including Mary Gray and the foresaid Charles McCullich her husband) pay £6 13/4.

Dr. Garnett, in his *Tour through part of the Western Islands* in 1798, observes that great numbers of herring were caught in the district 'and would have been sold to advantage, but the greater part were suffered to rot for the want of salt.' He explained that the duty on salt was so high that herring could not be cured, and the Government had agreed for it to be sold duty free for the purpose of curing fish only.

But this privilege requires so many forms, that it is impossible to comply with them and fish to advantage. In order to procure salt for the purpose of curing fish, those who want it are obliged to go to Oban, and at the customhouse make oath, that the salt they purchase is for curing herring only; they must at the same time give a bond, which is not discharged till they take the herring, and what salt may remain above the quantity allowed for a certain number, to Oban. They may be obliged to go to the custom house for a few baskets of salt, and return with the little fish they have cured, or perhaps with the salt without any fish at all... The want of salt is likewise severely felt by these poor people, when they lay up their winter stock of provisions; and it is scarcely to be wondered at that they should yield to the temptation of smuggling, to which they are in a manner forced by imperious necessity.

Another excitement probably involved every man, woman and child in the district, and the Kerrera people were well to the fore, and stood loyally together. This was in 1796 when a Liverpool ship was wrecked at the entrance to Loch Spelve, Mull. Dunollie describes it in a letter to his son in Edinburgh:

Dunollie
12 Jan 1796

Dear Patrick,

Since Sat last was little rest upon this coast from Luing to the extreme point of Lismore, the coast of Mull from Cregan to Duart gathering the wreak of a Liverpool outward-bound to the West Indies loaded with a cargo of dray goods suitable for the West Indian Market such as soap, candles, butter and immense quantities of muslins of all kinds, cloaks, shoes, boots medicines. She was broak at the entrance to Loch Speil, yr was a vast number of boats for several days gathering part of the cargo floating upon the surface of the sea betwixt all the way from Easdale to the point of Dowart and great quantities were castashore all of which has been pilfered by the people … My Kerrera Ladies will be so decked wt muslin I'll not know them. What of the wreak came ashore the people picked up in the night time with lantrons…

Feb. 5th 1796 We have had a Justice peace Court at Oban these 10 or 12 days … in deponing the people that was thought to have a part of what was thrown a shore, got floating upon the surface of the sea, or dragd out of the wreak.

The tennants of Kerrera were the first depond were willing to give upon oath what they got or had in there custodie ych would not be received unless they gave up what they know oyrs got, ych, I would not do, they were ordered to be sent to Inverery which accordingly was done with a party But the Judges thought proper to send ane express after them and return them.

Feb. 12 1796
The Oban Congress only broak up yesterday after being together 14 days. They will collect a great deal of goods. Sandie Cadelton at Inverery has got a power from the owners to be sole manager of the whole of the subjects recovered. The Ferryman's servant at Port Kerrera was impris'd in a Garet in Oban, and fettered for being unrulie and sent from Oban for Inverery under a Guard of the Volunteers and still fetter'd … but returned. You'll inform Mrs. Mac that I employed Mrs. John Stevenson to purchase a piece of muslin for her and ane oyr for Bess MacDowell at the Oban Roup of the goods saved of the wreak.

Between the bays of Barnabuck and Slaterach there is a cave known as the 'Fugitive's

Cave'. It is possible for a man to lie hidden on a ledge above eye level, and for a fairly casual searcher to miss seeing him.

Before 1857 there was not a regular Police force in Scotland, and the search and apprehension of a wanted man might devolve on a private individual. There is a list, undated, but probably made in the early decades of the nineteenth century of 'Tenants of Patrick MacDougall of MacDougall Esqr who have nrolled themselves to assist in Quelling and Disturbances in the County.' There are thirty three names under the heading 'Farms on the Main Land', and these are followed by twenty-six under 'Farms on the Island of Kerrera:

Angus McInnes	Peter McCulloch
John MacDougall sen.	Allan MacDougall sen.
John MacDougall jun.	Allan MacDougall jun.
Angus MacKinnon	Colin McCowan
Charles MacKinnon	Malcolm Livingston
Archd Ferguson	Duncan McCulloch
Hugh Livinston	John MacDougall
John McCallum	Donald MacDougall
Malcolm Livingstone	John Livingston
John MacLean	Duncan McCowan
Angus MacDougall	John Brown
Archd MacDougall	Dugald McCoag
Donald MacInnes	Hugh MacDougall

There is a footnote: 'As the whole tenants and their Sons fit for Service with the Crofters and Cottars have inrolled themselves it is to be understood that the number called out at one time will be at the option of the Proprietor.'

The following correspondence relates to the escape of a man wounded in the clash between the Radicals and the military at Bonnymuir, Stirlingshire, in April 1820. Duncan MacNeil of Colonsay, later Solicitor General and Lord Advocate, wrote to his uncle, Patrick MacDougall of Dunollie:

Glasgow 10 May 1820

Dear Uncle,

I have been in this city investigating some of the Radical proceedings, and have learned that a Radical who was wounded at Bonnymuir in the action with the King's troops is at present in <u>Kerrera</u>. It is <u>extremely</u> desirable that he should be apprehended and for that purpose I send you a warrant by a Magistrate of the County, having endorsed on it a concurrence by a Magistrate of Dumbartonshire and a blank concurrence by a Magistrate of Argyllshire which you as a J.P. can sign.

It will be necessary to set about the thing quietly and without the delay of an hour as the fellow's friends here are raising a subscription to carry him to America. He is a native I understand of Argyllshire, his real name is Black, he was bred a printer in Glasgow, and when last seen wore a short blue coat and dark pantaloons. If he is really in Kerrera or anywhere in your neighbourhood you will have no difficulty in securing him and transmitting him in sure custody either to Inverary or Glasgow… [a detailed description follows].

On receipt of this letter Patrick 'immediately sent Angus Sinclair, Messenger, with a Confidential person that knew the island well and upon the strictest search no such person was either heard of or seen there.' Patrick goes on: 'It then occurred to me that he might be on the Island of Lismore… since a number of the inhabitants were of the name of Black, so I despatched a Boat from Oban with a Confidential person whom I directed to be very circumspect in going about this business. He learned that Black had been there about ten days before, but was not on the island, he however reasoned that he was lurking betwixt Benderloch and Muckairn.'

Patrick then sent an express to the Sheriff in Inveraray for advice. The Sheriff told him to send the warrant to Ardchattan or Barcaldine 'who I am sure will do all in their power to ascertain if Black is lurking in that part of the Country and take measures to apprehend him'. He goes on 'As there appears no certainty where Black may be found sending a party from this to search would create such alarm that in all probability the fellow would make his escape, whereas either of the gentlemen I have mentioned might be able to lay hold on him before he takes the alarm.'

Dunolly, sending the correspondence to Ardchattan confided 'this business has been rather troublesome to me owing to my present state of health (he was seventy-eight) being confined to bed mostly for a fortnight with my old tormenting complaint of the Gout'.

Later he reported back to Glasgow, explaining he had sought help from the Sheriff 'who was of the opinion that it would be improper in him to take any active part as it might create an allarm'. He concludes 'I have not heard what success Ardchattan has had, but I fear Black has left this country if ever he was here. I have made every exertion in my power in the business and as I seem a little money out of pocket for expences please inform me how I am to be refunded'.

Extract from letter to John MacDougall of Dunollie from his factor, John Robson, 10 February 1832:

You will see from the Papers that Cholera has appeared at Kirkintulloch within 7 miles of Glasgow and that some cases have appeared in Glasgow which has alarmed us very much here. The Magistrates have written to the Officer of

Customs at Glasgow and I have received Orders to put the Quarantine Questions to all vessils from the Clyde and if the least Symtom of Disease appear to order them to the nearest Quarantine Station. I sent Fletcher the Constable to Inspect and Report the state of the Tenants on your property. I sent him in preference to employing the Ground Officer as he could direct them what they ought to do much better having more experience. He says they are much cleaner than he expected to find them but still there is much to be done, he thinks it will require 60 Barrels of shell lime to go over them all. I intend getting the lime how soon the weather permits and have it distributed amongst them. He has made out a list of the whole and the number of persons in each family. He has ordered them to put all their Dunghills at a distance from their houses, to clean themselves and their bed clothes and to put clean straw in the beds which they have all promised to comply with.

We are using every precaution that can be suggested to prevent or avert the virulence of the disorder should it unfortunately get amongst us. But our funds are getting low, and little prospect of getting more.

A lady recalled her forbears speaking of how the lime was watered over everything as a form of disinfectant, before stronger chemicals were proved to be more effective.

On New Year's day, 1839, the *Albion* of Montrose, a two-masted square rigged vessel, was stranded on the Slaterach shore, and apparently every able-bodied man on Kerrera was employed to help to discharge the cargo.

There were four types of job offered: labourers, at 3/- a day, carters at 7/-, night-watchmen at 3/6 and day watchmen at 3/- the day.

The list includes two men from Ardchoirc, four from Ardmore, seven from Balliemore, including the blacksmith, seven from Barnabuck; two from East Gylen, four from Gylen and four from Gylen Park, including the weaver, five from Slaterach, two from Upper Slaterach and two from the Mill.

Part of the labouring was removing tallow, but the main cargo is not mentioned. Of the thirty-nine men employed, fifteen also worked as carters, some 'cearting tallow', and one MacKinnon, mason, spent a day with a boat loading tallow. Nine also worked as night-watchmen; Malcolm Livingstone at Balliemore took twenty-four nights, and Alexander MacKinnon of Slaterach eighteen, but it is clear two men kept watch every night. Employment lasted until January 27th, and altogether the Kerrera men earned a wage bill of £82 2/-, presumably paid by the owners of the vessel

Although most of the Kerrera settlements still have an inhabited house on the site, there is a row of roofless ruined houses which belonged to a family involved in the life of Kerrera for much of the nineteenth century.

The old road from Slaterach down to the mill continued westwards along the shore from Slaterach bay to these houses, marked on the map as Leac. A tumble of stones of the district, gathered on green pasture land beside the sea to make homes for man and beast, stimulates the imagination, and is a challenge to probe into the past, delve among the records, and to bring to mind the people who here first saw the light of day, who here lived and worked, had the good moments and the tragedies of life, and who died in course of time.

Such a family were the MacKinnons of Leac. Mr. Lachlan MacKinnon brought his family to Kerrera in 1811, and with his mark signed an agreement to take a quarter share of the farm of Slaterach. However, in the following year when one of the partners left, a new agreement was drawn up which made the three remaining tenants – John MacDougall senior, John MacDougall junior and Lachlan MacKinnon, pioneers in a new type of farming by which the shared cultivations and communial settlements gave way to apportioning the land in three divisions on which each tenant built his house, byre and barn. Lachlan MacKinnon was allotted Runalich (*Rudha na licè*) and there he built the dwellings before he died a few years later, about 1817, leaving his widow and at least two of a family, Angus and Alexander.

When his widow died in the 1860s 'she was supposed to have been at least a hundred' and tradition suggests she latterly lived in the little single roomed building a few paces from the main houses. It was a West Highland custom, in some townships, to build such a dwelling for an elderly person where they could be cared for by the relatives as needed, but could be independent and perhaps leave more room for a growing family.

Young Angus took on his father's portion of the farm, (his name is on the rent roll of 1817) and later married Lucy MacDougall, probably a daughter of the Slaterach MacDougalls, and in the autumn of 1826 she presented him with twins. Concerning them, Sophy MacDougall of Dunollie wrote in 1845 to her brother-in-law, Advocate in Edinburgh:

> I promised to ask you if by any chance you know of an opening for a youth who writes a good hand and prefers driving the quill to the plough – I told his mother situations were less numerous than applicants, but that I would name the thing to you. The aspiring youth is Angus MacKinnon's eldest son – the first boy born on the property after our marriage, and who with his twin sister are the Chief's and my name children – John and Sophia. He is a fine lad and very steady.

Sophy went to work in the 'big hous' at Dunollie, then moved to Glasgow. She married a MacMillan, and returned to Oban, where she lived in Ulva Cottage. Years later, as a widow, she boarded some of the Oban High School pupils from the Outer

Isles. In a letter written about the turn of the century, she looked back on her Kerrera days, and bewailed 'the modern Board school system of Games – lawn tennis etc., for the girls being such a waste of time and strength bringing no return like work'. She believed labour would be far more interesting as well as profitable, as she had found in her life in Kerrera. Or, as the motto on the porridge bowl has it – 'There's no fun like work'.

The MacKinnons had at least two more sons and their tragic death is recorded on a gravestone in the burial ground at Kilbride:

Erected by
ANGUS MACKINNON
BARNABUCK
IN MEMORY OF HIS SONS
LACHLAN MACKINNON AGED 38 YEARS
AND ALLAN MACKINNON AGED 28 YEARS
WHO DEPARTED THIS LIFE
7th September 1865

Tradition tells the story of how the two had set out from the Leac houses for Oban with a load of potatoes for sale. When their mother looked from her window and saw

Twentieth-century potato harvest

the returning boat rounding the Shepherd's Hat island, she hung the tattie pot on the hook, to boil for their dinner; but apparently neither the boat nor the boys were ever seen again.

Six years later their mother, Lucy, joined them in the burial ground. Five years before this their father had taken on the tenancy of Barnabuck, and tradition has it that after the tragedy he moved out of the Leac houses, which then remained empty and became ruins, and lived at Barnabuck. During his time on Kerrera he had done much of the building of Balliemore school, and he was to become the last tenant of the Barnabuck ferry, and one of its last innkeepers; also the last tenant of the Slaterach mill. He left Barnabuck in the 1880s, and went to live with his daughter Sophia MacMillan at Ulva Villa, where he died in 1889 at the ripe age of ninety-four.

The foregoing notes tell something of the family which raised the Leac houses that fell into ruin after their departure. Much could be pieced together about the many fine Kerrera families who lived in houses built on the sites used by generation after generation, and who added something to the richness of the island community.

Celebrations

Life, however, was not all work, and the community united to celebrate national occasions. Perhaps the greatest event was the Peace Celebration after World War I. The school had a day's holiday on 15 November 1918 to commemorate victory, but the real celebration was the following summer, when a general holiday was observed on Monday 4 August on the island in commemoration of Peace. The gathering was the largest ever held on Kerrera.

> The proceedings were opened fittingly by the holding of a brief thanksgiving service conducted by the Rev. T. Knox. Thereafter Colonel MacDougall of MacDougall reviewed the experiences of our country during the period since August 1914, and paid an eloquent tribute to our Scottish, and especially our Highland regiments.
>
> Games suitable for young and old were indulged in with great zest, and although no records were made in time or distance for races, jumping and hammer throwing etc. the performances were both creditable and exciting. Football was taken part in with much vigour, the contesting sides retiring with one goal each to their credit, and a wholesome regard for the virility of their opponents.
>
> Perhaps in no department was there keener competition than in baking and butter-making, and the judges had a difficult task so high was the standard reached by all.
>
> On the highest point of the island a large bonfire was lit at 11 pm precisely by Mr. MacKenzie of Barnabuck, the oldest tenant. A large number of people gath-

ered at the close of the day in the school, and for some hours longer merriement continued in song and dance. It was a red letter day in the annals of the island, and one which will keep green for long the signing of Peace with Victory.[2]

Yet twenty years later the lights were to go out over Europe in the blackness of World War II.

Celebrations of various Royal occasions pulsated through Britain, and their vibrations certainly reached Kerrera. In the summer of 1897 'Tuesday was observed as a holiday by order of the School Board of Kilmore and Kilbride to celebrate the Diamond Jubilee of Queen Victoria... The gathering of teacher and pupils at Dunollie had to be postponed for two days because of bad weather'.

Five years later came plans for the Coronation of King Edward VII – 'How vividly I recall the year of the Coronation 1902, when I was presented with a New Testament for "general excellence"' writes an ex-scholar seventy years later. Owing to the King's sudden illness, most of the pre-arranged celebrations were postponed; but not so the trip in the little paddle steamer the *Princess Louise* to Dunstaffnage Castle arranged for the scholars by Kerrera's representative of the School Board, Mr. Archibald MacIntyre. In consultation with her captain, Captain Patterson (who lived near Hutchison's Monument) the little ship drew in at the ferry pier, and the children had their outing

A decade later, the teacher and two scholars were invited to represent the school at the joint Service conducted by Oban's Ministers in St. Columba's Parish Church (now, alas, no more) to mark the King's funeral. A special holiday, lasting from June 16th to 26th, was decreed to mark the Coronation of King George V and Queen Mary in 1911. Twenty-five years later the islanders celebrated the Silver Jubilee with a grand tea in the school, bedecked red, white and blue, and silver medals for the scholars. The following year the Educational Board installed an innovation in the school – a wireless set – and one of the first broadcasts was the announcement that the King's life had drawn peacefully to its close. They listened with amazement to the Proclamation of the Accession of King Edward VIII as it was actually taking place in London.

A maple tree was planted in the school grounds in May 1937 'to the Glory of God and in commemoration of their Majesties King George VI and Queen Elizabeth' followed by presentations of Coronation Bibles, mugs, savings banks and a grand Social for all in the evening. Sixteen years later, and this time it was a siberian spruce that was planted to honour the young Queen Elisabeth – more Coronation mugs – how many survive to become collectors pieces? Then there were sports in the field at Ardchoirc, followed by a dance in the big barn. Later the bonfire was lit – then supper for all at Ardantrive.

In 1938 a letter was circulated among school teachers and others from the local authority inviting suggestions for suitable dates for annual local holidays, for the mood seemed to be changing towards those breaks in the working routine. They had been called 'Days' – a day to stop work and celebrate, at least in theory, a special event: Victoria Day, later Empire Day, a day of children's sports and pride in Britain's far-flung Empire; Games Day – the Argyllshire Gathering in Oban, Scottish sports and crafts, but even more a foregathering of friends from all parts: Fast Days, to underline the significance of the approaching Communion Sunday.

> May 15 1896: No school today, Friday being the Communion Fast Day.
> Nov. 6 1896: Thurs. being the Fast day, no school

Until about the end of the reign of King George V, the school closed each year on the Thursdays and Fridays prior to the Kilmore Communion Sunday in May or June, and again in late October or November. Then it closed only for the Thursday Fast day; but in the 1960s the Fast days were replaced by a local holiday to be held on a Monday, and the link with the Communion tradition was lost.

Until at least 1920, Old New Year's Day, January 12th, rather than New Year's Day January 1st, was celebrated as the holiday on the island, and although the school had re-assembled after its Christmas vacation, it closed again for that day. A letter dated January 1830 to Dunollie, who was away from home, from his factor begins:

> I now sit down to give you an account of our proceedings for the Holiday. I sent for the two Ground Officers, and after stating to them your wish the tenants should get an allowance of Whisky on Old New Year's Day, and after consulting with them they thought it best that the Kerrera tenants should meet at Port Kerrera and the Mainland at Cleigh.
>
> I gave each of them an order for three gallons of Whisky, the one to Cleigh and the other to Port Kerrera, and I understand they had plenty.

The men folk went celebrating and first footing round the island, often ending up at Gylen Park, where Ceilidh and dancing went far into the morning hours. With a fiddle hanging on the wall of many Kerrera homes, music was no problem for social occasions, and the island fiddlers were often joined by players from the mainland.

There are interesting accounts of the community's efforts to provide a piano for the school, which would help the children and also the island's social gatherings. They are of special interest because they tell of the care, work and enthusiasm which went into gathering the required amount of money, a sum which nowadays could be found without much effort.

> Feb 9 1906: A most successful concert was held in the school tonight, the object being to raise funds to procure a musical instrument for the benefit of the scholars. A number of the children took part in the concert along with their parents and friends.

Miss Rodger, the schoolmistress, had put her own piano in the school meanwhile, and 'found it a great help for singing and drill'.

The concert was followed by another: 'The Committee have now to hand the sum of £5. Then ex-Provost MacCowan (of Kerrera connections) chaired a concert on 29 June – 'Fund now £7 3/6.' Successive concerts raised it to £9 0/1, then £10 11/7. The target was £11 11/6, and a donation of £1 completed the sum. It was lodged in the North of Scotland Bank, by the Concert Committee, Among its members were Miss MacRae (of Balliemore), Mrs. MacCallum, Miss Rodger, Messrs. Andrew MacCallum, Dugald MacIntyre, Allan MacDonald, Allan MacInnes and John MacKinnon, assisted by others including Neil Munro of Oban and Mrs. Angus MacIntyre of Glasgow.

> 10 May 1907 – the piano came on Thursday; it has been placed in the school by the Concert Committee.
> 5 July 1907 – A social meeting was held in the School tonight to give friends an opportunity of seeing the Piano.

Although the Committee could now retire with the satisfaction of having achieved their object, a number of 'Trustees', headed by Miss MacRae, were appointed to be responsible for the Piano's welfare. However, 'the best laid plans' – and there comes a rather sad little entry in the School Log of November 1913: 'The Piano was tuned during the week. Zinc was put on the botton of it as a mouse had got in and destroyed it.'

On September 2 1972 the community gathered at the school to celebrate the centenary of its erection, and of the first Church Service held in the building.

Centenary, 'what does it mean?' asked the six scholars, ages five to ten in the poem they had jointly composed for the occasion.

> Lots of people here today
> Some have come from far away
> Some from Kerrera all around
> Some have even crossed the Sound

We're all here this Saturday
To celebrate the Centenary
Centenary? What does it mean
A hundred years this school has seen.

Here it's stood through rain and sun
Children worked and had some fun
People also come to pray
Each and every fourth Sunday.

The MacDougalls built this Church and School
To give us knowledge to the full
So have a lovely day today
Sing, talk, be merry and be gay.

Like the day of the first Service in 1872, the weather was idyllically fine; as then, there 'was a large assemblage of the people of the island and others'. They spanned many links with the past hundred years. Those present included landlord and factor, tenants and former tenants, ferryman and postmistress; former teachers had crossed from Mull and Lismore, had relatives present or had sent greetings; former pupils of all the decades of the century and greetings from those of the last – all were represented.

The Service of worship and thanksgiving was conducted by the Minister of the parish of Kilmore and Kilbride, the Rev. John MacLeod, assisted by Fr. Wynne.

Round the walls were photographs of former scholars from 1899, as well as examples of the present pupils' skills. There were photographs of familiar island occasions – cattle boarding the cattle boat; a good catch of salmon; haymaking and harvest; the school entry for the rural choir at the Mod. On exhibition were rugs made from Kerrera sheep; and not least, the Bardic Crown by permission of *An Communn Ghaidhleach* won in 1962 by Angus MacInnes former pupil. His good wishes, and part of his winning poem were read.

Presents were handed over by Madam MacDougall of MacDougall to the tenants, to the scholars, including the traditional Gospels, and mementoes, with a sprig of the island's white heather attached, to the guests.

The Island hostesses provided a wonderful tea of homebaking, and after the centenary cake was cut and eaten the company went outside to relax on the grass and enjoy the ceilidh provided by former pupils, and members of the Oban and Lorn Strathspey and Reels Society, with Piper, fiddlers and accordionist. Among the songs, former pupils sang '*Cruachan Beann*' in tribute of Mr. Peter MacIntyre, teacher, at whose jubilee it was sung in 1896.

During that sunny afternoon, as the music became dreamily nostalgic, crates of peaches were handed round. Though the peaches, unlike many of the company, could not claim to have been grown on Kerrera soil, they were sent by one of a family whose roots were for long deep in Kerrera's life – respected tenants, farmers, salmon fishers, scholars, member of School Board. For Miss Jessie MacIntyre, formerly of Gylen Park, had been a pupil of the teacher in charge when the school was built, and her glowing gifts seemed symbolical of the occasion – they bridged the hundred years.

Before the company parted, the 'large assemblage of people' clasped hands, surrounding the building to sing 'Auld Lang Syne'. It was truly a gathering of old aquaintances who encircled their church and school, – a day of memories to be remembered.

Kerrera Church and School. We celebrate its Centenary, 2 September 1972

XIV FOUNDATIONS

Dry land, occupying an extensive area which now includes the island of Kerrera, appeared many million years ago; the future island's early history is written in her rocks.

For those with knowledge and imagination it can be read as from pages of a book – its great moments of chaotic upheaval and submersion; its calm periods of slow sedimentation with the formation, from time to time, of suncracks and prints of raindrops in muddy deposits.

The three great ingredients of the world's fabric, the metamorphic, igneous and sedimentary rocks, are all represented in Kerrera. The metamorphic rocks are mainly slates; the igneous rocks include basalt lavas and dolerite dykes; the sediments comprise breccias, conglomerates, sandstones and shales.

Kerrera's stratified rocks were deposited at two periods widely separated in time; late pre-Cambrian to early Ordovician and Lower Devonian (Lower Old Red Sandstone). The older rocks were folded, metamorphosed (re-crystallised) to form schists, slates etc., elevated and deeply eroded, before the deposition of Old Red strata. In Kerrera, where Lower Old Red Sediments overlie eroded metamorphic rocks a period of some two hundred million years is left without visible trace. Only the thin line of unconformable junction remains to represent the missing years of geological history.

Beautiful examples of the line of junction are to be seen west of Gylen Castle on the southern shore, and at the north-east point of the island, *Rudh a' Bhearnaig*, where Old Red conglomerates lie unconformably on folded and contorted slates.

The youngest rocks of Kerrera are the numerous narrow basic dykes intruded in Tertiary times, some 300 to 400 million years after the Lower Old Red Sandstone period.

If some of Kerrera's houses are presently roofed with local Easdale slates, certainly the island is floored with this rock whose history goes far back in geological time. In the dim past of some 400 or 600 million years, accumulations of mud were converted to shale. In the course of time, under the influence of heat and pressure deep down in the earth's crust, shale was converted to slate The slate was later elevated along with associated metamorphic strata, and became exposed to erosion. An uneven platform of metamorphic rocks was thus eventually formed. At localities in Kerrera where erosion has removed superposed deposits of Old Red Strata, we can now walk on a platform composed mainly of slate. Slate may thus be said to form the foundations of the island.

The dead black graphitic, pyritous slates of Kerrera are usually accompanied by bands of black limestone and of fine grained quartzose strata. This assemblage has been assigned by geologists to the Easdale group of the Dalradian schists. This ancient slate group occupies most of the northern and narrower half of the island. In the southern half the group is mostly overlain by later sediments. A strip on the south-east coast is, however, well exposed and exhibits the constant inter-banding of black slate and black limestone.

The Lower Old Red sediments and lavas were formed some 300 or 400 million years ago, at a late stage of the prolonged Caledonian mountain-building movements when as already mentioned, the basement Highland rocks had already been folded, metamorphised and elevated. Climatic conditions were probably semi-arid and and continental. The sediments are regarded as having formed as screes and outwash fans, (often conglomeratic) derived as erosion products from hills or mountains composed of Dalradian metamorphic rocks, and in part as finer products of erosion, deposited in inter-montane lakes. Primitive forms of fish lived in these lakes; early forms of plant life are believed to have been restricted to lake margins. On Kerrera, mainly in the broader southern half, but also in two or three localities in the north, including Barr Dubh (314 ft) are great cliffs of conglomerate of Lower Old Red age. Pebbles of various kinds are set in a matrix of coarse grit. Such deposits are popularly called Puddingstone.

Hugh Miller, the stone-mason of Cromarty, whose valued researches on the rocks of this period are classic, sailed down the Sound of Kerrera in July 1843 and wrote:

> with its border of Old Red conglomerate resting on the clay slate of the district… we could mark the peculiar character of the conglomerate, which in the cliffs washed by the sea, when the binding matrix is softer than the pebbles which it encloses, roughened instead of being polished, by the action of the waves, and which along the eastern side of the Sound here, seems as if formed of cannon-shot of all sizes bedded in cement.[1]

The breccias, of which fine examples may be seen north and east of Eilean Orasaig, consist of unassorted pieces of quartzose and calcarious material, belonging to the slate period, with a few chips of the slate itself. They represent screes of the old land surface, for their angular edges indicate they are not waterworn or much rubbed in transport.

On the southern coast are cliffs and beds of sandstone flags and shale. The shales give special clues to past incidents; they show, on flat surfaces, suncracks made as the original mud dried out, and pittings made by ancient raindrops. Specially fine examples are also on the south-western coast, where the shale is red. The shales also contain fossils; plant remains and casts of the primitive fish *Cephalaspis lornensis*, with a head shield shaped like a saddler's knife. An early form of millipede has also been found (*Kampecaris obanensis*).

The volcanic activity of Lower Old Red Sandstone times took place at more than one stage. In Kerrera the lavas were mainly erupted after the deposition of some 400 ft of sediments. The lower inner parts of a flow might retain their heat for some time after eruption, while the upper layers were blown into froth by escaping gas.

The prevalent type on Kerrera is a fine-grained basalt either compact or slaggy; Where compact it is dark grey when freshly fractured; when slaggy a pale purplish grey with elongated steam-holes, indicating the direction of the flow.

A narrow trough-faulted band of much shattered lavas, with slates on its western side, extends southwards along Kerrera's eastern coast as far as the vicinity of The Horseshoe Bay; over this stretch the eastern boundary fault of the trough is under the Sound of Kerrera. Further south the lavas are faulted against slates, both to the west and to the east. On the south coast, at *Port a' Chroinn*, the western boundary fault throws the lavas against Old Red conglomerate. An isolated mass of lava overlooking The Horseshoe Bay, rises to form the highest point on the island (617 ft).

Another lava outcrop covers an area of about eight acres south of Port Phadruig on the south-western coast. Here may be seen beautiful examples of columnar jointing defined by angular shrinkage cracks formed as the molten basalt cooled.

A feature of Kerrera's rock formations is the presence of numerous geological dykes; these are of Tertiary age and are thus the youngest rocks of the island (about 50 million years old). The dykes, composed of basic rock such as dolerite were formed by lava driven upward, by subterranean magmatic pressure, along a series of sub-parallel fractures with a general north-westerly trend. This fracture system was developed in relation to the Mull tertiary volcanic centre, and the Kerrera dykes form part of the Mull 'dyke-swarm' which extends far to the south-east.

Individual dykes have parallel sides, and thus form narrow wall-like rock bodies. The dykes were intruded into relatively cold country-rock and thus cooled more quickly at their edges than in their centres. These 'chilled edges' are of relatively fine grain as compared with the dyke centres because the quick cooling gave less time for crystals to grow.

There are many examples of varying breadth, to be measured in inches only, or in feet. In some cases the lava has been worn away leaving the fissure empty save for remnants of the dyke at its base, but with signs of exposure of intense heat on the bounding walls. In other cases it is the older rock that has weathered away, leaving the dyke upstanding. There are fine examples in the north, near Hurchison's monument – one with a large V-shaped cleft in it – and in the south below Ardmore farm. Gylen Castle overlooks three dykes traversing the promontory below its courtyard.

Sir Archibald Geikie, in his *Scenery and Geology of Scotland* (1865), makes the

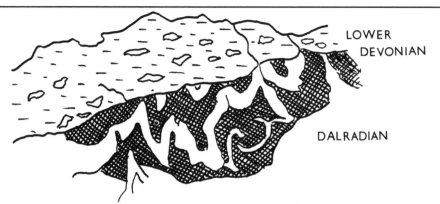

LOWER
DEVONIAN

DALRADIAN

'Where "Old Red" conglomerates lie unconformably on folded and contorted slates.'

The Earth heaved and quaked
the foundations of the mountains shook
smoke rose – devouring fire and searing heat
thick clouds dark with water came out of the radiance
hailstones and glowing coals.
The Lord thundered from heaven
He shot forth lightning shafts
and sent them echoing
the channels of the sea-bed were revealed –
the foundations of the earth were laid bare.
Then deep from the earth you shall speak
From low in the dust your words shall come
Your voice shall come from the ground like
the voice of a ghost,
And your speech shall whisper out of the dust,

intriguing suggestion that if we could gently depress the land for some twenty or thirty feet we would actually bring back the old outlines of the Scottish shores before the last upheaval had begun. Kerrera as we now see it, and for that matter the mainland coasts, is seen at 'low tide' – a tide which went out thousands of years ago, and has so remained. Were it to flow back overnight, the island off north-west Kerrera, *Eilean nan Gambhna*, 'the Shepherd's Hat' would lost its brim under the water. In fact Geikie's picturesque description of the 'raised beaches' of Scotland so aptly fits the scenery of this low land fringing parts of Kerrera's coast it is appropriate to quote from its passages:

Among the more marked changes which have influenced the scenery … since the close of the Glacial period are the raised beaches. Round the west coast a terrace having a height of about forty feet above high watermark winds as a green platform along the dark rocky coast of Argyllshire. It probably dates from the latter part of the Glacial period for arctic shells have been found in it.

It was succeeded by a lower and later terrace… which runs at a height of about twenty to twenty-five feet above high watermark. As it has yielded in several places works of human fabrication it must be of later date than the time when man became an inhabitant of this island.

… This green terrace runs as a flat selvage of sandy gravelly or clayey ground varying in breadth from six to seven miles to a few feet. It rises from twenty to thirty feet above high water and is composed of horizontal layers of sand, gravel or clay, often full of littoral shells, the whole having being laid down by the sea.

Along the inner margin of the terrace the ground usually rises as a line of shelving bank or precipitous cliff just as a shelving bank or steep cliff shoots upwards from the sea. The inland cliff that bounds so many portions of the terrace is not infrequently scarped into clefts and creeks perforated with long dim caverns.

Moreover the resemblance to a sea cliff goes still further, for the terrace itself is often dotted with prominent crags and worn pillars of rock, like the tangled covered skerries and sea stacks that roughen any wild beach open to the full swell of the Atlantic. These inland rocks, whether on the terrace or rising steeply from its inland edge, are feathered over with ferns and ivy and trailing briars; they are tinted with mosses and lichens and gay with many a bud and blossom, luxuriant bunches of harts' tongue hang from the roofs of the caves.

But divest the rocks of all this tapistry of verdure, strip the terrace of its mantle of … (vegetation), its highways … and seaports … and you then lay bare a sandy flat that ends at the foot of a gentle slope or at the base of a line of bleached and wasted rocks. You in fact reconstruct an old coast line' and there can be no more doubt that the sea once rolled over that terrace and broke against that cliff, then that the waves are breaking over the beach today.

Instead of the level (pasture) of the terrace, imagine a tract of sand or mud; for the mosses and lichens, ferns and flowers, substitute a shaggy covering of seaweed; let the tides come eddying across the terrace among the rocks and the cliff; and you thus restore that old coastline to the condition in which it existed at a comparatively recent geological period.

Geikie's vivid reconstruction of former ages seems to add to an appreciation of Kerrera's 'raised beaches'. The whole length of the island's eastern shore is fringed by raised beach deposits and there are local occurrences on the western coast-line. The most extensive tracts are in the north, near Ardantrive and at Slatrach Bay.

Whatever clues to Kerrera's past may lie beneath its green turf, not very many appear to have been disclosed.

At the north end, opposite the Maiden Isle, at the point named *Rudh a' Bhearnaig* – the point of the gap – (that great cleft in the dyke) the survey map indicates a burial ground 'Clad a' Bhearnaig'. For want of firm information, this site has caused much speculation, for there are indications that there were dwellings of some kind in the area.

A century ago rather less of these indications were below turf, and visitors noted down what they had seen. Angus Smith, in his *Loch Etive and the Sons of Uisnach* (1879), claimed to 'see clearly the remains of the houses. There are evidently oblong dwellings, and the collection of dwellings is surrounded by a wall. At the extreme north there is a very solid projecting building which suggests a watch tower, just on the point where it would be useful.'

William Keddie, in his *Highland Tour – Glasgow to Oban* of about the same period adds:

> A space of land, roughly estimated by pacing to measure about forty-five yards in breadth and the same extent in length, is distinctly inclosed by the remains of a wall about four feet in thickness. The space inclosed is sub-divided into squares, also defined by thick walls, forming apparently a series of distinct dwellings, access to which is provided for by two large openings in the external walls. In one corner of the inclosure there is an elevation resembling the remains of a cairn or tower; a similar eminence. although less well defined, occupying a corresponding angle of the inclosing wall on the same side, and both having the same seaward aspect.

Early in the twentieth century Mr. Dugald MacIsaac of Oban excavated an artificial mound near the farm of Slaterach and found two kists. Some years later two urns from these were sent on loan to the National Museum of Antiquities of Scotland, where they presently remain. The Museum made the following report in their *Proceedings of April ll 1932:*

FOOD-VESSEL AND CINERARY URN FROM KERRERA, ARGYLL.

Two short cists, formed of slabs set on edge, were unearthed, one containing a food-vessel and the other a cinerary urn. The graves lie practically alongside each other, a few feet apart.

> One grave, measuring 4 feet 5 inches in length, 1 foot 3 inches in breadth, and 2 feet 2 inches in depth, contained a food-vessel of brownish yellow ware' measuring 43 inches in height, 6 inches in external diameter at the mouth, 6 inches at the shoulder, and about three inches across the base. The vessel is encircled by two mouldings, each decorated by a single row of maggot impressions. A similar

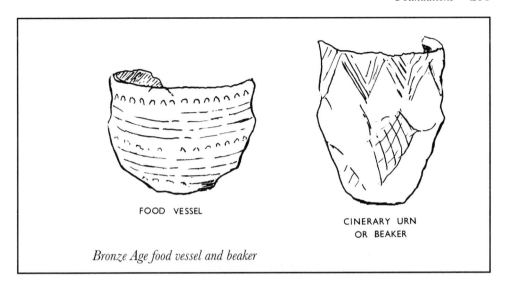

FOOD VESSEL

CINERARY URN
OR BEAKER

Bronze Age food vessel and beaker

line of these markings appears under the rim. The rest of the wall is decorated by transverse rows of broad roulette impressions about 4 inch apart. On the top of the lip, which is bevelled sharply on the inside, are maggot impressions set radially. More than three-quarters of the vessel survives. Seven water-rolled pebbles of cream-coloured quartzite were also found in the cist.

The other grave, which was also formed of slabs set on edge, measured 3 feet 3 inches in length, 2 feet in breadth, and 2 feet 2 inches in depth. It contained a cinerary urn of brownish yellow clay, measuring $7\frac{1}{4}$ inches in height, $5\frac{3}{4}$ inches in external diameter at the mouth $6\frac{1}{4}$ inches at the widest part, and $3\frac{1}{2}$ inches across the base. It is encircled slightly above the centre by a single cordon, the upper part being nearly vertical. The top of the rim, which is 5 inch broad, is bevelled on the inside, and decorated by impressions of a triangular pointed instrument, forming a zigzag line in false relief. On the exterior of the wall are incised hatched lozenge patterns, a large lozenge in the centre, with the lower and upper halves of other two just under the rim and above the base. The vessel has been restored and about three quarters of it survive.

REFERENCES

Introduction
1. MacFarlane W., *Geographical Collections Relating to Scotland*, Edinburgh 1907

Chapter I
1. Johnstone Rev. J., (editor) Norwegian account of Haco's expedition against Scotland. Trans. From the Flatyon and Frisian MSS. *Scotland Under her Early Kings, 1782*
2. Anderson A.O., *Early Sources of Scottish History AD 500 – 1286*, Edinburgh 1922
3. *Acts of Parliament of Scotland VII*
4. Grant K.W., *Myth, Tradition and Story from Western Argyll*, Oban 1925
5. Dunollie papers as dated
6. Bayne J., *The Jacobite Rising of 1715*, 1970
7. Fergusson Sir J., *Argyll in the Forty-Five*, London 1951
8. Dunstaffnage MSS

Chapter II
1. Groome F.H. (ed), *Ordnance Gazetteer of Scotland*, London 1901
2. Loder John de Vere, *Colonsay and Oronsay in the Isles of Argyll, Their History, Flora, Fauna and Topography*, Edinburgh 1935
3. Garnett Dr. T., *Observations on a tour through the Highlands and part of the Western Islands of Scotland*, London 1798

Chapter III
1. Loder's *Colonsay*
2. Garnett's *Observations*
3. *Ibid*

Chapter IV
1. Barnard A., *The Whisky Distilleries of the United Kingdom*, 1887
2 –4 Garnett's *Observations*
4. Loder's *Colonsay*

Chapter X
1. Garnett's *Observations*
2. Haldane A.R.B., *Three Centuries of Scottish Posts*, Edinburgh 1971
3. Correspondance C Reeves P.M.G. 1823
4. Petition to Sir Edward Lees P.M.G. c 1856
5. Haldane's *Three Centuries*
6. *Oban Times*, Feb.1867
7. Haldane's *Three Centuries*
8. Faujas Saint-Fond B., *Travels in England Scotland and the Hebrides*, 1799 translation
9. Garnett's *Observations*
10. MacLeod N., *Reminiscences of a Highland Parish*, London 1871

Chapter XI
1. McKerral Andrew, *Kintyre in the 17th Century*, Edinburgh 1948

Chapter XII
1. Faichney A. M., *Oban and District Around*, Oban 1902
2. *Oban Times*, 1865
3. Notes from the copy of sermon he gave me 1967

Chapter XIII
1. *Oban Times*, Aug 1915
2. *Ibid.*, 1919

Chapter XIV
1. Miller H., *The Cruise of the Betsey*, Edinburgh 1858

"Where not mentioned, sources of information from Dunollie papers"